What Is an Editor?

Saxe Commins in his office

What Is an Editor?
Saxe Commins at Work

Dorothy _{Berliner} Commins

The
University of
Chicago
Press

*Chicago and
London*

Acknowledgment is gratefully made for
permission to include or reprint letters or
portions of letters of the following people:
James A. Michener; Stephen Spender,
copyright by Stephen Spender, reprinted by
permission of The Harold Matson Company,
Inc.; Sinclair Lewis, by permission of Paul
Gitlin, attorney for the estate of Mr. Lewis;
Elliot Paul, permission of Robert N. Greene,
trustee of the estate of Mr. Paul; W. H. Auden,
copyright © 1976 by The Estate of W. H.
Auden; John O'Hara, permission of United
States Trust Company of New York, executor
of Mr. O'Hara's estate; Eugene O'Neill, © 1977
by Yale University; Isak Dinesen (Karen
Blixen), permission of The Rungstedlund
Foundation; William Faulkner, permission of
Jill Faulkner Summers; Budd Schulberg; Frank
Sullivan; Albert Einstein, permission of Helen
Dukas, trustee of the literary estate of Professor
Einstein; Walter Van Tilberg Clark; Maurice
Valency; Richard P. McKeon; Robinson Jeffers,
permission of Donnan Jeffers; Irwin Shaw;
Robert Haas, permission of Donald S. Klopfer;
Henry Steele Commager; Perry Miller,
permission of Mrs. Perry Miller.

The University of Chicago Press, Chicago 60637
The University of Chicago Press, Ltd., London

Library of Congress Cataloging in Publication Data

Commins, Dorothy Berliner
  What is an editor?

  Includes index.
  1. Commins, Saxe.   2. Editors—United States—
Biography.   3. American literature—20th century—
History and criticism.   I. Title.
PN149.9.C6C6   070.5'092'4 [B]   77-81716
ISBN 0-226-11427-9

For my children
Frances Ellen Commins-Bennett
Eugene David Commins

Contents

Illustrations

Prelude

The letters presented here are but a part of a voluminous correspondence carried on over a period of nearly four decades between Eugene O'Neill, William Faulkner, Sinclair Lewis, W. H. Auden, and many others, with their editor, Saxe Commins. These letters, together with the other documents presented here, are a selection from hundreds of papers belonging to Saxe Commins and now cataloged and stored in the Princeton University Library. This gathering is representative of that large collection and demonstrates the relationship Saxe had with his writers, some of whom are among the most important writers of our time. That relationship was always a very close and personal one, perhaps unique in the annals of editor and writer relationships. So much was done so closely in the kind of strict privacy that writers preferred and the editor honored that the letters are but the tip of the iceberg.

It may be said here that the absence of correspondence with some of the people mentioned throughout the book is explained by the fact that communication was often carried on verbally during the many hours the authors spent in Saxe's office or in our home. But the letters which do exist are of great interest because they show clearly a kind of relationship between editor and author which was extraordinarily fruitful.

In our present world, and certainly in any future one that we are able to imagine, it seems extremely unlikely that precisely the kind of personal relationship exemplified by the way Saxe worked with his writers will ever exist again. In that sense this gathering has already some historical value, representing a great period in which American literature came of age. The work of a few dedicated editors, including Saxe Commins, was a potent if invisible force in this remarkable period.

Saxe Commins was a reticent man, self-deprecating and modest to a fault. Typical of his modesty is that while he kept and preserved many letters from his writers, he did not see any reason to save copies of most of his own letters to them.

As an editor, he was bold and imaginative and possessed a deep intuitive sense which often enabled him to draw forth that subtle idea or that graceful phrase which an author was struggling so desperately to bring to the surface. This quality, combined as it was with loyalty and devotion, was given unreservedly to all the authors with whom he worked.

Editing as practiced by Saxe Commins demanded a sure sense of literary style and a wide and deep knowledge of literature, but it also required a mastery of the many practical crafts of publishing, from the design and production of books to their appropriate promotion. A natural teacher, Saxe Commins lectured and talked informally with many groups of writers and students on all aspects of publishing; and indeed, for a period of four years he taught a course at Columbia University.

When Saxe entered publishing, arriving at his true vocation in his mid-thirties, there was no prescribed or formal way to train for his role. Yet he was always anxious to pass along to the new generation of editors what he had learned by trial and error. In a sense, this book contains that process of education and growth as shown through his own work and the reactions of his writers. It is more than a memoir, then, and though I have included a brief outline of his life, the book is not intended as a biography or a scholarly accounting; rather, it is a portrait of a man at work and a chronicle of an amazing period in the history of American literature.

The reports and letters included here show how an editor in a commercial publishing house functions. But it might be informative to look at what Saxe considered the job to be, as he was preparing a series of lectures to be delivered at Columbia University. (At times Saxe could be didactic.)

Now what is an editor? To know what an editor "is," it becomes necessary to inquire into what he has been and what he became. He is first of all a worker, proud of his craft, sensitive to ideas of all kinds and responsive to them; he is discriminating against ineptitude, inaccuracy, misinformation, nonsense, and humbug; he fights for talent, for the free interchange of opinion and the widest possible dissemination of information. He is resourceful in the use of all the available techniques of the graphic arts, and all the means of communication. He is nimble in his thinking and his guessing and prophesying. He prays that he will be lucky.

The editor is called upon to play many roles, because with each new manuscript he is confronted with a new set of ideas, the projection of a new personality and the necessity of adapting himself to a new form. His is therefore a flexible mind, ever remembering that each new book with which he deals is an entirely new entity.

Saxe was also self-effacing.

Almost everyone who reads is an editor, since—one way or another—everyone responds to ideas, has notions of his own about the matter and manner of a book, and is tempted to make revisions as he goes along in accordance with his own background, judgment, prejudices, and critical acumen. It might even be said that the editor is any semiliterate who reads with a pencil in his hand.

And Saxe believed in being practical, though this wartime letter to an admirer is obviously written out of very strong personal feelings.

It is I, and, through me, Random House, who owe you more than thanks for your deep understanding of what we are trying to do. But first of all, let me clarify to you my modest role in all the meaning Random House has to you. My colleagues would set up a derisive snicker at the notion that I am a business-man; I am merely a working editor who has accumulated a set of naive concepts about publishing. In my book, the first principle of publishing is the communication of ideas. Let the economic determinists cry from now until doomsday that the profit motive is paramount; I still insist that the printed word is a living,

sacred thing and is all that St. John said it was: "In the beginning was the Word, and the Word was God." Let the theologians
interpret the word "Word" to mean Christ if they will, and that
is all right with me. But this is not to say that publishing can
exist outside the frame of our time and the limitations it imposes.
Above everything it is essential to be a practical publisher and,
if you like, a commercial one. And I hold a very strong brief even
for the commercial publisher. He serves his function in the very
real world and helps to shape, perhaps in a small way, the future
our children will know. This is not vague idealism; it is the
ultimate reality, and the only reality I know. I like to believe that
good books, by your definition and mine, can make or lose as
much money as bad books can make or lose. The notion that
commercial success is a result of compromise is a cheap fallacy.
Once the principle is established that both good and bad ideas
are marketable and either may prove financially rewarding or
penalizing, the choice, it seems to me, is obvious.... [Letter
written January 5, 1944, to Kenneth Melvin, A.P.O. 361,
Pacific Area]

That he couldn't stop being an editor is shown in a letter to
Howard Fast about a book Random House didn't publish and Saxe
didn't edit.

I read *The American* at one sitting on the day train from
Rochester.... Your book aroused in me a mixed feeling of real
admiration and some disappointment. Your narrative powers
have never been so sure. Schilling's story about Parsons is told
with sustained power and even Altgeld's listening to it con-
tributes to the drama of the whole scene.

The prologue, with its development of Altgeld's background
and environment, is completely convincing. What worries me
very seriously is the huge gap in time and in exposition and in
revelation between his boyhood and when he becomes judge.
The hiatus is noticeable even to the casual reader, I imagine, and
it left me dissatisfied. Then, too, there is a similar omission to
clarify the means by which he rises from his judgeship to become
Governor of Illinois. I thought more could be made of the conflict between Altgeld and Grover Cleveland, especially since
Altgeld had Cleveland dead to rights on constitutional grounds.

It delighted me to see Bryan made such a nincompoop with a
gift for resounding phrases. The question is whether Bryan,
historically, wasn't really a boy wonder with some integrity who
became corrupted by his egomaniac dream of power. I wish, too,

that more had been made of the Pullman strike. It would have given you an opportunity to concentrate a little more on the simple and heroic figure of Gene Debs. . . .

Even on the train, I couldn't overcome the editorial habit of picking up a few little items, but I haven't my copy here to refer to the page numbers. As I remember them, they go something like this: once or twice you have Altgeld clutch the rostrum. That's the neatest trick of the week. What you mean is that he clutches the lectern.

Somewhere there is a typo which gives "same" for "some."

Also you use the word "inferred" when you meant "implied." Then there is the mention of the Teddy Bear in reference to Roosevelt. The Teddy Bear came into popularity as a toy long after Roosevelt was president and even after he returned from his exploration of the River of Doubt. . . .

I'd like to talk with you some day about the physical appearance of the volume. [Letter of June 26, 1946, to Howard Fast]

But of course W. H. Auden said it best and briefly. "Efficiency of mind and goodness of heart are rarely combined in equal measure, but in Saxe they were."

1 Beginnings

Saxe was a slender, tense fellow, about five feet eight inches tall, with a fine brow and dark hair. At work he wore glasses, and sometimes when he looked up they slid down past the bridge of his nose. He was not given to dressing in the lastest fashion. Oh, those hats of his! He was quite fond of wide-brimmed felt ones, either black or brown. When he slapped one on his head, it gave him a rakish look. In time the hat would begin to look shabby. If I suggested buying a new one, he'd look at his hat and ask, "What's wrong with this one?" I would point to its floppy brim. "Oh that! Don't touch it. I like it that way."

He had been a chain-smoker since his college years. Later he took to pipe smoking. In his childhood he developed a keen interest in sports which lasted throughout his life. His favorites were swimming, tennis, skating, and baseball.

He was a natural student. When he finished high school, it was decided that the family's small resources would be used to further his academic schooling. He decided to study medicine and enrolled at the University of Pennsylvania. But when he had concluded his undergraduate courses and had almost covered the first year of his medical training, he had shattering news from home. His older brother, Harry, had been stricken with tuberculosis and had to be sent to live in Arizona. The family would have to pool their resources to pay the medical expenses. Moreover, Saxe would have to either quit college or accelerate his program. Since he had acquired some basic knowledge in medicine, he decided to transfer to dentistry at Pennsylvania.

Even at the beginning of his college years, Saxe would go to New York whenever he had a free weekend. There he would join his sister, Stella, who had married Edward (better known as Teddy) Ballantine, a gifted painter, sculptor, and actor. They lived in Greenwich Village in an atmosphere of quiet and charm, far removed from the bustling New York only a few blocks away. Not the least of the attractions of the village was its low rentals, and consequently young talents drifted to this secluded section of the city.

On one of these weekends Saxe met John (Jack) Reed, the fiery young rebel and crusader. Reed, the son of a United States marshal in Portland, Oregon, had entered Harvard and had soon become a conspicuous figure for his opinions, his scorn of rules and traditions, and his flamboyant personality. When he got to New York (about 1913), Reed's journalistic talent found an outlet in the *New York Globe* and the *Metropolitan Magazine.* He roamed the city, picking up items concerning ethnic groups and facts about social discrimination. He gave emphasis to the predicament of the dislocated aliens. He was quoted as saying, "Within a block of my house was all the adventure in the world; within a mile was every country."

Reed became identified with the causes of the disinherited. His reports on strikes and the conflicts that grew out of them brought him considerable public attention. At about this time Eugene O'Neill met Jack Reed and was intrigued and captivated by Reed's flaming idealism. Reed's dedicated spirit was later to lead him beyond the borders of reality, when as a correspondent to Russia after the Revolution of 1917, he remained there only to become a tormented and disillusioned convert. Yet he concealed his doubts and did not permit them to break down the enthusiasm with which he wrote *Ten Days That Shook the World.*

It was through Jack Reed that Saxe first met Eugene O'Neill. Their encounters were brief, but in the summer of 1916, while visiting in Provincetown, Massachusetts, Saxe had occasion to spend many hours with O'Neill. Gene was then engaged in writing the one-act plays which were to comprise the *Glencairn* cycle. During that summer the first of the three plays, *Bound East for Cardiff*, was produced in a ramshackle little structure that came to be known as the Wharf Theatre in Provincetown.

Gene found in Saxe a good listener. They would discuss at length the books they had been reading, such as Max Stirner's *The Ego and His Own* and Nietzsche's *Thus Spake Zarathustra*, all heady stuff, diluted a little with a sprinkling of the Romantic poets.

The most verbal champion of Stirner's book in those days was Terry Carlin. Terry had come to New York from Chicago, bringing a reputation as a complete dissenter. In New York, Terry could be found almost any night in the back room of a saloon on Sixth Avenue and Fourth Street called Hell Hole. Here Terry Carlin shouted his renunciation of every kind of conformity. Among his audience would be Hippolyte Havel, a true Bohemian who would lend encouragement to Carlin's long discursive monologue by adding his own colorful remarks denouncing the bourgeoisie.

It was in a setting of this kind that Gene placed the people and events of the only short story he ever wrote, "Tomorrow," which appeared in *The Seven Arts* magazine. The same scene and theme were later developed in *The Iceman Cometh*, with Terry Carlin as the prototype for Larry Slade, "the foolosopher." The plan for *The Iceman* crystallized in O'Neill's mind in the late 1930s, after he had been awarded the Nobel Prize.

When Saxe finished his formal schooling, he established a dental practice in Rochester, New York. It flourished and he was extremely busy, but this did not cut off his association with his literary friends. At this early period, he was obliged to squeeze his contact with the writers he admired into weekend trips to Manhattan. But even then, it was with Eugene O'Neill that he would most often spend his vacations. Gene was married to Agnes O'Neill at the time, and Saxe stayed with them in Provincetown, Massachusetts, Ridgefield, Connecticut, and Bermuda. Of a particular visit to Bermuda, Saxe noted:

> At the invitation of Gene O'Neill, I visited his home in Hamilton, Bermuda, in April 1926. He was then living in an old eighteenth-century mansion, surrounded by spacious grounds.
> During the two weeks of my stay, Gene and I frequently discussed the work upon which he was engaged, as we had done before, on my previous visits to Provincetown, Massachusetts,

and Ridgefield, Connecticut. On this occasion, Gene had begun the groundwork for his play *Strange Interlude*. He wrote undisturbed during the mornings; our afternoons were spent bathing and bicycling; and in the evenings we went for long walks.

At that time *An American Tragedy* by Theodore Dreiser had attained immense success and was being discussed everywhere. I recall our talk, on one of our walks, of that book and Gene's first reference to his new play, afterwards named *Strange Interlude*. He said that Dreiser had written the novel of an unexceptional man, whereas he was at work on a novel in dramatic form of an exceptional woman. His play, according to the very meticulous outline contained in his notebooks, indicated the manner in which he would extend the device of masks used in his previous play, *The Great God Brown*, to the use of asides which would indicate the duality of thought and spoken word of his characters.

It was the working out of this problem that he devoted himself to at the time of my visit. I was shown several drawings of the proposed stage settings which O'Neill had made in his notebooks. The manuscript of every one of his plays contains such drawings, as a help in orienting his characters on the stage. I recall, too, our discussions concerning the revolutionary length of the play.

Before Saxe left Bermuda, Gene told him he would like to purchase the house in which he was living, called "Spithead." When Saxe returned to New York, he immediately contacted the people who controlled the Bermuda estate.

Little did Gene know then, that in less than two years he would no longer live in Bermuda. When he bought "Spithead," he and Agnes were most enthusiastic about their plans to renovate the interior as well as the exterior of their house. It would be home to them for most of the year.

While Gene kept steadily at work on *Strange Interlude*, he was wondering whether the Theatre Guild would do this play. He felt thwarted and frustrated at not having found producers for *Marco Millions* and *Lazarus Laughed*. In the fall and winter of 1926 Gene spent some time in New York, seeing people about these plays. On being assured by the Guild that they would do *Strange Interlude*, he returned to Bermuda buoyant in spirit, and immediately began to work on the play for production. Thinking a change would be good for Agnes, for him and the children, he rented a cabin at

Belgrade Lakes, Maine, for the summer months. It was a fateful move.

Gene had met Agnes Boulton, a young widow, in 1917, when she came to Greenwich Village to further her writing career. She was not a tyro. From the time she was seventeen, she had written and sold a number of stories to various magazines.

At the very start of their relationship, Gene was attracted to her. There was something lovely about the bone structure of her face—a fine setting for her gray blue eyes and brown hair. In 1918, after an ardent courtship, not without its difficulties, they were married. Those were the halcyon days, rich and warm and eventful. It was Gene's second marriage, and from it issued Gene's two children, Oona O'Neill Chaplin and Shane Rudleighe O'Neill. But differences began to pile up which played havoc with their relationship. The break came after their summer in Maine.

From now on, it seemed as though the Furies had intervened, determined to steer the course of Gene's destiny.

At Belgrade Lake, Maine, he encountered Carlotta Monterey. He had met her before, when she was cast for the role of Mildred Douglas in his play *The Hairy Ape*, produced in April 1922. During the four years that had elapsed she had divorced her third husband. Beautiful in an exotic way, with her dark luminous eyes, her black hair tightly drawn back, her head held high, giving her an imperious look, she was a striking figure wherever she went.

She was the daughter of Christian Nielson Tharsing, a Dane who had settled in California. Her given name was Hazel Nielson Tharsing. At thirteen she was sent to St. Gertrude's, a Catholic academy. Her classmates soon found that she obeyed her every impulse to dramatize situations beyond truth and reality. Later, when she was training for the stage, she abandoned her given name and assumed that of Carlotta with the added name of Monterey, after that city in California, situated near the Bay of Monterey.

When the summer was over at Belgrade Lakes, the O'Neill family returned to Bermuda. Agnes knew Gene's interest in Carlotta was not transitory.

On January 27, 1928, just before *Strange Interlude* was to have its first performance, this telegram reached Saxe: "Invitation first performance of *Interlude* will be next Saturday instead of Sunday. See you then. Gene."

Saxe did see Gene after the performance. Gene then told him that

Carlotta had made plans for their escape. They sailed for Europe on February 10, 1928.

I first met Saxe through the Ballantines, whom I knew slightly. At that time Saxe was still studying medicine, and as a very young girl (aspiring to be a pianist) I was quite awed. In the brief conversation we had, I asked if he had ever witnessed an operation. "Why, yes," was the quiet reply. I ventured further by asking, "Do you think you could arrange for me to see an operation?" This must have floored him completely, but he was game! The next day we met at the Roosevelt Hospital.

Most of that experience left an indelible imprint on my memory. We were seated in the top row of a small amphitheater that was already filling up with students. The lights were dimmed as an anesthetized patient was wheeled in toward the center of the amphitheater. When the surgeon and his assistants came in, a huge light was lowered over the patient. The surgeon then proceeded with the operation, talking all the time in a language I did not understand, nor would I today. I must have turned to Saxe with a questioning look, for he whispered, "The man has a badly fractured shoulder blade."

We hardly said a word as we walked out. With a brief goodbye, we went our separate ways, Saxe back to medical school and I to my studies in music.

We renewed our acquaintance in 1927 after a lapse of seven years. About this time Saxe made his first appearance as an author in his own right. Having become interested in Freudian psychology, he and a Rochester friend, Lloyd Ring Coleman, wrote *Psychology: A Simplification*. It was published by Boni and Liveright in 1927.

When at different times Saxe came to New York, there were evenings of dining and the theater. Saxe was a delightful conversationalist. How we laughed as we recalled the operation incident! On his return to Rochester, there would be an exchange of many letters.

When Saxe came at Christmas time, a German brass band was playing in a courtyard near my studio. They were going through their repertoire of carols. While the musicians were puffing away at "O Tannenbaum, O Tannenbaum," with some off-pitch notes as they reached the high registers, Saxe asked me to marry him. It was then that he told me that he had long hoped to give up the practice of dentistry and enter the world of writing. We began to plan. Saxe would continue his practice until the beginning of May. I would go on with my teaching and playing until that time. We would guard our savings so that we could spend a year abroad. We were married on December 24, 1927, without pomp of any sort. I could not help thinking that my beloved mother, were she living, would have planned it differently.

Time winged past and in June we left for England. Saxe was delighted to leave his dental practice behind, though he kept in close touch with one patient, Eugene O'Neill. Our stay in England, while brief, was truly a rich one. We visited the Lake District, the land of the poets Saxe had always loved, and made several other small excursions. Then we moved on to Paris where we found a tiny attic studio in the rue Falguière. It consisted of one large room that served as living room, dining room, and kitchen, with a little stairway that led to a balcony bedroom.

We had hardly been in Paris two weeks when a letter came from Gene urging Saxe to visit him in Guéthary. It turned out that Gene wanted Saxe to help him with *Dynamo*, the play he was writing at that time, and to see to some other complicated literary commissions for him in Paris. Saxe wrote to me from Guéthary: "Will you make inquiries about the rental of a large Underwood typewriter? It need not have the French keyboard. Find out how much it costs for three months. My portable is not good enough for the job I have to do." In a letter received shortly afterward, Saxe referred to another play Gene was working on: "It's after one in the morning. I've been reading the play, though in rough draft. It's magnificent, another enormous stride forward in his inexhaustible genius. Just you wait. Mark my prophetic words, it will be a tremendous sensation, greater than the others, or I quit as a prophet." That play was *Mourning Becomes Electra*.

In the meantime, I received a letter from an old friend who had heard of our marriage and suggested we might like to live in his apartment during our stay in Paris. Leon Gordon was a successful commercial artist who had become nationally known for his billboard ads: the tilted cup of Maxwell House Coffee that was "Good to the last drop"; the well-dressed young man wearing an Ide collar; the executive in a tailored suit made by Hart, Schaffner and Marx.

Leon maintained a modern duplex apartment furnished with the beautiful things he had gathered in his travels. I went to see it. Centrally located at 11 rue Schelcher, it was indeed lovely. Certainly it would be a luxurious change from the atelier we were then occupying. Soon after Saxe returned from southern France, we decided to move to the apartment. We found and rented a small grand piano, a Bechstein, and I soon set a schedule for daily practice. Saxe began to work steadily on Gene's manuscript.

One day while Saxe was about to take the elevator to our apartment, another passenger stepped in. When Saxe reached our floor, the man asked, "Can you tell me who plays the piano on your floor?" Saxe, somewhat taken aback, said, "I think you are referring to my wife's playing. I hope she is not disturbing you." "Oh, no, no, no! On the contrary, do ask her to keep it up! The music stimulates me in my work."

The men introduced themselves. He was Myron Nutting, an American painter whose studio apartment was right above ours. Before long we were exchanging visits with Mr. and Mrs. Nutting. In the course of our friendship, Mr. Nutting did a drawing of Saxe. He also did a sketch of me at the piano, preliminary to a painting he completed later.

On one of our visits, Mr. Nutting showed us a drawing of James Joyce. We learned that the Nuttings and Joyces were close friends. One afternoon the Nuttings said the Joyces were coming to tea. Would we like to join them? Of course, we were excited at the thought.

When we arrived, Mr. Joyce was seated. When he rose to greet us I noticed he was very slim and tall, wearing very thick, dark-colored glasses. His hands were pale and slender, and as he extended his hand in greeting, his face almost broke into a smile, but it was quickly arrested. What impressed me most was his manner of speaking. His enunciation was clear and precise, quite distinct from the English normally heard.

Joyce, Myron Nutting, and Saxe sat together while I talked with Mrs. Joyce. She fascinated me. Her hair was reddish brown and wavy. Her complexion had that lovely fairness often seen in redheads. She was wearing a simple dark brown dress which hung almost to her ankles. A ropelike belt went around her waist. One of the guests was saying to her, "Nora, there is so much talk going on about *Ulysses*. Surely the ban will have to be lifted soon and Jim's book will reach out everywhere. You must be very proud of him."

Mrs. Joyce looked at her for a moment and said, in the most delightful rich Irish brogue, "Indeed, I'm proud of Jim. He's a good man, a very good man, but he's got such a dirty mind." Saxe soon found his way to Sylvia Beach's book shop, Shakespeare and Company, on rue de l'Odéon. It drew him like a magnet, since it had been the gathering place for T. S. Eliot, Ezra Pound, Gertrude Stein, Sherwood Anderson, Ford Madox Ford, Ernest Hemingway, and others. There Saxe met again the young poet Hart Crane, whom he had known in New York through Saxe's sister Stella. Saxe brought him to our apartment for lunch. We would have liked to have gotten to know him better, but he returned to America, and eventually we heard the shocking news that he had committed suicide.

Our apartment soon became a place to visit. M. Eleanor Fitzgerald (Eugene O'Neill's guardian angel, whom he always called "Fitzi") brought Margaret Anderson, a vibrant woman who played such an important part in the publishing of *The Little Review* and who fought so zealously to further the publication of Joyce's *Ulysses*. People came from America and people came from England. Some stayed for weeks.

Now that *Dynamo* had been carefully gone over and typed, Gene wrote to Saxe: "Another favor. Will you mail the script to Madden [his agent] exprès recommandé?" Two copies went off to the Theatre Guild as well.

Gene was in a state of nervous tension. The situation between him and his estranged wife Agnes was still unresolved, and it looked as though it would not be settled for some time to come. He and Carlotta were eager to get away to distant lands, preferably to the Far East, to escape the constant strain of legal negotiations between Gene's lawyers and Agnes's, to say nothing of inquisitive reporters trying to pry into their lives.

Finally they did get off on the much longed-for trip, and on October 7, 1928, a note reached us from the boat. Carlotta wrote, "After the boat had left, I went into Gene's cabin to help him arrange his things and there and then we found the cable from the Guild saying they accepted *Dynamo*—all of them, and wished Gene 'Bon Voyage.' I had worried so long and was so at end [*sic*], I wept like a fool and could have died! But it was a divine sendoff."

We had messages from them from Saigon, Singapore, French North Africa, Morocco, and then a worrisome period of silence. In

early November a card came from Carlotta postmarked Hongkong
saying, "If you want noise and confusion come here. We are going
to Yokohoma because the Tropics is not healthful for either of us.
In Shanghai on Friday for three days—am glad we came, but
Europe best to live in."

Soon after the New Year, Carlotta wrote, "Here we are back in
Europe, and in spite of illness and rotten newspaper men, we had a
rich and marvelous experience. We have taken a lovely villa at Cap
d'Ail." Carlotta closed the letter by saying, "We hope before very
long to see you both, either in Paris or here."

The winter had been unusually harsh and had caused considerable suffering to many people in France. News from home was
quite alarming. Economic conditions pointed to serious trouble.
The voice of fear was echoed in every country in Europe. We heard
Americans in Paris say, "Perhaps we'd better go home." I, too,
began to worry, but I tried to conceal my anxiety.

We did go to the O'Neill's at Cap d'Ail. What a house that was!
While Gene and Saxe walked in the lovely garden, Carlotta showed
me about. Her cupboards were full of absolutely beautiful clothes,
linens, and jewels gathered on their Far Eastern trip. She then told
me she didn't have to go to Paris for her clothes. Poiret and
Mainbocher had mannequins made of her figure, and a bootery in
London had models of her feet. All she had to do was select the
material and design of her clothes and shoes and they would be sent
to her.

This was a glimpse into a world I never knew existed and for
which, I must confess, I had a momentary craving. But I was more
concerned with what Saxe and I might face on our return. We had
already written to Leon Gordon, telling him we were planning to
return to America in early June. By return mail, Leon asked us to
dismantle his apartment and have all the contents shipped to his
address in America. He, too, was beginning to feel the first sting of
depression that would soon grip America and the world.

What a time for Saxe to begin his career as an editor! But when
we returned to our apartment in Paris, Saxe found a letter from
Gene.

Well, I've been thinking over what services I can burden you
with in God's (?) country but I don't seem to grab on to much—
except that I can give you a line on what brand of chatter to
hand out to all and sundry of my friends who are doing so much

heavy worrying about my domestic future and the state of my artistic soul, etc. Of course, as far as how I am happy, etc., you can simply tell them the truth—that I am happy and doing no repining. My plans for living abroad henceforth you can divulge but not where I intend making my home. Say that I am undecided about that but probably it will be in France. Don't say anything about my gorgeous Renault—make it a small Renault. As for my plans for this coming summer, say that C and I are planning a honeymoon trip somewhere—probably to Greece— that was the last you heard. Say that I'm on a new play—not one of the trilogy—and you've heard the idea for it but it's a dead secret. Add that although I may have it finished by next season, it is doubtful if I shall want it produced then as I am determined to give more time to my stuff in future. Add to that whatever you may have gotten from all I told you that night as to the change in me in regard to living and working. Say that the failure of *Dynamo* left me cold—that I was not satisfied with it when I read it over on returning from the East and have worked on it for the book, putting in two new scenes I had originally planned for it. Lay emphasis on the change in my state of mind— my new-found content, etc. I rely on you, Saxe, to do all you can to set this boy right on all the bunk that has floated about.

There followed a list of people to whom the playwright sent regards, complaints, and requests. At the same time, Gene had written his publisher, Horace Liveright, recommending Saxe Commins as editor.

The Fall of Liveright

Soon after our return to America in June 1929, Saxe learned what a precarious state the house of Liveright was in. There were many reasons, and one must begin with Horace Liveright himself.

His personality was a composite of many traits, often in conflict with each other. He could be superbly generous, advancing large sums to authors, much of which was never earned. He could be cruel. He had a respect bordering on reverence for a gifted writer, yet he could treat a lesser one with disdain. He could be blatant and shallow in his egotism, yet he had a longing to be respected for what he was trying to accomplish, and his accomplishments were remarkable. At seventeen, while working as a clerk in a Philadelphia stockbrokerage, he wrote the prose and lyrics for an opera called *John Smith*. It actually went into rehearsal, but his backer went broke just before the opening. After a number of years of successful bond selling in Wall Street, he quit, lured away by his great interest in books. An opportunity came his way in 1917 when Albert Boni, who had had much publishing experience with his brother Charles, suggested to Horace Liveright that they join in publishing reprints of the classics—mostly modern. Liveright was very receptive to the idea.

This undertaking flourished, and grew from a dozen or more

titles to several hundred, and became one of the most popular
reprint series in the book world, the Modern Library. So successful
was this venture that Boni and Liveright soon began to publish
other books. Boni was eager to introduce and promote the works of
established European writers. Liveright was all for new books,
books that gave voice to current thought in America, and he was
willing to gamble on new talent. This difference in objectives
inevitably caused friction between the two men, and there came a
time when the breach could not be bridged. Boni left and Liveright
was free to advance his own ideas. But that freedom carried with it
the need for huge sums of money. Then began what became a
pattern: the acquiring of vice-presidents who could supply enough
financial backing to support Liveright's ideas—and what ideas they
were! In the midst of such long-established and unchallenged
publishing houses as Dodd, Mead and Company, Harper and
Brothers, Charles Scribner's Sons, and a number of others,
Liveright proceeded to open the doors to such authors as Theodore
Dreiser, Sherwood Anderson, Hart Crane, Robinson Jeffers,
Eugene O'Neill, Ernest Hemingway, T. S. Eliot, Ezra Pound, and
William Faulkner. Was there ever such a list in contemporary
literature in any publishing house in America?

Liveright fought against censorship. His battles with the Vice
Society in New York and the Watch and Ward Society in Boston
have gone on record. He helped to unshackle book publishing from
the hidebound traditions that held it in restraint.

What then brought the brilliant career of this important publisher and colorful personality to such an early end? There were a
number of contributing factors. For one, Liveright's interest in the
theater became his siren. He gave lavish and extravagant parties for
theater people and would-be patrons and dreamed of sponsoring
superb performances. He actually invested in quite a few shows.
Alas! They failed almost at their openings.

Liveright was warned that the well was running dry, and when
he looked about for a new vice-president, none came forward to
replenish it. He turned to Wall Street, hoping desperately to recoup
his losses. But, as he soon had to admit, the stock market was
"disastrous" for him. This, even before the crash in 1929.

In a letter to Eugene O'Neill in July 1930 he told of his plan to go
to Hollywood, ostensibly to present a carefully selected list of
books that would be good material for the talkies. But what

Liveright did not tell O'Neill was that he was no longer in control of
the publishing house he had founded. Earlier that year it had been
taken over by Arthur Pell, who was determined to restore the
firm's finances. Most of the staff remained; jobs were scarce.
Salaries were reduced to a minimum. New quarters were found at
31 West Forty-seventh Street, much smaller and certainly less posh.
The editorial staff was headed by Thomas R. Smith, an erudite man
with a true sense of literary values. Manuel Komroff, whose
friendship with Eugene O'Neill was of long standing, was both
editor and production manager.

Such was the state of affairs when Saxe came to present himself
at Liveright's—now called Liveright, Incorporated. It was immediately apparent to Saxe that he should seek work elsewhere. But
where? Some weeks later he ran into Donald Friede, a former
vice-president of Liveright's whom Saxe had met when Saxe's book
Psychology was published in 1927. Friede had recently joined
Pascal Covici in founding a publishing house, and he suggested that
Saxe accept a position in the editorial department.

Although a little heartsick not to be at Liveright's, Saxe soon
began working at Covici-Friede. In a short time he was entrusted
with some of the firm's important publications. For example, he
worked on Chaucer's *Canterbury Tales*, translated into modern
English by William Van Wyck and illustrated by Rockwell Kent;
Frank Harris's famous biography of Oscar Wilde, which included
Bernard Shaw's estimate of Wilde and also the hitherto unpublished final confessions of Lord Alfred Douglas. Saxe also worked
on C. F. Bulliet's profusely illustrated book on modern art, *Apples
and Madonnas*, and on *My Thirty Years' War* by Margaret
Anderson of *The Little Review*.

Saxe quickly found himself confronted by the many problems
that inevitably plague an editor. There was, for example, Valentine
Thomson, the daughter of a former French Minister of Marine
Affairs and a colleague of Aristide Briand. She came to Covici-
Friede with her manuscript about Briand, which was immediately
signed up for publication. Saxe felt that this book was not only
important but timely, because of the recent Kellogg-Briand Pact,
which repudiated recourse to war as a solution to international
controversies.

Meticulously checking the facts in Mlle Thomson's manuscript,
Saxe was appalled to find many factual errors and told the lady so.

She fought stubbornly over each correction and suggestion, and when Saxe pointed, toward the end of the book, to a flagrant statement that he could not possibly overlook, Mlle Thomson became so infuriated that she decided to call in someone else to assist her with the final pages of the book. Shortly after the book was published, not only Mlle Thomson but also the friend who had given her some minimal editorial assistance were awarded the Ribbon of the Legion of Honor by the French government.

I was in Rochester at that time (1930) awaiting the birth of our first child; Saxe wrote all this to me and ended his letter with "after all my work! Now laugh this off, if you can."

Interesting as all of these books were, they hardly sold. The market for books, as well as for everything else, was deplorable. It was a period in which fear spread into every phase of life and brought much suffering. I felt that I had to do something to supplement Saxe's paltry salary, especially now that we had a daughter, Frances Ellen.

In these years David Sarnoff, a friend of my parents, was establishing radio networks throughout the United States. I went to see him, and a few days later came his message, "Get busy and outline your program." For eight weeks each Sunday morning I played with the American Pro Arte Quartet. Then I began a series of programs entitled "Movements from Celebrated Sonatas for the Piano," which went on for thirty-nine weeks. I was asked to repeat this series. This I did soon after our son Eugene David was born.

Nearly a year after Saxe went to Covici-Friede, where he was none too happy, the opportunity came for him to transfer to Liveright's. Manuel Komroff was resigning his position there so that he could devote all his time to writing his own books. O'Neill sent his congratulations from Paris.

I was tickled to death to learn . . . that you have landed with Liveright. Your work there ought to be very congenial, as I know you will like all the bunch there. I know how you must have felt at the other place . . . It was fine of Manuel to use his influence with Liveright's in your behalf. Manuel, as I have always said since I first met him, is one rare person. His success with *Coronet* has pleased me more than anything I know of in a very long time.

Gene went on to accept Saxe's offer to handle his affairs at Liveright's.

Yes, there is something you can do for me at Liveright's—and
thus save a lazy man a letter. Alexander King has written to
me—a very hectic sort of note—in which he tells me he is dying
of cancer of the kidneys, but he hopes to live long enough to
finish the illustrations for *Lazarus Laughed*. Well, somehow I
suppose I ought to be awfully sorry, but something in the tone of
the letter makes me believe that Alex has heard how down I am
on his last illustrations for *Anna Christie* and that he is giving
me a little sob story to work on my sympathies. People with
cancer usually do not go writing letters about it to men they
hardly know. Or if they do, they shouldn't.

   At any rate, I want you to tell Pell I do not want King doing
any more illustrations—and I especially don't want him doing
Lazarus Laughed.

Though the period at Liveright's was a brief one, from 1931 until
the time of the firm's reorganization in 1933, Saxe was extremely
busy and happy. One of the first manuscripts he tackled was by
Professor Knight Dunlap of the Department of Psychology at Johns
Hopkins, *Habits: Their Making and Unmaking*. Then he worked
with Sherwood Anderson on his *Beyond Desire* and *Death in the
Woods*. Out of that experience came a warm relationship that
included Sherwood's wife Eleanor and me. It was ended only with
Sherwood's death in 1941.

From the time Saxe first met Robinson Jeffers in 1933 and worked
with him on his *Give Your Heart to the Hawks*, there flowered a
relationship with Jeffers and his wife Una. Saxe also worked at this
time with such fine writers as John Chamberlain (*Farewell to
Reform*), Horace Kallen (*Individualism*), and Peter Freuchen
(*Eskimo*).

I will never forget the evening when Saxe brought Freuchen
home to dinner. He was a tall, big-boned man with a long red
beard. Over cocktails before dinner, Saxe and Freuchen were
engaged in lively conversation, and I watched Freuchen as he kept
stroking his beard. He must have noticed this and asked simply,
"You like it?" Without much ado he pulled out of his pocket a small
pair of scissors and proceeded to snip off a piece of his beard and
hand it to me! After he left, I looked at the cutting and for the life of
me didn't know what to do with it!

Though manuscripts continued to be read, edited, and printed,
every person at 31 West Forty-seventh Street knew the future was
grim, and try as he might, Arthur Pell could no longer ward off the
impending financial crisis of Liveright.

Gene proved the kind of friend he was in a letter written from Sea Island, Georgia, in May 1932:

> About that jack [a loan]: Don't be a nut! I'll be "uneasy" if you think of paying it before 1942. Otherwise uneasiness on that score won't visit me. Forget it, Saxe! I tore up your meticulously businesslike note long ago. No such things exist between you and me. And I really owe that money to you for your service as Doctor Commins in Rochester long ago. So, in fact, in short, and finally, go to hell with your damned nonsense! I'm your friend, ain't I? That used to mean that what's mine is yours—and I'm old-fashioned.
>
> It's rotten about your having to take a cut—but I suppose it's on the cards these days. Wait until this income tax the great minds at Washington are contriving takes its cut at me next year—and we can go out with tin cups together! However, I'll have this home down here—and it's a peach!—paid for—and there are plenty of free fish, shrimp, and oysters around.

Yet if either of the friends had ever thought to balance accounts, it would have been difficult.

Saxe himself describes the fall of Liveright and how he and O'Neill made their escape and found a new home built on a firmer foundation. What follows is taken directly from Saxe's copious notes:

> When I brought the completed manuscript of *Mourning Becomes Electra* to the Liveright offices in 1931, there was a general dismay over the title. The then editor-in-chief, Thomas R. Smith, looked at the sheaf of papers, concentrated on the title page, played for a while with the long black ribbon on his spectacles, cleared his throat as a preliminary to uttering a shattering profundity, shook his white-thatched head and exploded the word "meaningless" with an implied exclamation mark at the end of it. As on cue, the editorial assistants and the publicity director embellished the verdict with even stronger adjectives, both commercial and semantic.
>
> Not until patient explanations were offered that the verb in the title was a synonym for "suits" rather than the active word for coming into being, were they relieved of their perplexity. Even then they grudgingly admitted that it made some sense, but not enough to identify such an exploitable property. They insisted, as publishers habitually do, that a book title must smite the beholder in the eye, whether it applies to the contents or not, and must, above all, be easily remembered.

The Liveright firm, as everyone knew but would not openly admit, was teetering on the brink of insolvency and it was hoped that the publication of the new O'Neill play would postpone the disaster for a while.

Fighting for that postponement with every stratagem at his command was an accountant, the new owner of the Liveright publishing company, Arthur Pell....

Pell counted heavily on the sale of 100,000 copies of *Mourning Becomes Electra* and not without reason or precedent. If this could be accomplished, the plus would replace the minus....

Strange Interlude had been one of the most phenomenal commercial successes in the history of modern play publishing. Approximately 110,000 copies, in the trade edition alone, had been sold, a figure no play by anyone but Shakespeare had attained until then. *Mourning Becomes Electra* became Pell's hope of coming out of financial mourning known by its mournful color as in the black. His subordinates merely hoped that the play would produce a lighter shade of red.

I had been working with O'Neill in his home in Northport, Long Island, and in subsequent visits worked on the galley proofs of *Mourning Becomes Electra*, omitting any mention of how much the publication of the play meant to the survival of the Liveright company. This reticence was not so much discretion as it was the lack of certainty about the danger signals; it would add to his anxiety on the eve of the publication and production, to learn that the work on which he was engaged so long might be jeopardized. So the matter rested.

Mourning Becomes Electra was produced and published in November 1931. Its immediate success eased the financial difficulties for a time. Alas, the earnings from the publication of the play were not enough to prop up the tottering house indefinitely. Matters went from bad to worse in 1932, after the brief respite provided by O'Neill's play, but we struggled along on its momentum until another stroke of publishing luck made a national best seller of *Washington Merry-Go-Round*, a savage critique of the Hoover Administration which at the moment was in as perilous a state as our own little regime, since both tried to ride out the depression.

In 1933 as that depression was approaching its nadir, our salaries were cut in half and from all sides creditors were clamoring for some sort of settlement from Pell. [Insolvency was imminent.] There was only the question of how long it would be postponed.

As O'Neill's editor I was very concerned about the large sums of money due O'Neill in royalties from *Mourning Becomes Electra* and his other plays. Worry impelled me to call a meeting of the principal stockholders and to place an ultimatum before them. Either a certified check covering all of O'Neill's royalties would be given to me within twenty-four hours or I would announce on the book page of the *New York Times* that O'Neill had decided to transfer his publishing program to any one of the five leading publishers of the country.

It was a staggering threat which . . . could be carried out, for I had a virtual power of attorney in O'Neill's behalf and had been authorized specifically to exercise my own judgement, as his editor and in the protection of his royalties.

Late that afternoon a certified check for the full amount due O'Neill was on my desk. The reason for the alacrity with which they submitted to my seeming blackmailing threat was that an announcement of O'Neill's intention to change publishers would precipitate bankruptcy proceedings among the many creditors. . . .

With the check safely in my possession, I took the train for Sea Island, Georgia, where Gene and Carlotta had established themselves in manorial style in Casa Genotta, a large home, architecturally Spanish, near the Atlantic shore, its name compounded from the given names of its owners to sound somewhat Iberian. On my arrival I merely turned over the check to Gene, saying as little as possible about the circumstances under which it had been obtained.

My visit was brief but pleasant. Gene brought a football and we spent many hours on the hard crusted beach throwing it back and forth. We swam often, I near the surf and he far out of sight in the ocean. We went for long walks along the shore, reminiscing about the old times and old struggles and a now romantically recalled poverty. Our companion on these walks was Blemie, a Dalmatian of aristocratic canine lineage, idolized and pampered by Carlotta and protected by Gene. Blemie's food was shipped from New York after consultation with animal dieticians. Special steel instruments were made for scaling tartar from his teeth. He slept in a made-to-order bed in the upstairs hallway. Sheets on this bed were changed at frequent intervals and a monogrammed blanket was provided for his comfort.

When I walked alone on the beach with him, it gave me a perverse pleasure to see him stick his aristocratic nose in the debris washed up by the sea or the offal of less privileged dogs. Years later, when he died in Danville, Contra Costa County, California, where the O'Neills were living in Tao House, . . .

(then it was the oriental period of their constant migration, after they had abandoned their French chateau near Tours), Blemie was buried on the estate with ceremonial grief and heart-rending wailing. A tombstone with a touching inscription was erected over his grave and Gene wrote an elegy in very lyrical prose for the departed dog.

From the isolation of Casa Genotta on Sea Island, with all its opulence, I returned to New York and its anxieties over little more than survival. On my arrival it was all too evident that the Liveright creditors were organizing to deliver the coup de grace. The blow came with suddenness and a fierce bitterness in April 1933, when Van Riis, the printer who staggered under a load of $280,000 due him, Herman Chalfonte, the paper supplier, and the Ace Paper Company, constituting the necessary legal triad, filed suit. The sum due authors in unpaid royalties added up to more than $150,000.

Pell could not stem such a tide of debt, although he marshalled all his forces. . . .

Arthur Pell emerged from the reorganization in control of all the remaining assets of the Liveright Company. In that list of assets was one item that provides an ironic note to the death scene. To particularize on this single item requires a discursive section characteristic of the writer who was involved. He, Theodore Dreiser, owed the decomposed company $17,000 for unearned royalties. These, by way of explanation, are monies advanced to an author until he can complete a work. . . . The weight of evidence was in favor of Pell and against Dreiser.

In the decade of the 1920s, when Horace Liveright was in possession of his senses, or more particularly his flair for sensational publishing, . . . virtually every best seller list was crowded with titles published under the Liveright imprint. In a single season Gertrude Atherton with her *Black Oxen* jostled Emil Ludwig and his *Napoleon* for national leadership. *The Story of Mankind* by Hendrik Willem Van Loon was cheek by jowl with Anita Loos's *Gentlemen Prefer Blondes*, and *Flaming Youth* by Warner Fabian (who in real life was Samuel Hopkins Adams) was compelling nationwide attention. Into this mixed company of successful writers came Theodore Dreiser who hitherto had to console himself for the apathy of the public with the approval of a few critics. His *An American Tragedy*, to his great surprise and profit, became a sensational best seller.

In one of his inspired moments, Horace Liveright had suggested to Dreiser that he write the story of a murder committed at Saranac Lake by one Chester Gillette, a lad grown up in abject poverty. Young Gillette had fallen in love and impregnated a girl from his own social and economic stratum. When he caught a glimpse of life a reach above his own position and dared hope to win the love of a maiden with a little more grace and a great deal more money than his first girl could even hope to possess, he was confronted with the problem, so to speak, of evading the issue. His solution had the fault of simplicity, he merely induced his first love to go with him for a canoe ride on Saranac Lake and there he hit her on the head with a tennis racket until she fell overboard and was drowned.

To Horace Liveright this was the perfect if bare outline of a plot that would reveal the predicament of the most ordinary of young men trapped in a common but all-too-human situation which could end in no other way than tragedy. What was the background of this young man? What was his psychological and social conditioning? Dreiser, taken by the idea, was confident that he could answer these questions in full and unsparing detail. He set to work in his lumbering manner to write the long, relentless, and powerful novel, in his unrelieved, naturalistic manner, about the simplest of American men in one of the oldest of the eternally human plights that brought in its wake his downfall and his death.

Upon its appearance, *An American Tragedy* immediately became a huge critical and financial success. Dreiser had the grace to inscribe one of the first copies to come off the press to Horace Liveright. Over the autograph he wrote an acknowledgement of his indebtedness to his publisher for providing him with the central theme and plot and outline of the novel. Horace was of course touched by this evidence of generosity.

As time went by and the book became more and more popular, Dreiser approached Liveright and asked him whether he thought there would be a possibility of selling it to a motion picture company for twenty or twenty-five thousand dollars. Liveright promised he would try, but instead of asking that sum he would attempt to get forty thousand dollars. Dreiser was elated and loudly sang the praises of his publisher—for the moment his agent.

Liveright, a shrewd trader, succeeded in raising the price not to forty thousand, but to ninety thousand. The contract for *An American Tragedy* was drawn up. But before the picture could be ready for production, a revolutionary event occurred in the movies. *The Jazz Singer* by Samson Raphaelson, with Al Jolson in the leading part, was made and shown; it was the first talking picture and, at a stroke, the silent movies virtually became obsolete.

Never having foreseen the possibility of talking pictures at the

time the contract for *An American Tragedy* was drawn up, the
so-called party of the first part had failed to mention this in the
agreement. Because of this lapse, the motion picture company
was obliged to buy the rights to the property all over again.
Dreiser was not only jubilant, but he was also very rich. At a
luncheon to celebrate his newly acquired wealth, Liveright
reminded him of the first modest proposal and his reaction when
Liveright suggested the doubling of the original price. Now it had
multiplied almost eight times. Calculating what the agent's
commission would have been, if there were an agent, Liveright
laughingly said Dreiser's debt to him would easily run into five
figures. Thereupon Dreiser picked up a cup of coffee and threw it
into Liveright's face!

Before this time, while *An American Tragedy* was at the height
of its popularity, Dreiser proposed a new novel to Liveright; it
was to bear the title *The Stoic*. Arrangements were immediately
made whereby the author was to receive a stipend of $100 per
week as an advance against royalties ultimately to be earned by
this embryonic but still highly putative novel. Announcements
of its forthcoming publication were printed in catalogue after
catalogue, season after season, but no manuscript was in
existence. My conscience is still disturbed because I wrote an
announcement describing a book no one had even seen. In 1947,
fifteen years later, *The Stoic* was published under the Doubleday
imprint as a posthumous novel, born two years after the author's
death.

In the early 1930s, however, the weekly payments of $100 had
accumulated until they aggregated $17,000—and still no manu-
script. Promptly and conscientiously, Horace Liveright had paid
the weekly sum and it was continued even after he was ... out
of the business he had established and conducted so brilliantly, if
erratically. After the Wall Street crash in 1929, broken in spirit
and in health, his money lost and his prestige faded, humiliated
and abandoned, Liveright was forced to relinquish the publishing
house that bore his name.... Wild ventures in the stock market,
the theater, in Hollywood—all went against him and brought
about his downfall. His friends ignored him, his flair was
gone—he was unwanted and dispossessed. Within a few years,
he was dead.

In 1933 ... all the assets of the [reorganized Liveright firm
were bought] for five cents on the dollar. One of these assets,
now transferred to the new owners, was the $17,000 advanced to
Theodore Dreiser for the still undelivered manuscript of *The
Stoic*. The foremost American realist could discharge this obligation in one of two ways; he could repay the money or submit the

new novel. Unfortunately for him, no such manuscript was then in existence. Accordingly, Pell sued and asked in his bill of particulars for the money or the novel. The court having learned that there was no manuscript, had no alternative but to order Dreiser to meet his obligation and turn in $17,000.

Dreiser set up a hue and cry, wrote articles on the infamy of the courts, stooped to virulent anti-Semitic attacks and let himself be used as a figurehead by American communists. His appeals to the public and more persistently even to the courts were unavailing. The verdict stood and he had to pay the full sum. He could well afford it. His income and investments were enormous!

At that particular time Dreiser was at work on a book that in a manner reversed the title of his most successful novel and was published as *Tragic America*. Working with him was not exactly a rewarding collaboration. He was obstinate, truculent, and totally lacking in courtesy. There was always the dread of what he might say in a moment of pique and, afterwards, the even greater dread of what the critics were always certain to say about his inaccuracies, his ponderousness of style, and his juggernaut assault on the simplest of declarative sentences. Grammar was violated and syntax slaughtered.

Insistence upon realism does not preclude carelessness. While editing *Tragic America* I flagged twenty-seven references that were either manifestly or suspiciously libelous. It is part of my job to call such passages to the attention of the author and publisher, so that they would at least be aware of the possibility of law suits and perhaps heavy damages. The usual procedure in such cases of possible libel is to consult a lawyer expert in the field of literary infringement and learn from him whether the questionable reference comes within the meaning of the law. Generally his decision is based upon his own confidence in his ability to defend what might be considered libelous in a court of law. Damage done by a word or phrase or a passage or even the entire context is difficult to determine, but an egregiously harmful statement is usually omitted or modified. Even the truth under some circumstances can be libelous.

When Dreiser saw the twenty-seven passages I had marked for possible libel, he erupted into a volcanic rage, demanding that I be dismissed at once and calling me names that even he wouldn't allow to be printed in his novels. My only defense was that I would have been remiss if I had not at least marked the dubious passages which might or might not cause trouble and that no harm could come from being cautious or even captious.

Then I suggested that, to be on the safe side, we should submit the manuscript to Gustavus Myers, author of *History of the Great American Fortunes*, from whom Dreiser himself had obtained much of the material for his book. Myers, a gentle and meticulous man and the author of many books that undermined the reputations of numerous men in high places, had never been involved in a libel suit, in spite of the explosive nature of his revelations.

Dreiser was amenable to the suggestion and we arranged with Myers that he examine the manuscript for libelous statements, for an honorarium of twenty-five dollars. His report uncovered not twenty-seven libels, but thirty-four, seven of which I had overlooked. As anybody could have foreseen, *Tragic America*, when published, received a well-deserved chastisement from the critics and a shrug of indifference from the American public.

There is no gainsaying that Dreiser was a pioneer in the American literary movement in realism, even if this movement arrived in our country twenty-five years after the battle for it had been fought and won in Europe. His *Sister Carrie* certainly marked a decisive event in the history of the native novel at the turn of the century. Against the stern taboos and prejudices of that time and even against the attempt at censorship on the part of his own publisher, more to the point the publisher's wife (Mrs. Frank Doubleday), Dreiser struggled almost single-handedly for the right to interpret through the novel a truthful, if stark, reflection of human experience.

It is possible that Frank Norris, if he had lived longer, would have earned the honor of freeing the American novel from its heavy burden, for *McTeague*, *The Pit*, and *The Octopus* prepared the way and gave direction to Dreiser's work. It would be difficult indeed to dispute Dreiser's earnestness of conviction and his clumsy but irresistible power. It does not follow, however, that a novelist of historic importance and a writer of great influence need be a man of character or sensibility. If the realist influence does nothing else for an editor, it shatters the romantic illusion that a writer must perforce be an able thinker and a discriminating critic of his own or other's works. Association with men whose gifts outweigh their mentalities or characters raises many marginal queries about the sense and sensibility of some men of letters.

It was in this atmosphere of tension, suspicion, and conflict that the Liveright [insolvency] proceedings reached their climax. Just before the end came, all employees were given notice of dismissal, salaries were abruptly stopped and the seemingly rational activities required for giving form to ideas in books came to a dead end.

I consoled myself that O'Neill had collected all his royalties
just before the debacle and that Dreiser would have to pay the
$17,000 he had garnered on the promise of producing a manu-
script that was still the figment of a blurb-writer's imagination.
Unfortunately for all the other authors under Liveright's banner,
they were able to realize only [a very small] percent of the
royalties due them.

To a writer whose earning powers at best are meager, such a
settlement is just short of a catastrophe. Most severely punished
were Drew Pearson and Robert Allen, authors of *Washington-
Merry-Go-Round*. Their topical political book, published
toward the end of the Hoover Administration, had had an
enormous success. It caught the public fancy because it reflected
the nation's dissatisfaction with a regime that compounded its
ineptitude with indifference. More than 100,000 copies were sold
to a public avid for revelations about the powerless party in
power. The authors received approximately one-twentieth of the
money due them.

Quite as severe was the penalty imposed on the Liveright staff;
it was [disbanded]. T. R. Smith, editor-in-chief, an old man now,
still believing in the genteel tradition of publishing, was shorn
not only of his security, but also of his dignity. Without any
financial resources or prospects, he could only look to a bleak
future; he was unwanted. For a while he subsisted on the sale,
item by item, of his library, preponderantly volumes of erotica.
All the passion spent, he died in loneliness and abject poverty.

Julian Messner established his own publishing company and
Leane Zugsmith devoted herself to free-lance writing. Louis
Kronenberger, by far the ablest member of the group, became
drama critic for *Time* and the author of many distinguished
books on some principal figures of the eighteenth century. It was
my good fortune to work with him several years later in another
place and in happier circumstances. His many-faceted, sparkling
mind earned my profound admiration.

Aaron Sussman, that anomaly in advertising, an idealist,
established his own agency and is now the representative of the
world's leading publishers. Albert Gross, Liveright's production
manager and the most companionable of men, created a place for
himself with the firm of Coward-McCann and continued his
interest in Yiddish literature as critic and translator. He died of a
heart attack only a few years after the reorganization.

My own outlook was somewhat brighter. Virtually every
publisher in America hovered over the Liveright legacies, eager
to inherit whatever of value of the company's assets. The most
desirable of these reside in the continuing contracts with estab-

lished authors and this property, so called, becomes free under
bankruptcy. That is to say the writer is then at liberty to choose a
new affiliation. Existing contracts are abrogated and the author
can seek the shelter of a new home.

The most highly coveted "property" at that time and under
those circumstances was Eugene O'Neill. Out of generosity and
loyalty he made it plain that he would sign no contract without
my counsel and consent. Furthermore, he wanted it stipulated in
writing that no arrangement to publish his plays could be made
unless the agreement included a clause which guaranteed me a
job as his editor and a general editor of the company of his choice
for the duration of his contract. To this latter condition, I
raised an objection on the ground that I might conceivably
embarrass him and that he should not under such circumstances
be bound to me or I to him. O'Neill saw the reason of this
precaution and agreed that a literary alliance is, at best, a
hazardous venture. He insisted, however, that I remain his
editor.

At once virtually all the publishers in New York began to court
me. I went to Sea Island to lay before Gene all the offers that had
been made and tried to assay their worth in terms of advantage.
My preference was for Bennett Cerf and his company, Random
House and the Modern Library. The reason for that choice was
that I had known Bennett professionally during the Liveright
days and recognized in him the potential of an imaginative,
resourceful, adventurous and most trustworthy publisher. From
my first meeting with his partner, Donald S. Klopfer, I was
impressed by his quiet competence, his reliability, and his good
sense. Subsequently, through a quarter-of-a-century of daily
association I was to learn of his many attributes, not the least of
which is his complete selflessness.

O'Neill suggested that Bennett fly down to Sea Island to
consummate the arrangement and this was done in an atmosphere of mutual trust and friendliness. With the signing of
the contract, a separate agreement was drawn up which provided
for my employment as a general working editor for Random
House for a three-year period, and I began my work on
9 July 1933.

Thus was born the trade publishing activities of Random
House and thus began a relationship that endured for twenty-five
years, a time of struggle and passion and growth, until the
infant, come into maturity, is now a formidable figure in
its field.

3 Early Years at Random House

When Saxe joined Random House as an editor, their catalog for fall 1933–34 had already carried the following carefully worded announcement about James Joyce's *Ulysses*: "Provided that this book is cleared by the courts, it will be published in November 1934 in a complete, unabridged edition, with a new introduction by James Joyce. The directors of Random House are sparing no effort to remove the ridiculous ban on this great book, and a favorable verdict is confidently expected." *Ulysses* was published in 1934, complete and unabridged, with a reprint of the historic decision by Judge John M. Woolsey, whereby the federal ban on the book was removed once and for all. *Ulysees*, of course, became an immediate best seller.

One of the first projects with which Saxe was involved at Random House was Gertrude Stein's *Four Saints in Three Acts*, which was published in late 1934. The play had been set to music by Virgil Thomson, and the operatic version was presented in New York earlier that year.

It is difficult not to be bewildered, to say the least, by *Four Saints'* total disregard of accepted form. Gertrude Stein's insistent and repeated statement that in all her writing she has striven to

create the perfect sentence, leaves one wondering where in her
works it is to be found. Here are the opening lines from *Four Saints
in Three Acts*:

> To know to know to love her so
> Four saints prepare for saints
> It makes it well fish
> Four saints it makes it well fish
> Four saints prepare for saints it makes it well fish it makes
>   it well fish prepare for saints

Of course no book of hers could be edited. The most Saxe could
do was to make sure everything she said went in and see to the
pagination in logical sequence. For example, the title reads *Four
Saints in Three Acts*, but suddenly, toward the end of the book,
there appears act IV, containing scenes II, III, IV, and V. When
Saxe, a little puzzled, called Miss Stein's attention to this, she
looked at him and said, "My dear, you simply don't understand."

She and her devoted companion, Miss Alice B. Toklas, toured
the United States in 1934–35, and wherever they went they were
given the red-carpet treatment. On their return to New York, Saxe
asked Miss Stein what she thought of Hollywood. Miss Stein
replied, "I have many opinions about Hollywood, but what is more
important is that Hollywood has had its first glimpse of a real
genius."

As was to be expected, there were many stories about her
floating about. One in particular was told to me by the ebullient
Bennett Cerf. "It was during this time when 'a rose is a rose is a
rose' was being quoted all over the country, so when I sent
Gertrude a small royalty check (and it was a very small one, in
fact), I had it made out to 'A Stein is a Stein is a Stein.' Back came
the check with a note from Gertrude that did not have to be
deciphered at all. It read, 'Dear Bennett, Cut out the nonsense and
send me a proper check immediately. Love, Gertrude.' "

Perhaps as a result of Hollywood's exposure to a "real genius,"
Saxe was offered a fabulous salary, a house with all its trimmings,
and the leisure to work undisturbed by a representative of that
colossus Metro-Goldwyn-Mayer. The reasoning was that Saxe
would be invaluable in redeeming and converting scripts into
motion picture material. Even at this early stage in his career as an
editor, his reputation had attracted the attention of one of the
moguls of the motion picture industry, perhaps the very one who

had glimpsed Miss Gertrude Stein and immediately run to discover
who her editor could be. Saxe was flattered but turned them down.

19 April 1935

Mr. Bertrand Bloch
285 Central Park West
New York City

Dear Mr. Bloch:
    I need not tell you that I was deeply touched by your
consideration in writing me as you did this morning. It was
extremely thoughtful of you to bear me in mind in connection
with the Metro project. However, in all fairness to you, and to
myself incidentally, I cannot and really do not wish to make any
change. Even if the Metro job paid more money and would give
me every assurance of permanence, I still would be obliged to
forego even a definite offer in view of the loyalty I owe Random
House. More important than anything else to me is the fact that I
am extremely happy where I am. The work is congenial and my
employers, Bennett Cerf and Donald Klopfer, are men for whom
I have the very highest regard and devotion. In the year I have
been with them they have proven time and again their faith in me
and I can do no less than justify that faith by continued loyalty.
    I want to make this very clear to you simply because, as I have
said, I was profoundly touched by your consideration of me. If
there is anything I can do for you, you have but to command.

Sincerely,
Saxe Commins

It is an editor's task to write a report on manuscripts that are
considered seriously for publication. When Gertrude Stein's *All
Wars Are Interesting* (the title was changed to *Wars I Have Seen*)
reached Saxe's desk in 1944, after France had been crushed and
Hitler had let hell loose on the world, Saxe read the manuscript
with a sense of outrage he could not restrain.

Manuscript: *All Wars Are Interesting*
Author: Gertrude Stein
Reader: SC

    No doubt we will publish Gertrude Stein's new book. No
doubt we will get a great deal of amusing and irrelevant
publicity. No doubt it will sell many copies to those who expect
another *Autobiography of Alice B. Toklas*. And there is no

doubt whatever that few who buy the book will trouble to read it through or examine with any critical sense what she tries to say. For once, I would like to try to put aside the usual scoffing at the impenetrability of Gertrude Stein's style and devote myself to the task of analyzing the essence of such thought as is hidden under the repetitious dress and the painful echolalia of her writing. The easier way would be to confess at once that it is impossible to find out what she is writing about, that she is mumbling to herself and that she is kidding the whole world. The harder way is to accept the challenge to get under her style and take a peek at—let's say—her substance.

To read through her entire manuscript is an experience similar to taking the drop-by-drop water torture. Repetitious sentences hammer on the brain with a monotonous thud that makes you want to scream in agony, and if you are searching for content analytically, the most that anyone can read at a time without shrieking with nervous exhaustion is ten to fifteen pages.

The professional thing to do is to examine this book without prejudice and try to arrive at some fair conclusions about the contribution in thought that Gertrude Stein has to make. Here is the evidence, stripped of all stylistic considerations.

Actually Miss Stein records life under German occupation which, on her own word, was not entirely unpleasant. To make her point, she has a theory that the twentieth century couldn't begin until the Germans were vanquished and thrown out of France. Everything prior to that belongs to the nineteenth century. The meaning of this is, according to her, that the nineteenth century was dominated by Darwinian ideas on evolution and that [it] belonged to some vague concept of realism. Non-realism now is finished with science and needs it no more. It is dismissed by a Steinian edict.

Mixed up with this misconception of the contribution of science is a vague concept of the differences between the medieval and the modern mind—none of which she troubles to make clear. Words and concepts are used casually and irresponsibly to suggest a philosophical position which is not a position at all but a succession of pronunciamentos made without any consistency or responsibility. At any rate, ideas are thrown out at tangents and buried in such a mess of verbiage that nobody except an editor would trouble to shovel it off.

She tells of the wars, which she has found interesting, beginning with the Spanish-American and Boer Wars, coming through the Russo-Japanese War, the First World War, the Spanish Civil War, and finally World War II. Not once is there a sense of

outrage or indignation or protest. Never is there a hint of the
social, economic, and political forces which were responsible,
but there is only the repetition and the insistence that this war is
"funny"' or "interesting" or "extraordinary." At the very worst,
this war is "disturbing." To her, wars are either "nice" or
"interesting" (page 5). Her conclusion of the grim tragedy that
France went under in six weeks is, "That is what makes them
changeable enough to create styles" (page 8). This is a summary
of her point of view on the fall of France.

At no time during the occupation did Gertrude Stein lack for
food or comfort. Her advice to French boys who were about to
be deported to Germany as slave laborers was as follows: "All I
could say was to try to study them and learn their language and
get to know their literature. Think of yourself as a tourist and
not as a prisoner" (pages 37–38). Later in the book it develops
that some of these boys escape and join the Maquis. Miss Stein's
interest in noting the activities of the Maquis concerns not so
much their courage and sacrifices, but her own untouched
reactions to the phenomenon of Frenchmen dying. Yet, in all
fairness, when she deals with the Maquis toward the end of the
book, one can guess that they were heroic, in spite of the
subjective account of them given here.

On the subject of collaborationists, she is incredibly tolerant.
Bernard Fay, who was given all the Nazis could offer, including a
very high post, is referred to by Miss Stein in this manner: "They
have just told me that Bernard Fay has gotten very fat, that must
be potatoes" (page 43). When Bernard Fay presents the Vichy
point of view, Miss Stein explains it with no sense of outrage
whatever (page 91).

On the question of anti-Semitism, especially in reference to the
Dreyfus case (see pages 55 *et seq.*), there is presented the most
utterly ridiculous nonsense, with this conclusion, speaking of the
Jews: "Anyway financially there is no sense in anti-Semitism. For
other reasons yes but financially now and today they are
insignificant."

When it comes to the question of Vichy, she just urges her
readers not to worry, the government of 1943 "can be anything
and if it is it can change to anything else and after all what
difference does it make except to the people in power. It certainly
does not make any difference to anybody else ever, certainly
not" (page 69). Her defense of Petain (pages 88 *et seq.*) is made in
the following terms: "I always thought he was right to make the
armistice, in the first place it was more comfortable for us who
were here and in the second place it was an important element in

the ultimate defeat of the Germans. To me it remained a miracle...." "Marechal Petain then did save France.... he was an old man and he just had to wait and he spent every day and all day waiting but very actively waiting, etc." (page 93). For further justification of Petain, see page 106.

On republics: (105) "The fashion is the fashion, and republics simply republican republics are going to be the fashion. You can see that the nineteenth century is dead, quite dead" (page 106).

Thus, on the subjects of the reasons for the war, the attitude of the collaborationists and the meaning of France's historical role, her thought, upon examination, is at best reactionary and at worst reprehensible. I have notes of instances too preposterous for credence in which she proves that England is at war because they made the mistake of naming their king George. All wars in which England participated broke out during the reign of a George (page 124). She seriously gives credence to the prophecies of St. Odile. Her superficial and really ignorant statement about German music associated with her success as a nation doesn't deserve comment (page 105). Nor do her dicta on jazz related to unconditional surrender which, she says, has nothing to do with war, make any sense (page 111).

On Laval, the worst she can say is that he has "fidelity but not loyalty" (pages 175–6). When she refers to the collaborationists as "poor darlings" (page 197) it's almost as serious as saying, as she does on page 94, that Europe is too small for a modern war. The facts here are more or less against her.

Of course, few people will trouble to seek the thought hidden in the rubbish heap of words thrown together incomprehensibly, but there is plenty of evidence, if one is foolish enough to try to dig it out, that Gertrude Stein has missed completely the meaning and the tragedy of the greatest cataclysm of history. All it did was to disturb her comfort!

Fortunately, her point of view will influence or persuade no one beyond the narrow circumference of her cult. To those who see in this war tragic consequences to the living and to generations of the unborn, the most charitable thing that can be said of this book is that it reveals the essential shallow mindedness of a woman who is indifferent to a world cataclysm while she remains absorbed in her own private word game—a word game that assumes no responsibility and is as emotionless and meaningless as it is at times offensive.

It's time a little moral indignation, instead of sycophancy, was aimed at Gertrude Stein.

Of course, the book was published in 1945, and the opinions of reviewers were indeed diverse.

I can imagine that a number of people will have their teeth set on edge by Gertrude Stein's recollections, *Wars I Have Seen*— just as I can imagine that others will enjoy the exercise of running through her sketchily punctuated but more lucid than usual sentences for the curiosity and amusement of seeing where her thoughts arrive. . . . The irritables will find plenty to fume at. In her first person singular Miss Stein is as discursive as she is egocentric. Her chronicle meanders rather like Salvador Dali on a bicycle; yet it is always clear in its focus, for in the meandering the world is seen to be revolving around Gertrude Stein. [Edwards Weeks, *Atlantic*, April 1945]

Miss Stein's narrative of her experience is beautiful and very moving in parts, with many marvelous simple stories. She is at her best when she creates an atmosphere of terror by little unpretentious strokes. Since 'it is very funny the way everybody and anybody may feel about anything,' we need not wonder to find that many funny things are also said by Miss Stein, who is not just anybody, about France and the war, which are not just anything. [Jean Wahl, *New Republic*, January 19, 1945]

Saxe never regretted having resisted the lure of Hollywood. As a matter of fact, he turned them down a second time—once again in his old role of ghost. As director of the Modern Library, Saxe's attention was arrested by the following letter.

17 December 1936

Mr. William Makepeace Thackeray
Modern Library
New York

Dear Mr. Thackeray:

We have read your recent book *The History of Henry Esmond, Esq.* and believe it possesses material adaptable for motion pictures.

We are recognized agents for writers at all studios and as such would like to represent you in the sale of both your own personal services and your literary products.

In the event you have already made a commitment to some agent for the above book, we nevertheless are impressed with your potential possibilities as a screen writer and would be interested in both your services and future stories.

We would appreciate your advising us by return mail whether or not you are represented here in Hollywood; and in the event that you are not and desire us to represent you, we would be happy to forward to you a copy of our agency agreement with writers for your information and guidance.

Cordially yours,

———

Saxe could not resist replying. He was sorely tempted to give as Mr. Thackeray's permanent address Kensal Green, a cemetery in the northwestern part of London:

Dear Mr. ———:

Thank you for your letter telling me that you believe my recent book, *The History of Henry Esmond, Esq.*, possesses material adaptable for motion pictures. This effort is a rather crude attempt, I fear, but I am now working on a novel which I think will be a natural for the pictures. I am thinking of calling the new book *The Virginians*.

I will be interested in hearing what you think of the title.

Sincerely yours,
William Makepeace Thackeray

The next years were to be banner ones for Random House. One book after another of vital interest in many fields was being brought out. Aside from the Theatre Guild anthology of current productions and the complete edition of sixteen Pulitzer Prize–winning plays, there were new editions of the old masters of poetry, drama, and essays: Pushkin, Blake, Donne, Coleridge, Hazlitt, and Shakespeare. Contemporary poetry was not over-looked with the poems of Robinson Jeffers, Louis MacNeice, C. Day Lewis, W. H. Auden, and Stephen Spender among those published. Saxe was much involved in all this work. Auden, Spender, and Lewis had been students together at Oxford University, and the three of them were Saxe's friends.

In the late 1920s the Soviet government inaugurated the First Five Year Plan, designed to transform Russia from a backward agrarian country to a forward-going industrial nation. To achieve the goals set by the plan, the people's strength and endurance was pushed almost to the breaking point. It was with the intent of recording his impressions of this period and the crucial years that followed that

Maurice Hindus, a journalist and author of five books on Russia, undertook a journey to that country. Before Hindus's departure, Saxe stressed to him how keen everyone was for an eyewitness report on the day-to-day life of the people.

A little more than three years later Hindus turned in his manuscript. He had named it *Moscow Skies*. Most eagerly, Saxe began reading. He pulled up short, however, when he came to a love scene. Hindus was describing a young man and his girl in a moonlit arbor, and the young man was saying, "My darling, I love you as passionately as I feel for achieving my quota of the Leather Cooperative." Saxe could not refrain from saying to Hindus, "Now look here, Maurice, you've been in love; I've been in love. One doesn't say such things at such ecstatic moments!" Hindus sat quiet for a while—then exploded! "What do you know about love? What do you know about the Russian soul?" "O.K.," said Saxe, "it's your book. But I urge you to think twice about that section."

Louis Fisher, the noted foreign correspondent and writer, spoke of having seen a good deal of Hindus in Moscow at that time and said of him: "Hindus has a tremendous capacity for warmth and affection. He participates in the sufferings and joys of others. Doubts frequently torment him, as they do all of us; but when they tormented him, he was disconsolate and grim and yearned for a heart-to-heart talk with a kindred spirit. In Markoosha [Mrs. Louis Fisher], Maurice occasionally found that kinship. They would then take down their souls and had a wonderful time."

For some time Saxe had been concentrating on building and expanding a publishing list devoted to the classics and to the physical and natural sciences. The first successful venture in the classics was the joint effort of Professor Whitney Jennings Oates of the Department of Classics at Princeton and Professor Eugene O'Neill, Jr., of the Department of Classics at Yale, in editing *The Complete Greek Drama* (two volumes), which was published in 1938. Out of this sprang a wonderfully warm relationship between "Mike" Oates and Saxe that never diminished. Saxe, of course, had known Eugene, Jr., since he was a youngster. Eugene O'Neill, Sr.'s, pride in his son's achievement was enormous. He often spoke of it to Saxe, saying, "He'll redeem his old man yet."

In the mid-1930s there was evidence that America was beginning to rise out of the desolate state of depression. With the election of Franklin Delano Roosevelt as president in 1932, there had been a return of confidence. During his first term (1933–36) Roosevelt had done much to mitigate the utter despair that had gripped the nation. In 1937, from these years and his years as governor of New York state, Roosevelt selected some of his notes and commentaries, his addresses and press conferences, and expressed the wish that they be published. He consulted with Judge Samuel T. Rosenman, who had been his counsel during his administration as governor in Albany. Judge Rosenman later wrote in a letter: "I interviewed several prospective publishing houses—Random House was the one selected. Mr. Bennett Cerf introduced me to Saxe, told me about his abilities and experience and said Saxe would be the editor. Thereafter Saxe and I worked very closely on every step of the preparation and final printing of the five volumes."

Twice Saxe was called to the White House for consultation with President Roosevelt. Despite a very tight work schedule, with a number of other books due to go to press, Saxe worked steadily on Roosevelt's papers. No week-ends for rest, no time off during the summer of 1937. This stupendous job was begun in the early spring of 1937, and in the spring of 1938 the publication of the five volumes was announced by Random House. The titles of the volumes were as follows:

1. *The Genesis of the New Deal, 1928–1932*
2. *The Year of the Crisis, 1933*
3. *The Advance of Recovery and Reform, 1934*
4. *The Court Disapproves, 1935*
5. *The People Approve, 1936*

Soon after the books came off the press, Saxe received a set from President Roosevelt with the inscription, "To my friend Saxe Commins from Franklin Delano Roosevelt," and a set to each of our children inscribed, "For Frances Ellen Commins," and "For Eugene David Commins."

In 1941 Saxe was working on Elliot Paul's *The Last Time I Saw Paris*. Elliot's *The Life and Death of a Spanish Town*, an intensely moving account of the horrors of the Spanish Civil War, had been published in 1937. In his letters to Saxe, Elliot's strong democratic and antifascist views are clearly revealed, as in this one written from Hollywood.

I have been over this so many times that now the galleys have gone away, I am in doubt as to whether three points have been made clear or whether they have been obscured or omitted in the shuffle.

1. I want to be positive that the item concerning Blum's partner's and his son's graft in connection with contraband supplies sold for exorbitant prices to the Spanish government is included.

2. I want to be certain that Henri-Haye's connection from the outset with the Cagoulards and his intimate relationship with Otto Abetz, the chief German spy in France, is specifically stated.

3. I wish also to be absolutely certain that our own State Department's connivance with Chamberlain to strangle the Spanish Republic by denying arms to the Republicans in contravention of all international precedent and decency is unequivocally set forth.

There are only two Fascist leaders left whom it is possible for our State Department and local Fascists to appease. Number One is Franco, Number Two is Petain, and true to form, our authorities and reactionaries and Catholics are as busy as bees appeasing this pair up to the last possible moment, which may occur before you receive this letter. It is just as sure that before this book is in print Franco will have joined the Axis wholeheartedly and Petain will have tried to turn over the French fleet and the French African army for Hitler's use, as it is that Random House still deals in books. Do not let anyone be deceived by Petain's talk about regrets and resignation. That is part of the show to preserve the French people's faith in the "hero of Verdun," while they are being hoodwinked by Darlan and Laval. There is so darn much appeasement going on everywhere that I will not be a party to it for the sake of prudence or to attract book clubs or gain large sales. I am sure Bennett will feel the same way about the situation if he understands it.

Please check up on these matters before the galleys are broken up into pages and do the necessary in case we have omitted references to the three other points I have just reviewed. The name of Blum's partner you can obtain from Jay Allen or Luis Quintanilla. Please do so.

I am getting increasingly anxious about Steinberg's sketches. I should have received them long ago, and if he is unable to do the job in time, please wire me instantly and I will have an artist here make the sketches so that I can check them before they are forwarded. I hope this will not be necessary.

P.S. Please tell Bennett that it may mean everything to us to get three sets of corrected galleys out here at the earliest possible moment. I have two influential producers definitely interested in

making a picture and as soon as I have a chance to talk with
Orson Welles I am positive that he can be added to the list. To
get action and competition I must have these proofs for my
personal use, in addition to the work being done by William
Morris. The producers in question are Victor Saville of MGM
(*Goodbye Mr. Chips, A Woman's Face*, etc.); Lewis Milestone,
who releases through RKO (*All Quiet On The Western Front,
Farewell To Arms*, etc.).

Orson is very friendly and receptive to ideas and needs new
material not of the run-of-the-mill. I think, in this one instance, I
shall break my life-long aversion to salesmanship and do a little
scouting on my own.

That was written at the end of December 1941, just a few weeks
after the United States entered World War II. Today, the indignation sounds as naive as the idealism. Only the jockeying to arrange
a movie sale (accompanied, of course, by a hatred of salesmanship)
has not changed.

Elliot, unlike many authors, was a generous man. In the same
letter he thanked Saxe for the "amazing job," underlining the
statement "I feel that I should name you as co-author of the book"
and going on to specify, "since it is as important to leave the wrong
things out as to put the right things in." In the latter connection,
Saxe had earlier advised Elliot against including certain material:

Because two-thirds of the manuscript is now at the composi-
tor's, you will see why it will be necessary for you to make
insertions in the galleys themselves. I refer, of course, to the
section on the couturiers or anything else you might want to add
to the chapter on Western Culture. My own feeling about it is
that fascinatingly as your tabloid history of dressmaking reads it
is piling Pelion on Ossa. There is a danger in this chapter of just
being encyclopedic and doing some injury to the unity of Part I
by the inclusion of wonderful material but a little afield. By this
reasoning you could also have a dissertation on wine culture,
mineralogy, and all the arts and metiers. My point is that I'd
rather see this chapter touch only the peaks, as it does, than to
make it a display of general information on subjects that in
themselves are damned interesting. However, you must be the
arbiter and there is time to include a section on dressmaking or
anything else when you get the galleys.

I come now to the diagrams indicating the swing of the
political pendulum from Right to Left. Graphic as it is, I honestly
do not believe that it adds much to the political meanings you

have conveyed in your prose. Included, it would give a text-bookish impression. It seems to me that everything you want to convey is so completely represented in the views expressed by your characters and, more especially, by the political alignment on the rue de la Huchette that the chart would be an author's intrusion. For this reason alone I urge you to let me exclude it.

While making these suggestions, Saxe could also write:

I am so obsessed by everything in the script that I am living on the rue de la Huchette twenty-four hours a day and nobody can find me at Random House or on Madison Avenue. I am convinced that all your readers will feel the same way. That's why I am so insistent on keeping the focus on the street and its wonderful people.

Elliot was a remarkable personality—most charming and articulate, a gourmet, a bon vivant with a heroic capacity for drink. After World War II he moved to a farm in Connecticut. Disliking telephones but wanting to have some quick means of communication with Saxe and Random House, he arrived one day, straining under a large wooden crate from which soft cooing sounds emanated. Saxe looked up through the glasses at the end of his nose.

"What have you there, Elliot?"

"What in hell do you suppose I've got? Carrier pigeons, that's what!"

A selection of O'Neill's plays had been published in 1932 by Liveright. Prior to the book's appearance, Gene had been very concerned about the choice of editor. He was aware that George Jean Nathan was eager to serve in that capacity. His friendship with Nathan dated back to the time when Nathan and H. L. Menken had been editors of the magazine *Smart Set*. Nathan had also been the drama critic of that magazine. Gene had sent them three of his early plays—*Ile, Long Voyage Home,* and *Moon of the Caribbees.* To Gene's utter surprise the plays were accepted for publication. *Long Voyage Home* appeared in the October 1917 issue of *Smart Set*, and *Ile* and *Moon of the Caribbees* appeared the following year.

Though Gene never forgot that Nathan had championed him in the early days, he did not let that cloud his opinion of Nathan as a critic. That it troubled Gene is evident in this letter to Saxe:

Dear Saxe:

This in haste to supplement my wire. I object to Nathan in this instance because when a volume including as many plays as this is put out it will stand in everyone's mind as representing the whole significant trend of my work—and, between us, I don't like leaving such a choice to Nathan. In spite of my friendship for him and my respect for his judgment along many lines, I by no means believe, or have ever believed, that he is any infallible critic of my work or has a comprehensive understanding of its inner spiritual as opposed to its material outer dramaturgical trends. He has too many (frankly confessed by him) blind spots. He is too Latin—rationalistic, skeptic, sentimental in the influences that have moulded his critical viewpoint. He is antipathetic to all plays with a religious feeling (he liked "Brownie" [*The Great God Brown*] for its other aspects), all plays involving any tinge of social revolution. He liked *The Fountain, Gold!*, and he despised *Lazarus*, totally misunderstood what I was driving at in *Dynamo*, thought *Hairy Ape* was radical propaganda and disliked it for that, considered *Desire* imitation Strindberg. I will say nothing about the many Nathan conceptions of life he had read into my plays and praised to my irritated amusement.

Don't misunderstand this as any panning of Nathan or any lack of gratitude for all the fights he has made for me. I'm only saying things about his criticism that I've often said in my arguments with him.

And on practical grounds I think with a case of this kind it's always a mistake to do the obvious thing that everyone accepts without interest as predetermined. Nathan is the obvious thing here. It's poor business, it has no imagination, no drama in it. The only comment on his clause and his foreword will be: "Of course, old stuff." And I think it's bad policy from Liveright's as well as my end to always have Nathan as a sponsor. If he were the only prominent "critic" who appreciated my works—but there are plenty of others—Krutch, Young, Altmore, Gabriel, W. P. Eaton, etc., etc.

My suggestion is to let me select ten plays. In a couple sentences of foreword—no more—I would say my selection was based on my good judgment and what the best critics all over this world had said about either production or the printed play. Then I would suggest that the Book of the Month ask one prominent American critic to do a short appreciation of a single play—ten critics for the ten plays—such appreciation to include a dire panning of the rest of my work by comparison, if this critic felt that way about it. I append a list of my selection of plays and possible critics for each play. This, of course, is tentative. By looking up your press records and old jackets you could probably add greatly to the list of alternative critics for each play. Let every critic appreciate his pet play as *the* best, that's the idea. Brown, for example, and Woollcott would probably say kind words about *Jones* or *Glencairn* if they were allowed to add that all my work since then has been trash. You get my idea? Difference of opinion, clash, argument ensuing, fresh interest and angles from the public and press standpoint—with my choice of the plays as the background.

If this thing is worth doing, it's worth doing well. Trouble is with any organization like the Book of the Month, too lazy to take trouble—do the obvious—and lose out.

Or if Book of the Month won't do this then I suggest choice of plays to be made from consensus opinion of one poet (Robinson Jeffers, say), one novelist (Dreiser or Lewis), one historian (Beard or Adams), one dramatic critic (Krutch or Altmore or Young or—endless list of possibilities), and one psychologist (White or Jelliffe or—another endless list) and our publisher (?). And Nathan do the foreword.

The above second suggestion is just a dashed-off suggestion and may have nothing to it. What I'm after in this suggestion is to get away as far as possible in the choice matter from arbitrary choice by one dramatic critic whose opinion is already well known followed by foreword by same critic. Sabe? The list of plays is to be submitted to parties to have all long plays on it except ones I barred. Of course, it's doubtful if you could find one person in each class who had read or seen the plays! But some other scheme along these lines might be thought out. The good point about such a consensus scheme is that no one but the boobs would regard such a selection as having any real artistic authority! Whereas it would be interesting and comment-provoking.

But I suppose this is all useless talk. The contract is signed, isn't it?—and that's that—and the Book of the Month will do the obvious thing, entailing the least amount of effort, thought, and imagination.

As ever,
Gene

6 Marco Millions—Atkinson or John Macy or Gabriel
9 Strange Interlude—Nathan or Littel or Krutch or . . .

10   Mourning Becomes Electra—Krutch or Young or Mason
       Brown
 2   Emperor Jones—Brown or Woolcott or Eaton
 3   Hairy Ape—Young or Gabriel or Eaton
 1   Glencairn—Woolcott or Anderson or Brown
 8   Lazarus Laughed—Mumford or De Casseres or Krutch
 5   Desire Under the Elms—Barrett C. or Krutch or Gabriel
 4   All God's Children—Lewisohn or Nathan or Krutch or . . .
 7   Great God Brown—Nathan or Krutch or . . .

Select critics who are also authors of books by preference—give
them credit for that authorship under their article.

The result of O'Neill's unhappiness was a compromise. O'Neill
himself became editor, *Glencairn* was scrapped, and the plays were
presented in chronological order. The book was entitled *Nine Plays
by Eugene O'Neill.*

4

Eugene O'Neill: *Ah, Wilderness!* to *Long Day's Journey into Night*

Mourning Becomes Electra, which appeared in 1931, had been the last of Eugene O'Neill's plays to be published by Liveright. After its successful production, the O'Neills left New York, where they had been renting an apartment, and moved to Sea Island, Georgia, into a house that they had had built on property fronting the ocean. Gene began work on a theme that had been haunting him—the failure of materialism and science to bring man the spiritual peace he was seeking—and which had drawn him into an exploration of religion. He tried to incorporate his ideas into a play which he then called "Without Ending of Days" and which in its final form was to be called *Days without End*. But the work was arduous and disappointing. The writing had become too involved, too personal.

In a letter to Saxe dated January 3, 1933, he wrote:

"Without Ending of Days," on which I have sweated blood, has reached a third draft—and there it seems likely to stop forever unfinished. It has run itself into all sorts of blind alleys and exhausted me mentally and physically to the point where I've had bad nervous indigestion—a new one for me! I am thoroughly disgusted with it. See no way out and think I will junk the damn thing—see what it looks like a year or two years from now—and after a rest now, start at something else. I have plenty

Sea Island, Ga.
Jan. 3rd 1933

Dear Saxe:

Just to add a word or two to what Carlotta has written you re "Ah, Wilderness!". The sub-title really indicates in exactly what spirit this simple, sentimental comedy — with undertones, oh yes, with undertones! — was written, and the nostalgia for our old lost simplicity and contentment — and youth! — it expresses. I woke up one morning with this play fully in mind — never had had even a line of an idea about it before — title and all. Immediately laid aside "Without Ending Of Days", on which I was laboring, and started writing this. It simply gushed out of me. Wrote the whole damned thing in the month of Sept. Evidently my unconscious had been rebelling for a long time against creation in the medium of the modern, involved, complicated, warped & self-poisoned psyche and demanded a counter-statement of simplicity and the peace that tragedy troubles but does not poison. The people in this play are of the class which I get least credit for knowing but which I really know better than any other — my whole background of New London childhood, boyhood, young manhood — the nearest approach to home I ever knew — relations, friends of family, etc. all being just this class of people.

And, of course, there is the intention in the play to portray the startling difference between what we Americans felt about life, love, honor, morals, etc. and what we are conscious of feeling today.

I got immense satisfaction out of writing this play — and I feel a great affection for it — so great that I don't know whether I'll ever subject it to the humiliation of production or publication — For me it has the sweet charm of a dream of lost

Letter to Saxe from Eugene O'Neill, January 3, 1933, concerning *Ah, Wilderness!* and *Without Ending of Days*

youth, a wistfulness of regret, a poignantly melancholy
memory of dead things and people — but a smiling memory
as of those who live still, being not sadly dead.

If you know what I mean —

Not that any of the people in this play are
portraits of real people. Rather they are each portraits
of many people.

Secrecy in this case, Saxe, above all others! Don't
let a soul know a damned thing — even that you
have it! You will appreciate why.

"Without Endings Of Days", on which I have sweated
blood, has reached a third draft — and there it seems
likely to stop forever imprisoned. It has run itself into
all sorts of blind alleys and exhausted me mentally &
physically to the point where I had bad nervous
indigestion — a new one for me! I am thoroughly disgusted with it. See no way out and think I will
junk the damned thing — see what it looks like a
year or two years from now — and after a rest now
start something else. I have plenty of other ideas, God
knows. The whole experience with this opus has been
very discouraging. I've worked so damned hard on
it and given so much intense thought & energy — with
such confusing results! But I suppose that's all in
the game.

I'm enclosing a check with which I want you to
get something as a gift for my translator-supervisor from
me. You will know what she would like. I would not
insult her by attempting to pay her for her kindness
but I would like to show my grateful appreciation
some way. Please express my immense gratitude to her
when you write! She has been a peach about this
and I will never forget her kindness! Would she like
a complete set of my books, duly inscribed & autographed,
do you think? If so, send them to me from Liveright.
Charge to me, give me her name & I will do the
rest.

Carlotta joins in love to you, Dorothy & the kids.

As ever,

Gene

of other ideas, God knows. The whole experience with this opus has been very discouraging. I've worked so damned hard on it and given so much intense thought and energy—with such confusing results! But I suppose that's all in the game.

In the same letter, he joyously tells Saxe about another play, *Ah, Wilderness!*

I woke up one morning with this play fully in mind—never had had even a hint of an idea about it before—title and all. Immediately laid aside "Without Ending of Days," on which I was laboring, and started writing this. It simply gushed out of me. Wrote the whole damned thing in the month of Sept. Evidently my unconscious had been rebelling for a long time against creation in the medium of the modern, involved, complicated, warped & self-poisoned psyche and demanded a counter-statement of simplicity and the peace that tragedy troubles but does not poison. The people in the play are of the class which I get least credit for knowing but which I really know better than any other—my whole background of New London childhood, boyhood, young manhood—the nearest approach to home I ever knew—relatives, friends of family, etc., all being just this class of people.

And, of course, there is the intention in the play to portray the startling difference between what we Americans feel about life, love, honor, morals, etc., and what we are conscious of feeling today.

He got, he said, "immense satisfaction out of writing this play—and I feel a great affection for it—so great that I don't know whether I'll ever subject it to the humiliation of production or publication." In the end, however, both *Ah, Wilderness!* and *Days without End* were produced and published. In fact, the printed texts appeared simultaneously with the production of the plays by the Theatre Guild of New York in 1933. Soon afterward, *Ah, Wilderness!* was engaged in a forty-week tour throughout the country, with George M. Cohan in the leading role.

Days without End, which Gene called a modern miracle play, aroused considerable controversy because of its religious content.

The O'Neill's Sea Island home did not prove to be the idyllic retreat they had hoped it would be. The sultry, stifling summers, with their dampness that enveloped the interior as well as the exterior of their house, were more than they could endure.

The fall of 1936 saw them on their way to the Northwest, in the direction of Seattle. For a time they thought they would establish residence in the area of Puget Sound. Surely, here they would find the privacy they were seeking.

They had hardly been there a month when word reached Gene that the most coveted award, the Nobel Prize, was about to be bestowed upon him. Soon the O'Neills were deluged by reporters, cables, telegrams, and every kind of message, and of course the people of Seattle wanted to pay homage to their distinguished visitor. But the O'Neills evaded them all and set off for California.

During their stay in San Francisco, Gene was quite ill and had to be hospitalized for a long period. That imposed rest, however, did much to bring about a good recovery. Even the tremor of his hands subsided considerably, so much so that he became more than eager to get started on a work that he so intensely felt had to be written—*The Iceman Cometh.*

The O'Neills bought a tract of land in Danville, Contra Costa County. While Carlotta busied herself with architects and builders for their new house, Gene immersed himself in the writing of *The Iceman Cometh.* When he reached the final draft in 1940, he showed it to Saxe, who was a visitor in their new home, Tao House.

Gene and Saxe went over the draft word for word. Then Saxe typed it and took it back with him to be placed in the Random House vault.

Soon Gene undertook the tormenting task of unburdening himself of the sad, tragic saga of his family. In the writing of this, Gene undoubtedly was undergoing every phase of purgatory, as is evident in his letters to Saxe. These letters began to arrive in a steady stream, urging Saxe to pay another visit. Gene wrote, "I am feeling lousy, cum laude, to say nothing mentally." In another letter he said, "Be sure and come—seeing you again would be worth more than an ocean of medicine to both of us semi-invalids in Tao House." Saxe went in January 1942, and his notes on O'Neill contain the following account of his visit.

Another Journey

A letter from Gene dated 4 November 1941 read in part: "I've written no less than seven—count them!—detailed outlines for non-cycle plays this year. All grand ideas, too, I think. But I can't seem to decide which I want to do first. Too much

Sea Island,
Ga.

Jan. 1933.

Dear Sara:

I've wanted ever since to write the note inscription in "Zenda," to come — and stay well, to say — to Mrs. ... ideas at once. I remember too well now from all you used to say about her. Up to your letter, I hadn't placed her as David's niece, wife of Maurice.

Thanks for what you say of "The Silversmith." I have been bewildered by arguments to prove or ... what — I feel. You see, it's not a simple little play, no moving effect of great tragic drama, and its whole importance and really depend on its conveying a mood of memory, its quiet, its

Letter to Saxe from Eugene O'Neill, January 1933, concerning *Ah, Wilderness!*

distraction in the air. Too much tragedy. And my health uncertain. It's hard to settle down to the hard labor of day-to-day plugging at one thing. Want you to read *Long Day's Journey into Night*. Better than *The Iceman Cometh*. Best thing I've done or ever can do, I believe. But it will have to wait until you come here. Only one typed copy—and anyway this is a play I don't want to send anywhere or have anyone read for the present, except three or four people. No one except Carlotta has read it." At the end of the letter, Gene added, "Try and come out!"

Just before the beginning of the Second World War, and for several years preceding, O'Neill had put aside the most formidable undertaking that he had envisioned as the nine plays which were to constitute the Cycle that was to cover a little more than a century of American life. He was then possessed with the idea that possessions debased and corrupted their possessors and finally dispossessed them. What he had already written—one full play, *A Touch of the Poet*, outlines and notes running to 125,000 words, scene sketches and snatches of dialogue—had been shelved for more insistent work. There was indeed too much distraction, too much tragedy and always, uncertain health.

Of the non-Cycle plays, the two which have since contributed most to the O'Neill revival are *The Iceman Cometh* and *Long Day's Journey into Night*. Among the lesser plays of that period are *A Moon for the Misbegotten*, published in 1952 and produced in May 1957, and a one-act play, *Hughie*, still in manuscript form.

The earliest opportunity to leave New York for California came in January 1942. Arrangements were made at Random House whereby I could remain with the O'Neills until work on the manuscript of *Long Day's Journey into Night* would be completed and I could return with the finished play.

At Oakland, California, I was met at the railroad station by Herbert Freeman, a one-time South Carolina football player and for many years man servant, chauffeur, and family retainer of the O'Neills. He had been with them since their Sea Island days and was worshipfully devoted to Gene. When we arrived at Tao House in Danville, Contra Costa County, I was greeted with cordiality, with a shy warmth from Gene and a visible relaxation of her habitually imperious manner by Carlotta.

For the sixteen days of my visit rain fell almost constantly and we were virtually prisoners in a palace. When the sun appeared from behind the grim clouds for a little while, we walked about the spacious estate up a narrow trail to the crest of a hill from which there was a spectacular view to the northeast of mist-veiled Mount Diablo, an imposing mountain peak of the coastal range. We seldom ventured beyond the trestled entrance to the road leading to the house.

Only twice did we leave the grounds. The first time was when Gene was driven to Oakland by Freeman for treatment by his physician and I went along for the ride, and the second when we celebrated the completion of our work with a dinner party for three in San Francisco. Otherwise we remained in isolation and devoted ourselves during the daytime to our labors, I at typing four copies of *Long Day's Journey into Night* from the version mentioned in Gene's letter. This typescript bore many interlinear additions and corrections in Gene's microscopic handwriting. While I pecked away with two fingers on the typewriter, Gene occupied himself with other scripts in his study and Carlotta, a compulsively fastidious housekeeper, busied herself with her own chores. By way of a break in this routine, I took Blemie, the pampered Dalmatian, for long walks in the rain so that he could add his drop to the deluge. At night we played "Sorry" for the standard stake of a quarter a game or we sat in front of the fire and talked about a remote world going up in flames. Such news as we heard on the radio was bleak and disheartening. America had been at war for a month and the bulletins from two fronts were then dismal. They repetitiously announced setbacks and withdrawals on land and sea. Rigid blackouts were in force on the West Coast for fear of Japanese assaults by sea and air.

A single item unrelated to the war was frequently interpolated between the official and unofficial communiques from Europe and Asia. When it came over the air, the dial of the radio was quickly turned off and we and the instrument remained silent. It concerned the recent marriage of Charles Chaplin to Oona O'Neill, an event which had been publicized as more of a national than a personal matter.

Oona had visited her father at Tao House a year or so earlier and at that time had created a most favorable impression, both for her young and startling beauty and the gentle shyness of her behavior. She had made her appearance after a separation of many years and seemed at first a stranger, but by the end of the visit she had so quietly and ingeniously overcome her own and her father's feeling of remoteness that little by little she was reinstated as a member of the family.

But what had occurred not long before my arrival transformed this newly earned admiration into fierce resentment and made Oona an unmentionable pariah in her stepmother's eyes.

We—Gene, Carlotta and I—were acutely aware as we talked

in front of the fire that we were cautiously circumventing the subject that had been so sensationally reported in newspapers and on the radio. What was uppermost in our minds remained unexpressed as we exchanged views about the progress of the war, especially in terms of how it had altered our previously held pacifist convictions, or talked on the circumference of ideas to avoid approaching the center.

Never one to repress her anger for long, Carlotta was the first to break the tacitly agreed pact and burst forth into a diatribe that began by quoting from *King Lear* and continued with some maledictions that were never dreamed of in Shakespeare's vocabulary. She bitterly blamed Oona's mother for exploiting her child for her own gain in a deliberately mercenary campaign. First it was to thrust the child into shameless publicity as a cafe-society celebrity and then to maneuver her into making what was then known as the "Number One Deb," a dubious honor which implied a marketable beauty and availability for a rich marriage. And now, to cap the whole odious program, according to Carlotta, the mother accomplished her goal. . . .

It was impossible to decide whether Gene was more embarrassed than miserable by these violent accusations; he was certainly concerned about the plight of his daughter. He disliked Hollywood and all its works, and in his eyes Chaplin represented a great artist who had been corrupted by the exaggerated importance given to the movies and their self-deluded stars. He remained silent while Carlotta elaborated on her bill of particulars against Chaplin and seemed to be brooding unhappily over the choice his daughter had made. As a matter of fact, he had seen little of Oona since she was a child and ten or twelve years of close association between father and daughter were lost to both of them. Her visit after so long a lapse made them both self-conscious and uncommunicative. Yet Oona must have carried it off creditably, if only by her childlike simplicity, and Gene filled with an unexpressed pride in the beauty of the daughter who was a stranger to him.

When talking privately with me he declared that fatherhood meant less to him than to most male parents because he had only remote emotional ties with his three children. He had not seen Eugene Junior until he was twelve years old and only felt the first stirrings of parental pride when his son began to make his mark as a classical scholar. As for timid Shane, his other son, he felt a hopeless bafflement and a distant kind of anxiety.

Shane had been a visitor at Tao House before my arrival and from all accounts, particularly Freeman's, a bad time was had by all. The confused and lonely lad, eager for his famous father's attention and affection, was ignored. Carlotta was aloof and insisted on rigid palace discipline. Only Freeman befriended the troubled boy. He would drive him into San Francisco, and Shane, free for a while from restraint, sought excitement and escape at the then current Golden Gate International Exposition. He even managed to shake off the benevolent watchfulness of Freeman in order to drink surreptitiously and a little ashamedly. Freeman, however, knew all the time what the boy was up to and kept it a secret to spare him remorse and, what is worse, a severe upbraiding from Carlotta.

Many after-the-fact authorities on human behavior are able to explain to their own satisfaction how the emotional disturbances of adolescence and maturity are born of infantile rejection. They speak sagely of traumas and hostilities, and they try to persuade the victim that a verbal catharsis will eliminate these poisons from the depths of the unconscious.

Whether the genesis of Shane's addiction to narcotics in young manhood had its early impetus in an unfulfilled need for affection and that severest of youthful deprivations, the sense of being unwanted, or even in a congenital strain that was reasserting itself after having skipped a generation, is all highly speculative. As persuasive a case can be made for simple and inexplicable accident and plain bad luck. For those who seek supernatural explanations, it is a poetic convenience to invoke the Eumenides and blame his plight on the pursuing furies. Whatever the origin, the penalty of suffering was Shane's.

Whether Eugene Junior's fate was worse or better, it at least had finality and a complete riddance of pain. He, too, had visited his father in 1941 and had brought with him his then wife, whose welcome at Tao House was a little less than cordial. She was a huge woman and, from Carlotta's accounts, none too orderly. That alone earned for her severe criticism.

At the time young Gene was under the stress of double trouble, academic and marital. When both were brought under the roof at Tao House, the tension was compounded. Carlotta, always outspoken, stirred up the simmering conflicts with her bluntness. Gene, however, retired beyond the barriers of silence, wishing that he could be left alone to work in peace and perhaps wonder privately about the triple problems of his children.

During his visit, Gene Junior was permitted to read the original version of *Long Day's Journey into Night*. He did so, to my certain knowledge, because on his return to New York he came to my office and mentioned it in great secrecy, confiding in me also about the unhappiness of his California holiday. After a bitter account of his treatment at Tao House, he unburdened himself to me of his accumulated hatred of Carlotta. Then, walking on Park Avenue, he took up where he had left off at my office the tale of his bitterness. Nonetheless he added that there was ample compensation for all his misery in the realization that his father had written by far the most deeply felt tragedy among all his plays, *Long Day's Journey into Night*. His praise was extravagant but manifestly genuine.

Not a word was said between us about his father's insistence that the play be neither produced nor published until twenty-five years after his death. He may or may not have known of the existence of a legal document bearing such a stipulation. If he knew, he would have mentioned it, since there was no secrecy between us concerning the play. The likelier possibility is that he did not know because he talked of the problems of producing and casting as if there were a great urgency in bringing the drama before the public. He certainly did not know that a legally worded statement was already reposing in the Random House safe, attached to the final version of the manuscript. It set forth Eugene O'Neill's wishes about posthumous production and publication a quarter of a century after his death.

Six years after Eugene Junior's death and after *Long Day's Journey into Night* had been published and produced in 1956, an interview with Carlotta in the *New York Times* attributed Eugene O'Neill's strict instructions about the play to the undue influence of his dead son who persuaded his father, while in California, to make the twenty-five-year restriction out of consideration of family sensibilities. At the time of the interview neither father nor son was alive and could not confirm or deny the allegation. The dead are beyond offering testimony.

It is hardly likely, in any case, that the son could have influenced the father who always made his own decisions in the theater and in his books. Certainly no word was said to me in the early months of 1942, when I was a guest at Tao House, concerning young Gene's having ever broached the subject.

Then was the time when I was given explicit instructions as to the means by which O'Neill would assure postponement of production and publication of *Long Day's Journey into Night* until twenty-five years after his death. More than once he made his wishes known to me in conversation, and before I left I was asked to have Mr. Horace Manges, attorney for Random House, draw up a document which would embody those wishes. This was to state in legal terms that the manuscript of *Long Day's*

Journey into Night should be sealed and kept in the custody of Random House until twenty-five years after the demise of Eugene O'Neill. This was to be my first task on my return to New York.

At that time the visits to Tao House of Oona, Shane, and Eugene Junior were in the past and mine was in the then present. The eye of memory in casting a backward glance captures images that are likely to be distorted. A defective instrument at best, the selective eye of memory chooses its own impressions. It compensates and corrects itself with the aid of hindsight and inevitably brings into play those psychological forces which bolster one's need for self-exculpation and even self-aggrandizement. It may well be that the tricks memory plays on us are defense mechanisms whose function it is to preserve what's left of one's egotism. In any case, what it sifts out of the past is usually what one prefers to remember.

To avoid that trickery of memory, adherence to a simple catalogue of facts about my own visit and its sequel may reveal something of the history of the play which in all likelihood will occupy the attention of literary commentators for many years.

My stay at Tao House was pleasant and congenial and made unselfconscious by affection. Gene and I worked steadily and, I like to believe, to good purpose. When questions were raised about vague or indecipherable words or phrases in his minute handwriting, they were answered patiently and painstakingly even if the queries were captious or preposterous. Discovery of an inconsistency or unconscious repetition or the suggestion of a transposition or change in syntax or accent always brought out how amenable Gene was to recommendations and grateful for a second, objective eye. He never seemed to mind how irrelevant or absurd an editorial comment might be because he was convinced that the chances of overlooking anything would thus be reduced. Unlike many writers, he was not so blindly in love with every word he had written that he would want to slur over possible imperfections in what he cherished most. Even observations which showed my own stupidity were welcomed because they provided an opportunity to explain and clarify intent and effect.

In this manner we worked together for more than two weeks and often during that time the subject of posthumous publication and production was discussed. *Long Day's Journey into Night*, he had become convinced, should be kept from the public until everyone involved, particularly the members of his family, was dead or old enough not to be hurt or even disturbed by it. After debating various lengths of time, he fixed a period of twenty-five years after his own death for publication and production. The time lapse settled, he asked me to have a legal statement embodying his wishes drawn up when I returned to New York.

Four typewritten copies were made of the play, two for deposit in Washington with the Register of Copyrights, one for himself and one for me to carry back to New York for safekeeping in the Random House vault. It should be explained that plays in manuscript form, unlike books of fiction and nonfiction, qualify for copyright as unpublished works and may be registered therefore at any time before publication.

Our task completed, I left Oakland on "The Lark" for Los Angeles on the night of 8 February 1942, carrying with me one copy of *Long Day's Journey into Night*. My stopover in Los Angeles was prolonged beyond my expectations because of a sudden death in the family and I remained two days longer than I had intended in order to attend the funeral. Immediately after it I left for New York.

There I consulted with Horace Manges, making known to him what O'Neill required, and asked him to draw up a document which would explicitly set forth his wishes concerning the post-humous publication and production of the play. When he had the statement formulated, it was mailed to O'Neill for his signature.

29 November 1945

Random House, Inc.
20 East 57th Street
New York 22, N.Y.

Gentlemen:

I am this day depositing with you, on condition that it not be opened by you until twenty-five years after my death, a sealed copy of the manuscript of an original play which I have written, entitled *Long Day's Journey into Night*.

I should like to have you publish this play under the same terms as those set forth in our agreement dated 30 June 1933 (in which you are referred to under your former corporate name of The Modern Library, Inc.) as amended and extended, except, however, in the following respects:

1. Publication shall not take place until twenty-five (25) years after my death.
2. No advance shall be payable prior to said publication date, at which time an advance of Five Thousand Dollars ($5,000) shall be paid.

3. Copyright in the United States and Canada shall be taken out in your name.
4. Where the term "Author" is used in our prior agreement, it shall, after my death, apply to my Executors or Administrators, to whom all payments hereunder shall be made.

If the foregoing terms are acceptable to you, will you kindly sign and return to me the enclosed copy of this letter.

Sincerely yours,
Eugene O'Neill

ACCEPTED: 29 November 1945
RANDOM HOUSE, INC.
By (signed) Bennett A. Cerf

On the return of this letter, signed, from California, it was attached to the carefully wrapped and heavily wax-sealed package containing the typescript of *Long Day's Journey into Night* and deposited in the Random House safe. There it remained undisturbed with a copy of a one-act play entitled *Hughie* for twelve years. No one was permitted to touch or move it. The secret of its contents remained sealed with the five people who had read it—the author, his wife, his son, the critic Russell Crouse, who was allowed to examine O'Neill's copy on the occasion of his visit to Tao House, and myself.

When, after his death in November 1953, Eugene O'Neill's will was probated in Boston on December 24 of that year, it was revealed that he had disowned his two surviving children, Shane and Oona, and had named his widow as his sole beneficiary and executrix. The sentence cutting off his two children read: "I purposely exclude from any interest in my estate under this will my son Shane O'Neill and my daughter Oona O'Neill Chaplin and I exclude their issue, now or hereafter born."

The reason for this exclusion was incomprehensible at the time and gave rise to surprise and wonder. But it was not long before the mystery was solved.

In mid-1954, Bennett Cerf, president of Random House, was called on the telephone by Carlotta O'Neill and asked whether he had read the copy of *Long Day's Journey into Night* which had been hidden for so many years in the company safe. To this he answered that indeed he had not because he was not allowed legally to do so and therefore he had never so much as seen nor opened the package; the seals were still intact and he had no intention of breaking them. In reply to this, Mrs. O'Neill said she wished he would read it at once because she wanted it published as soon as it was possible to do so. Before Cerf consented to read

it he wanted, he told her, to think about the matter and would
then call her back.

He immediately consulted with me and asked my views. I
suggested that he learn from our lawyer, Horace Manges,
whether this violation of a dead man's wishes would be legally, if
not morally, condonable, and second, that he insist upon a
public statement, to be printed on the jacket and within the book
itself, signed by the widow, to the effect that publication rights
were granted with her full authorization. The last suggestion was
offered with the view of averting the possibility that Random
House or Bennett Cerf might be accused of vandalism. We were
clearly faced with the alternative of undertaking publication with
clean hands or relinquishing our right to do so altogether.

When Cerf communicated this decision to Mrs. O'Neill, she
exploded with fury and vented most of her wrath on me,
accusing me of having instigated a plot against her, of having
ruined all the O'Neill plays on which I had worked with him and
charging me with about as many crimes as are included in the
penal code. To which, with characteristic loyalty, Cerf replied in
a letter that was as gratifying as it was bolstering to my vanity.
This letter alone, if I could live up to it, was a solace for my hurt
inflicted by the unforeseen termination of a nearly forty-year
friendship. For Cerf's act of devotion I hold him in high esteem,
but even in greater respect for his determination not to compromise his principles as a publisher by violating a dead man's
wishes.

We were shocked when we learned from our attorney that a
strict interpretation of the law provided that the instructions of
the deceased may be superseded by those of the *sole* beneficiary
and executrix of a will. Therefore Mrs. O'Neill was within her
legal rights if she caused to be produced and published a play for
which there had been a legal, if no longer binding, stipulation
against such a publication or production. There was no mention
of the restricting document or the wish itself in the will.

At last the mystery was solved. Now it became clear why
Eugene O'Neill had been *induced* to disown his two surviving
children. Had they been legitimate heirs in the eyes of the law,
the widow would not then have been sole beneficiary and the
claim, within a strict interpretation of the law, to the right to
produce and publish *Long Day's Journey into Night* before the
stipulated time, which would have been in 1978, would have
elapsed.

Astounded and bewildered by this development we could not
at first let ourselves believe that, legally or morally, such a

flouting of a dead man's wishes, explicitly stated in a signed document, would be permissible or justifiable. Unfortunately, we were laboring under moral illusions only, but our legal misapprehensions were more decisively against us.

Lawyers for Mrs. O'Neill overruled our naive contentions and confirmed the opinion of the attorney retained by Random House. That made it unanimous. Two distinguished members of the Boston Bar, successors to many colleagues who had been hired and fired by the relict of the playwright, called on Bennett Cerf to reach a determination about the publication of the posthumous play. Their errand was quickly accomplished; Cerf relinquished all rights to publication.

These counsellors were the successors to Mr. Melville Cane, poet and essayist and an able and trustworthy lawyer, one of the many who had served their terms and been rejected. Long ago Cane and I had had a brief encounter in which at first I was the victim of his client's wrath. He was to feel its lash much later.

For more than ten years Mrs. O'Neill and I had maintained in our joint names a large safe-deposit box in the Manufacturers Trust Company which had its banking offices at Fifty-seventh Street and Fifth Avenue. In it were stored many manuscripts, certificates of stock, mementos and some rather expensive jewelry. During the time the O'Neills lived in France and California, letters, cables and telegrams came to New York asking me to remove certain items from the box and ship them wherever they were at the time. Sometimes I was asked to add things to the contents of the box. But no article of mine was ever placed in this receptacle, nor did I ever have occasion to use it for my own purposes. The reason for the joint rental of the safe-deposit box was so that I could always have access to it and deposit or withdraw anything the O'Neills might request.

Once an anxious series of telegrams and letters came from Mrs. O'Neill. She was nervously concerned about the loss of some valuable jewelry. Reference to the inventory of jewels locked in the box revealed that they were quite safe and intact. Her telegram on receiving the good news expressed happiness, relief and gratitude at my having found them where they were all the time. There also came the request to ship all the jewels in the safe-deposit box in the bank to California by registered mail. This was done and the acknowledgment of their receipt was in the language of rejoicing.

During the first of two separations between the O'Neills—once when his arm was broken and then his leg—I received a peremptory letter from Melville Cane. He demanded that I

relinquish my key to his client's safe-deposit box and made the
statement that my access to it was not only questionable but also
suspicious. The implication was that I planned to make off with
its contents. To this letter I replied with a bitter reproach to him
for impugning my honesty and also with a full explanation of the
circumstances under which the box had been rented and used for
more than a decade. The key was enclosed with the letter.

Gene was in Doctors Hospital at the time convalescing from a
fractured arm. I brought him Cane's letter and the carbon copy
of my reply. He was furious. Then, with a broad grin on his face,
he asked me whether we had in our offices printed rejection slips
for manuscripts that were not worthy of a personal letter. When
I told him we had such standard forms and used them only for
the utterly hopeless manuscripts submitted to us, he said that
what I should have done was to let one of those printed rejection
slips serve as my answer to his letter.

Fortunately my little contretemps with Melville Cane was
resolved many years later when he was no longer Mrs. O'Neill's
attorney. He remembered our exchange of letters and at last
could explain why he had to act as a lawyer under the orders of
his client. He knew all along, he said, that I had never used the
safe-deposit box for my own purposes and was certain that I had
discharged my part of the bargain scrupulously. We later came
to respect each other with genuine understanding.

Now Melville Cane belongs to that growing company of
lawyers who were given rejection slips by Mrs. O'Neill. The two
gentlemen from Boston who called on Bennett Cerf about the
publication by Random House of *Long Day's Journey into Night*
were also honored in this manner and can now consider themselves alumni. They were succeeded by a constellation of
attorneys whose names on their letterheads are an awesome
directory. It was they who arranged for the posthumous publication of the play by Yale University Press, after Random House
had relinquished all rights to it, twenty-two years before Eugene
O'Neill had intended it to be issued.[1]

For several years prior to his death in 1953, Eugene O'Neill
had contributed manuscripts, notes, and correspondence to the
archives of the Yale University Library. After his death all his
papers were given to Yale for safekeeping and for the ultimate

1. Actually, the manuscript for the play and all publication rights in it were
given to the Yale University Library by Mrs. O'Neill, who authorized the
library to arrange for the play's publication. Mrs. O'Neill's attorneys drew
up the deed of gift to Yale, but the publication by the press was arranged by
the library. —D.C.

use of scholars. Under these circumstances and even if a quid pro quo was not involved, it was logical and certainly legal, regardless of the moral distinctions entailed, to override the author's living wish and have Yale University Press publish *Long Day's Journey into Night* with deserved success.

When the play was produced in 1956, first in Stockholm and then in New York, the question of the propriety of bringing it to the stage was overshadowed by the unanimous acclaim of the critics and the whole-hearted support of the public. O'Neill's own misgivings about the effect his work would have on the reputations of the dead and the susceptibilities of the living proved in the end to be baseless. The play was accepted, as it so richly merited, not as a rattling of skeletons in a family closet, but as a work of art dealing with a universal rather than a personal experience. It has been, from all accounts, magnificently acted and produced. I have never seen the play in whose history I was, in a strange sense, an unlisted member of the cast acting an anonymous role.

The Sequestration and Death of Eugene O'Neill

Secluded as the O'Neills were, they could not entirely escape the effects of the war. Their two Japanese gardeners were obliged to leave; the housemaid left to find work in a factory; and Herbert Freeman, the O'Neills' major domo, enlisted in the marines. Our Christmas greetings from them in 1943 included a postscript to Saxe from Gene: "Write us you're coming out! Your last chance! We've put the ranch up for sale. Too much of a burden and worry. It has us licked!" Several months later, after selling their handsome mountainside home, he and Carlotta moved to a hotel in San Francisco.

With the summer of 1944 came the Allied invasion of France and the beginning of the liberation of Europe. Gene, ever inclined to take the long view, was already thinking of the war's end and worrying over the sort of peace that might follow. He wrote to Saxe on July 12, summing up his views and apprehensions.

Are you looking forward to the approaching peace treaty with Germany, as a good liberal should—full of forgetfulness of the past and dopey visions of an end of wars? Imagine not! And neither am I. I fear they will not allow our article writers and radio commentators into the little locked room where the same old game is played by three or four professional swindlers—that is, alleged statesmen—who will sell the future of peoples down the river of power politics. My greatest hope for the coming little arrangement, if I had any hope, would be that we could bring Talleyrand back to life to be our representative. Then we could at least be sure that it would be the others who would come out of the secret little room without their pants and holding the sack! Dear old Talleyrand, Prince of Diplomacy! He came before his time. In this realistic age, he would have had unrestricted scope for his genius—and his intelligence, which his modern imitators so sadly lack.

Gene had been at work on *A Moon for the Misbegotten*. The first draft was written in the winter of 1941, and he continued to work on it, from time to time, as late as 1944, even though his prefatory note in the published play says that it was completed in 1943. Originally produced by the Theatre Guild in 1947, it ran into censorship trouble in its pre–New York tryouts, particularly in Detroit. Not only for this reason but because both the playwright and the Guild were dissatisfied with the cast, it was closed on the road and did not arrive on Broadway till revived (not by the Guild) in the 1950s.

O'Neill's letter of March 17, 1951, to Bennett Cerf and Saxe, giving them permission to publish *Moon*, along with *A Touch of the Poet*, was written while he was hospitalized with a fractured knee, and during a period of estrangement from Carlotta. Shortly before he wrote this letter, he had had Saxe remove all his manuscripts, including *Moon*, from his apartment and store them in Random House's vault. After the O'Neills were reconciled and moved to Boston, he had Saxe return all his scripts, including both *Moon* and *A Touch of the Poet*.

In 1952 he returned the script to Random House for publication.

9 January 1952

Random House, Inc.
457 Madison Avenue
New York 22, N.Y.

Gentlemen:
   In connection with my play *A Moon for the Misbegotten*, the manuscript of which has just been delivered to you on my behalf for publication pursuant to our agreement dated 30 June 1933 as renewed on 14 September 1951, I consent to such publication by you as soon as possible.

Very truly yours,
Eugene O'Neill

By the time the play was finally published, it had been close to
ten years that Gene had been unable to write. This was not because
of a psychological writer's block but the result of a physical illness.
A tremor of the hands which had afflicted him on and off since
childhood had become too severe for him to hold a pencil.
Although the doctors had diagnosed his ailment, which became
progressively worse, as Parkinson's disease, an autopsy performed
after his death revealed that Gene's affliction was due to a
degeneration of the cells of the cerebellum, a rare disease about
which very little is known. The autopsy findings left unsettled the
question of whether Gene had inherited the ailment. The initial
symptoms are generally trembling hands and speech impairment.

Gene tried using a typewriter and even tried to dictate his plays,
but, unhappily, it seemed that he could create only with pencil and
paper. It was another, perhaps the greatest, tragedy in a life that
was filled with tragedy. He was at the height of his creative powers,
his mind full of new plays, but he was thwarted, struck dumb so to
speak, by trembling hands.

Resigned to living with his tremor as best he could, Gene
returned with Carlotta to New York in 1945 for the publication and
the Theatre Guild production of *The Iceman Cometh*.

The following is an exerpt of Saxe's notes concerning this period:

The Captive

Before he was thirty years old, Edward Sheldon, author of
Salvation Nell, *The Boss*, *The Nigger*, *The Garden of Paradise*,
Dishonored Lady, *Lulu Belle*, and the most popular of all his
plays, *Romance*, was stricken with total arthritis. For the second
half of his life—he died at sixty—he lay completely immobilized
on a kind of catafalque in a pent-house apartment at Eighty-
fourth Street and Madison Avenue. He was also totally blind.

In spite of these terrible disabilities he maintained an active
communion with the friends of his better days and with newly
acquired admirers. To them he was a saintly figure, not so much
for his courage in the face of his private catastrophes, but for his
avid participation in the world from which he would not allow
himself to be excluded. His mother and a staff of nurses and
secretaries kept a constant vigil, fed him, read to him, maintained his enormous correspondence, attended his bodily functions, kept his muscles from becoming as rigid as his joints by
hourly massage and stood around-the-clock guard over the
living corpse. The mind, the voice, the ear and, above all, the

spirit were vibrantly alive after all else had died. Laid out in his raised bier, his rigid figure dominated a large room decorated in a vivid blue contrasted by the varicolored bindings of thousands of books that lined the walls and were heaped upon tables. A black domino mask covered his blank eyes. To maintain the appearance of being well groomed a simulation of a coat and shirt over his shoulders and a tie around his neck ended just beyond the upper end of his blankets. The flower in the lapel of his false coat was always fresh.

As Sheldon's body withered, his mind seemed to sharpen. Guided by information brought by visitors, by a world-wide correspondence of which his half was dictated, by books, magazines and newspapers read to him and by frequent use of the telephone, he kept himself acutely aware of the world of thought and action. In his youth, while still a student at Harvard University, he had written *Salvation Nell* for Minnie Maddern Fiske and it was a resounding success. This play and *Romance* earned huge sums of money, so that the staggering expense of his three decades of illness was adequately met. During the thirty years of rigidity and blindness, he sought compensation in a wide-ranging interest in people, ideas and letters. Many theatre-goers believed that he was dead, so long a time had passed since his last play was produced. His visitors, the elite of the theatre and the foremost literary figures of his time, came to gain sustenance from him rather than to bring sympathy.

When *The Great God Brown* was published, Sheldon, having had it read to him, dictated a letter of appreciation to Eugene O'Neill, who replied with genuine admiration and gratitude for the words of approval he so highly prized. Mrs. O'Neill had called on Sheldon several times and came away in awe of his bravery and the acuteness of his mind. What I know of him is based almost entirely on her reports after such visits. They occurred when the O'Neills had returned to New York from California in 1945 for the production of *The Iceman Cometh*. On their arrival they engaged a suite of rooms at the Hotel Barclay on East Forty-eighth Street.

At dinner there one evening I was witness to a painfully embarrassing display of cruelty and vindictiveness. It was not the first time that I had been made privy to domestic scenes of spite and violence on one side and a tormented meekness on the other. The origins of the sparks that detonated this explosion of malevolence could only be sought by an examination into the nature of evil.

Gene had brought with him from California a varied collection of manuscripts, the harvest of many years of intensive work. Principally they were finished plays, notes in long hand running to 125,000 words, tentative drafts, character sketches, scene divisions, snatches of dialogue, stage directions and the like for the nine plays of the cycle in progress on the general theme of the tyranny of possessions and the consequence to those possessed by them. Among the completed plays was *A Touch of the Poet* which dealt with the founder of the family that was to proliferate from his seed through many generations to become the symbols of O'Neill's pervasive theme of the havoc wrought by the passion for possession. Of incidental interest was the choice of the name of the leading character in *A Touch of the Poet*. He was called Melody, a man who had fought under Wellington in the Peninsular Wars and had migrated to Boston, there to establish himself as a tavern keeper. The name was given him after a talk we had long before the writing of the play about prizefighters remembered from our youth. One of them, a Negro lightweight out of Boston, bore the mellifluous professional name of Honey Melody. After repeating it many times and delighting in its euphony, O'Neill said it would be a fine name for a character he had in mind.

Our dinner was a dismal affair, eaten in silence and gloom. It was all too apparent from Gene's nervous anxiety and Carlotta's angry gibes that something serious had occurred. When the table was cleared I learned the cause of the tension; the manuscripts were lost. They had disappeared mysteriously during the day and there was no clue to their whereabouts.

We tried to recapitulate every event and every contingency from the time the manuscripts were last handled to the moment when it was discovered that they were missing. Gene was certain that he had not taken them out of the hotel suite when he went that morning to the offices of the Theatre Guild. He was sure that he had locked the door and delivered the key at the desk the few times he was obliged to leave the hotel. He recalled how he had packed the manuscripts in the trunk in California and how he reassured himself about their safety when his baggage was brought to their hotel rooms in New York. For a few days after that he simply assumed that they were where last he had seen them.

Carlotta disclaimed having seen the manuscripts at any time since they had left California and made matters worse by insinuations that Gene's memory was failing him, that he was growing senile and was less than aware of what he was doing most of the time. I ventured the suggestion that we make another thorough search of the suite and perhaps, like Poe's purloined letter, we would find what we were seeking in the most obvious of places. Whereupon we went through every trunk, closet, cupboard and bureau drawer in the apartment, all to no avail. Carlotta taunted us while we explored likely and unlikely places of concealment, omitting only an examination of the drawers in which she kept her lingerie and other items of a personal nature. When we stopped there, she insisted with growing resentment that we should not let delicacy deter us and she flung open the bureau in which she kept her underwear. Gingerly and embarrassedly we removed every garment, but still no manuscript came into view.

As the search continued, Gene's nervousness manifested itself in an uncontrollable tremor of his hands and a quivering of his lips. He was trying desperately to prod his memory and thus solve the mystery of the missing manuscripts, but he was completely blocked. Our systematic examination of the apartment convinced us that they had disappeared without a trace. We gave up the search and I went home.

Two days later when Gene and I were alone for a moment, he whispered to me that the manuscripts had been found and begged me to forget the entire unhappy episode. He explained, as if he were trying to condone a sick child's perverse behavior, that Carlotta had taken them out of the apartment and hidden them to punish him for reasons totally obscure to him. She knew where the manuscripts were during all the time of his torment and of the vain search. Only Strindberg, he observed grimly, would understand his predicament and know the motivations for such wantonly calculated cruelty.

When Edward Sheldon died in 1946, the O'Neills gave up their suite at the Hotel Barclay and rented and refurbished his penthouse apartment. The elevator door opened directly upon a large hallway, to the right of which was Carlotta's room, furnished with a canopied bed, a blue-black paneled mirror, an elaborate dressing table and deep closets for clothes. A glazed porcelain Chinese hip-high idol stood a grotesque guard at the foot of her bed.

Gene's room, farther down the hall, was austerely furnished. In the drawers of his natural-wood desk were kept his manuscripts. At this desk we worked on the texts and proofs of his plays. A Victrola and a cabinet containing many jazz records stood against the wall beside his dresser. In the hallway near at hand were ceiling-high shelves stacked with phonograph discs.

The large living room, where Sheldon held court from his

raised bier for so many years, served as a library and dining room. Its walls were lined with books and its tables covered in neat array with current magazines. A French door led to a spacious roof garden, canopied for about a quarter of its length with a large roll awning. From this roof could be seen the Metropolitan Museum of Art, Central Park and the towering apartment buildings that framed it to the west.

It was to this apartment, always associated with the living corpse of Edward Sheldon, that I came two or three times each week, either to work or to talk haphazardly about events and ideas and books and, for the most part, a past summoned to remembrance by a phrase or a name or any one of the accidental keys that open the locks of speech and thought and communion. Our own home at the time was on East Ninety-fifty Street, only eleven short blocks away, and with or without invitation we visited each other in neighborly fashion. Neither of us had many other visitors.

Where Ned Sheldon had lain in state as a procession of callers came and went, we, the seeing and living, sat in isolation with an invisible wall around us, believing hopefully that we could exclude the world. Gene, always seclusive, now built even higher barriers against intrusion. His physical affliction, Parkinson's disease, had advanced considerably and the tremor of his hands and his slowness of speech were so manifest that he became more and more conscious of the impression they made on others. To avoid explanations and apologies he withdrew farther and farther into silence and self-effacement. Occasionally I would bring my children to visit him and now and then he and Carlotta would come to our home for dinner.

On one of these visits Gene asked my wife if she could write out a melody or two which he wanted to use in *The Iceman Cometh*. They sat at the piano and Gene in his tremulous and uncertain voice hummed the "Rap, Rap, Rap, Tap, Tap, Tap" and the "Potato" melodies. Little by little they took form on the piano and a score was written out. These songs were used in the original production of the play.

Those were the quiet times. Friends and neighbors were at peace. It was the calm before a great storm. When it blew, the hurricane left a wake of destruction.

We were at dinner in the room in which Ned Sheldon's ghostly presence still lingered. Carlotta, Gene and I had moved to more comfortable chairs away from the table to drink coffee. The telephone bell rang and Carlotta answered it. The tone of her voice underwent an abrupt change when she heard the name of the caller; it was all too apparent that her annoyance was mounting. Holding her hand over the mouth-piece, she turned to Gene and said icily: "It's one of your friends. I won't talk to her." Thereupon she began to pace the floor nervously while muttering to herself.

Timidly Gene went to the telephone. All I could hear was his share of the conversation. It went somewhat like this: He said "Hello" and waited a little while. Then he said: "Of course, Fitzi, I'll do anything I can . . . Will one hundred be enough? I'll be glad to make it more . . . are you sure? . . . I'll mail you the check right away . . . Let's hope it's not as serious as you fear . . . Count on me." Then he hung up.

While he was talking, Carlotta continued her restless pacing of the floor, wringing her hands and working up a seething rage. She was close to hysteria, her eyes blazing and her voice hoarsely incoherent with words of imprecation. When Gene came away from the telephone, her rage had mounted to fury. All of Gene's former friends were roundly cursed, blamed for his illness and branded as parasites and hangers-on. Fitzi, particularly, was singled out as the worst miscreant, as a bum and scrounger who was interested only in preying on Gene. This was M. Eleanor Fitzgerald, the friend and consoler and steadfast encourager during the days of poverty and anonymity. Mildly and placatingly Gene tried to say that Fitzi had helped him when he was in need and now he could do little less than try to repay her for her many kindnesses. She was sick and in desperate need of help and even if she was all and more than Carlotta charged, he still was bound to lend a hand. Patiently he tried to explain that the call came from Mount Sinai Hospital, where Fitzi had been taken after suffering severe abdominal pains. At first glance the doctors suspected a malignant growth and there would have to be X-ray examination and perhaps even an exploratory operation. Meanwhile Fitzi had to find enough money to pay the deposit demanded by the hospital before admission to cover the initial costs of room, nurses, laboratory fees and the like. But Fitzi was without funds and in desperation she had called Gene and she was right in doing so, Gene tried patiently to explain. She had helped him when he had known trouble and the least he could do was to respond to the appeal of someone who had befriended him.

So reasonable a statement, instead of abating the storm, lashed it into an even greater fury. Carlotta cursed Fitzi in language that was far less than ladylike and gave special emphasis to a word that for her had the worst possible connotation—bohemian!

That epithet coming from Carlotta had an obscene inflection; it represented all that was evil and reprehensible to a person who made great pretensions to an aristocratic lineage. She, the lady, abandoning refinement, heaped abuse upon contempt for the people Gene knew during his days of struggle; they were criminals, blood-suckers, thieves, bastards, scum—and bohemians. As the tirade gained momentum, Gene tried vainly to defend them and himself, to explain old loyalties and to justify his past. This brought on another eruption.

I cowered in my chair, not saying a word and hoping against hope that a favorable opportunity for a quiet exit would present itself. It came when a servant entered the room to clear the coffee cups. I pleaded that I was tired, that I had to go to work early next morning, that my family were waiting up for me and stuttered in that vein as I meekly backed out of the room to the elevator. I walked a short distance to my home, embarrassed for having been a silent witness to a family upheaval and quite ashamed of myself for having made no effort to mediate the quarrel or, worst of all, for failing to speak up in behalf of Fitzi who had always been kind to me.

The following morning I was wakened early by a telephone call. It was Gene asking me to come over without delay to his apartment. On my arrival I saw no sign of Carlotta. I soon learned from Gene what had happened after I had left the night before. Immediately after the elevator door had been closed behind me, Carlotta renewed her attack on Gene's friends with increased virulence, heaping the major portion of her hatred on Fitzi. The outburst continued for a long time, a one-sided harangue in which the central theme was Gene's weakness and cowardice in tolerating his bohemian friends. He remained silent, but that silence lent fuel to the fire and at its height it culminated in an explosion of violence.

Carlotta rushed into Gene's room and lifted the glass that covered his dressing table over her head and crashed it to the floor where it broke into hundreds of splinters. Underneath this glass Gene had kept the *only* picture he had of his mother and himself as a baby. Carlotta, now at the summit of her frenzy, snatched the picture and tore it into bits, crying, "Your mother was a whore!"

This was the last straw. Gene slapped her face. Whereupon she screamed maniacally and ran to her own room. There she hastily packed a bag, dressed for the street and made a melodramatic exit, swearing she would never return.

Gene waited for dawn to call me. Soon after my arrival and

after having learned from him the sequence of events that led to the wild parting, we took counsel. First of all, someone would have to stay with Gene and we immediately thought of Walter Casey, a boyhood friend from New London and a man of unswerving devotion. Within an hour after we called him, Casey arrived with a handbag containing his clothes and toilet articles. He understood the situation without detailed explanations and began to take charge by preparing breakfast. I was then able to go to work and left for my office with a somewhat easier mind.

Within twenty-four hours we were aware of the presence of detectives assigned to watch the apartment and whoever came or left. Always in pairs, the sleuths stood guard on the street corner. They employed a mysterious system of waving white handkerchiefs, to what end none of us could guess.

Gene's remorse over the night's quarrel was pitiful and in a sense degrading. He reproached himself for having lost his temper and, because of that, his wife. There were, he pleaded, extenuating circumstances which we could not possibly understand. There was guilt on both sides and the marriage of two quiveringly sensitive people required an expansion of forbearance. It was he who should have exercised greater control and no matter what the provocation should have shown more tolerance.

The Parkinson tremor became more and more acute. Alarmed, we called Dr. Shirley Fisk, whose offices were nearby on Fifth Avenue. When he arrived we explained the entire situation to him. He prescribed sedatives and urged that someone remain at Gene's side twenty-four hours a day. He also recommended frequent cups of black coffee as a means of controlling the agitation of his arms and legs. But more important, Gene was to be watched constantly lest he come by an injury, accidentally or self-inflicted.

For ten days Casey and I alternated on sentry duty. We sat in the kitchen percolating coffee and trying to formulate plans for the future. Most of all, Gene insisted on discussing measures whereby he could learn where Carlotta was hidden. He wanted to hire a detective and actually did so, only to learn that his lady was, for the time, incommunicado at a mid-town hotel.

On the night of January 28, 1948, I became sleepy as the hours dragged by. At midnight I asked Casey whether he could remain in charge while I went home for some rest. He assured me that there was no need for me to wait, that he was certain that Gene would sleep well into the morning and that even he could retire for a few hours. So I went home, thinking of little else but the comfort of my bed.

I was awakened at six in the morning. Dr. Fisk was on the phone. He urged me to dress quickly and come over at once, for Gene had fallen a few hours before and broken his arm. The doctor had been summoned by Casey after the accident and he had found Gene on the floor of his bedroom with Casey leaning over him, afraid to move him lest he do him further injury.

While I was on my way to the apartment Dr. Fisk ordered a Keefe and Keefe ambulance. It arrived soon after I did and after the doctor had briefly outlined what had happened and what had to be done. Apparently Gene had tried to walk in the dark to the bathroom and had slipped on the highly glossed floor and fallen over a low stool, fracturing his right arm as he wildly tried to break his fall. Now all that could be done would require hospital facilities. At the moment he was in a semi-comatose condition because of the injection given him by Dr. Fisk but still suffering severe pain.

The ambulance arrived and Gene was bundled onto a stretcher and carried down the elevator. Its siren screaming, the ambulance, with Dr. Fisk and me seated beside Gene, drove heedless of red-light traffic signals to Doctors Hospital on East Eighty-seventh Street. While Gene was being trundled into the X-ray room, I registered for him, paid the ambulance fee and declared myself next of kin on the hospital admission form.

The X-ray plates revealed a compound fracture of the humerus. An orthopedic specialist was summoned and he and Dr. Fisk reduced the fracture and applied a plaster of paris splint from the shoulder to the wrist. In spite of the acute pain in setting and splinting the broken arm, there was no word of complaint from Gene. Only the haunted, melancholy eyes showed his suffering. Once in bed and made relatively comfortable by his French-Canadian nurse, he fell asleep under heavy sedation.

For a few days his only visitors were Casey and I, and we always came separately. Casey was reluctant to leave the apartment unoccupied because he was concerned most of all about the manuscripts in the desk drawers. Gene was especially worried about them because the elevator door opened directly upon the apartment and he feared that such easy access would tempt a thief—or somebody. He then asked me to have Casey take all the manuscripts out of his desk and bring them to Random House, where they could be placed safely in the company vault.

I did as I was asked and telephoned Casey. At about 11 in the morning he drove up in a taxicab to the Fifty-first Street entrance to Random House and with the aid of the driver carried in two cartons containing all of Gene's manuscripts. They were deposited in the vault and labels were attached to them on which were written notices that these boxes were not to be moved or opened by anyone but Eugene O'Neill or me. That done and the vault locked, Casey went back to the apartment.

I tried to do something about earning my pay. While thus engaged in the mid-afternoon my telephone bell rang. A blast assaulted my ear. It was Carlotta's voice. "What do you mean, you thief, by stealing my manuscripts! I caught you this time. I'll send you to jail. My detectives saw it all. They followed Casey. They know you engineered it. I know how to handle the likes of you!"

"Just a minute, Carlotta," I managed to interrupt. "I didn't steal Gene's manuscripts. Don't you know that he has been in Doctors Hospital for several days with a broken arm? He asked me to put them in a safe place. That is all."

"You are a liar, and so is Gene. He couldn't tell the truth. I don't give a damn what happened to him."

There followed a cascade of curses. The veneer of the lady had been rubbed off and the mind and the language of the show girl were exposed. The tirade became an outpouring of obscenities.

I tried to stop it by interjecting that she could say anything she pleased about me, but she had no right to revile Gene in this way. He was sick and helpless and unable to defend himself. These last days had been ghastly for him and now, alone in the hospital with a broken arm, he deserved the utmost consideration. Whereupon she reacted against me with all the hatred and evil she could compress into three words.

"You——bastard!" she screamed into the phone and banged her receiver into its cradle.

Stunned, I sat looking at the telephone in bewilderment and chagrin. Then I wrote out from memory as accurately as possible a transcript of what had been said over the telephone, omitting the grosser obscenities. That night at the hospital I showed Gene what I had written and asked him whether, under the circumstances, I was to come to see him again or stay away altogether. He read the sheet of paper slowly and then paused for a long time.

"Try to understand," he said. "She's sick, terribly sick. Don't you leave me too."

I promised I would not.

Many years have gone by since the catastrophe which began and ended with telephone calls. The first was from Fitzi asking for help from an old friend. The last was from Carlotta irreparably destroying a dubious friendship. I have never again heard Carlotta's voice since she screamed her last three whiplash words at me.

As Gene's arm mended and release from the hospital was imminent, Carlotta reappeared from her hiding place and made overtures for or was offered peace terms. At any rate, a reconciliation was effected and a plan to resume life together somewhere on the New England shore was considered. The apartment which for so many years had been a shrine for visitors to blind and paralyzed Edward Sheldon was now abandoned by the O'Neills.

They left New York in the spring of 1948 for Boston, where they stayed at the Ritz-Carlton while they looked around for a permanent residence. On July 26 Gene managed to get a letter to Saxe. He wrote that they had bought a home "right on the ocean" near Marblehead.

It is a tiny house with little rooms, the upstairs ones with sloping eaves—built in 1880. Reminds me of the first house my father bought in New London, also on the waterfront [when I was a kid]. We both love this new place. Of course, a lot has had to be done to modernize it ... and to thoroughly insulate it for an all year round home—our last. Everything is cut down overhead and makes it a cinch to run with just a cook. No car. We don't need one. The aim is to simplify living and gain as much security for our old age as is possible. I feel I shall be able to write again, and again have some roots—of seaweed—with my feet in a New England sea. It is like coming home, in a way, and I feel happier than in many years, although we are still stuck here in a hotel impatiently awaiting the completion of the work on the place.

As to health, we are both much better and will be better still when we are in our home. My arm isn't right yet and won't be for six months, they say, but it steadily improves. No swimming this summer, of course. But next year—! [Gene was overly optimistic, as he would never again be physically strong enough for swimming.] The tremor is better, too, but I'm just cursed with it for life, I guess, and the best to hope for is to circumvent it. This letter, for example, is written during a good spell, and it's not so bad, eh? And why complain when the world itself is one vast tremor.

Saxe wanted to write to Gene, or speak to him, but he knew that any letters or phone calls would be intercepted by Carlotta. She had made it clear when they had moved to Boston that most of Gene's friends were never to enter their home. This brutal severance of whatever ties Gene had was to take its toll later.

Nevertheless when Gene's birthday, October 16, was approaching, Saxe said to me, "Throughout the years I've never failed to greet Gene on his birthday, wherever he may have been. I won't fail him now. I'll send him a telegram and sign your name. Gene will understand." To our great surprise, I had a letter from Carlotta several days later saying among other things that Gene had asked her to thank me for the wire. "You were sweet," she added, "to remember him"; and at the end, as though she had never reviled Saxe and made threats to have the law on him, she said, "I hope things go well with you and yours."

At Christmas time over the next years we received greetings from Gene to all of us, but the script became so wavery, so nearly illegible, that it tore at our hearts. He had sent an inscribed copy of *The Iceman Cometh* to our son Eugene which read, "For Eugene, from a proud Godfather, Iceman O'Neill."

Shut off from nearly all his old friends, Gene lived like a recluse, secluded with Carlotta in the little house on Point O'Rocks Lane, Marblehead Neck, the little house they dreamed would make their lives whole again. But it was not to be.

All communication was cut off and even matters pertaining to Gene's work had to be transmitted through Miss Jane Rubin of the office of his literary agent, Richard Madden. I had been purged, as had all of his old friends and, most unfortunately as it turned out, his children, Shane, Oona, and Eugene, Jr. The son who bore his name was, more than anyone else, in desperate need of communication with his father.

Young Gene was then undergoing a time of adversity. His three marriages had failed miserably. His academic career, in the beginning rich in promise, was in decline. He had given up his post at Yale University as an Assistant Professor of Greek and the Classics, a position he had attained after a notable scholastic record as an undergraduate. The promise, unfortunately, was greater than the performance, and both he and the university were disappointed.

An opportunity to make a genuine contribution in his field arose when Random House undertook the publication of all the extant Greek dramas in a variety of translations. Whitney J. Oates, Professor of Classics at Princeton University and since

July 26 '48

Dear Saxe:

Much gratitude for the inscribed book. I feel as if I'd read it already, you've told me so much about it, but I know I will have a new pleasure in reading it.

The big news with us, which I meant to write you long ago, is that we had the good luck to get in first on the sale of a house right on the ocean near Marblehead — first sale of waterfront property in its vicinity for many years. Carlotta bought this out of her reserve fund. It is a tiny house with little rooms, an upstairs ones with sloping eaves — built in 1880. Reminds me of the first home my father bought in New London, also on the waterfront. We both love this new place. Of course, a lot has had to be done to modernize it — as the kitchen, etc. and to thoroughly insulate it for an all year round home — our last. Everything to cut down overhead and make it a cinch to run with just a cook. No car. We won't need one. The aim is to simplify living and gain as much security for our old age as is possible. I feel I shall be able to write again, and again some roots — of seaweed — with my feet in a New England sea. It is like coming home, in a way, and I feel happier than in many years, although we are still stuck here in a hotel impatiently awaiting the completion of the work on the place.

As to health, we are both much better and will be better still when we are in our home. My arm isn't right yet and won't be for six months, they

---

Letter to Saxe from Eugene O'Neill, July 26, 1948, concerning the O'Neills' new home near Marblehead

The Ritz-Carlton
Boston 17, Massachusetts

Cable Address
RIZCARLTON-BOSTON

Telephone
KENMORE 5700

Overlooking one of the World's most beautiful parks, the Public Garden

say, but it steadily improves. No swimming this summer, of course. But next year —! The tremor is better, too, but I'm just cursed with it for life, I guess, and the best to hope for is to circumvent it. This letter, for example, is written during a good spell. and its not so bad, eh? And why complain when the world itself is one vast tremor.

All best to you, Dorothy & the kids —

Ho ever,

Gene

P.S.
Remember me to Bennett, Haas, Klopfer

1938 the closest friend I have had in a lifetime of magnificent friendships, was chosen for the task of editing the two-volume work and together we suggested the name of Eugene O'Neill, Jr., as his collaborator in the compilation which would bear the title *The Complete Greek Drama*. O'Neill, Jr., was to be responsible for the comedies of Aristophanes and Menander, and Oates for the tragedies of Aeschylus, Sophocles, and Euripides. Of the forty-seven plays in the 2,500 pages of the two books, Oates edited thirty-three, with Prefaces, Introductions and Notes, and O'Neill fourteen. The volumes, when published, were received with exceptional critical and general-reader enthusiasm and were highly successful commercially.

Through the good offices of Professor Oates, young O'Neill was tendered a place in the Classics Department at Princeton in 1947, but the experiment, after a year's trial, did not succeed. He then drifted from one institution of learning to another, including Fairleigh-Dickinson college in Rutherford, New Jersey, and the New School for Social Research in New York, and dropped gradually in status until he reached the bottom of the academic ladder.

A bearded giant of a man, perhaps six foot three in height and massively built, he had a basso-profundo voice of which he was inordinately proud. He made himself believe that with a little training he could become Chaliapin's successor. With his resonant voice to recommend him, he sought engagements with radio networks and actually found some radio assignments as a reader of books for the benefit of the housebound. He also appeared occasionally on the program known as "Invitation to Learning," a weekly half hour informal discussion of the world's great books. Always in need of money, the earnings he came by so infrequently and precariously were never enough for his needs. Let it be said for him that in the face of heartbreaking discouragements he tried his skills at whatever presented itself and never betrayed his love of scholarship.

He had bought a small piece of land near Woodstock, New York, on the Ohmayo Mountain where he hoped to build a home. It carried a mortgage of $4,000, sponsored by the endorsement of his father. The time came when the mortgage was due for renewal and all that was required was a re-endorsement. That formality, he was confident, would be observed without difficulty. As the due date approached he made every possible effort to communicate with his father, but to no avail. Letters remained unanswered, telegrams were ignored, telephone calls never went beyond the vigilant monitor and guard at Marblehead. In a panic he appealed to whoever might have access, but every avenue of approach was blocked. He persuaded W. E. Aronberg, O'Neill's attorney in New York, to intercede but his messages were intercepted and never relayed to the father. Desperate, the junior O'Neill tried to raise the money by appeals to his friends, but they were as impecunious as he.

He came to my office on Thursday, September 21, 1950, to seek my counsel, even though he knew that I had been forbidden communication of any kind with his father. He told me of all the stratagems he had used to break through the barrier and how he was always repulsed and turned back. His hatred of Carlotta was almost maniacal; it was she, he insisted, who was the cause of his desperation. If only he could have the mortgage renewed and find some work, his problems would be on the way to solution. He was a scholar of considerable reputation among his peers; he had a voice of deep sonority and great appeal; he was a strong man and could do manual labor. He asked me to try to induce five or six book publishers to underwrite a radio program in which he could offer thumbnail comment and criticism of current books in a weekly broadcast. This was indeed clutching at a straw, for even if he was qualified by scholarship, voice and judgement, the problem still remained to bring five or six publishers into accord, a thirteenth Herculean labor. Nonetheless I promised to do what I could and actually explained the proposal to a few publishers, all of whom merely wondered whether I had taken leave of my wits.

When he left me on that Thursday, there was no way of foretelling from his despair that it would carry him as far as it did. On the following Monday afternoon at about three o'clock, a telephone call from Woodstock brought the hysterical voice of Frank Meyer, a neighbor of young Gene and the man from whom he had bought his land, crying out: "Gene has just killed himself. He slashed his wrists and ankles. My wife found him dead at the bottom of the stairs in his house."

Would I notify his father?

In my own panic dread of such an assignment, trying either to evade the delicate task or to act as rationally as possible, it seemed to me then that a doctor or a lawyer should be asked to perform it. I forthwith telephoned Bill Aronberg to convey the shocking news and to seek his advice more than to shift the burden onto him. He said without hesitation that it was his duty as O'Neill's lawyer to notify him of the disaster. After all, he was, he said, on a retainer and this was his responsibility, not mine. He promised that he would telephone Marblehead and then call me back to report how the father withstood the shock.

A half hour later his call came and I realized at once from the tone of his voice that he was disturbed and blazing with anger. He said he wanted to give me a verbatim report of his long-distance conversation.

When Carlotta answered the telephone, Bill Aronberg said: "Hello, Carlotta. This is Bill Aronberg. I have terrible news for you. Try to be brave and break this gently to Gene. Young Gene has just committed suicide."

Whereupon Carlotta answered: "How dare you invade our privacy?" and slammed the receiver down. That was the entire conversation.

Young O'Neill was beyond insult and injury. No inquest could reveal that he died as much from a thwarted effort at communication as by his own hand. A note found near his body tried to convey a sardonic if somewhat theatrical last message of bluster and defiance. It read: "Never let it be said of an O'Neill that he failed to empty the bottle. Ave atque vale!"

Less than five months after young Gene had written his final hail and farewell, Bill Aronberg, still Eugene O'Neill's lawyer, Lawrence Langner, director of the Theatre Guild, and I were involved in what Carlotta chose to call a conspiracy to kidnap and transport her husband from Salem, Massachusetts, to New York City. Also implicated in the "criminal conspiracy" was the late Dr. Merrill Moore, physician and psychiatrist and the only begetter of thousands of sonnets.

The sad episode had its beginning in Marblehead in the first week of February 1951. What I know of that act in the tragic drama that was his life came to me from Eugene O'Neill's own lips as he lay immobilized in a bed in the Salem Hospital. This is what I learned from him when I was summoned to his bedside:

On the cold February night of the 5th he and Carlotta had had a quarrel, the nature of which he would not divulge. At any rate, to escape her wrath, he explained, he walked out of the house, coatless, and wandered in the darkness about the grounds of their Marblehead home, following the path that led from the door to the road. The night was colder than he at first thought and he decided to return for an overcoat. As he approached the door he mistook one of the stones, sharply angled at the top, which lined the driveway for a shadow. Unheedingly he stepped on it and fell, stunned by a sharp pain in his knee as he lay sprawled on the ground. On trying to rise, he discovered that his leg would not support him and fell again. He realized at once, from the pain and his inability to flex his leg that serious damage had been done to his knee.

He began to call for help. There was no answer. For an hour he lay on the roadway, helpless and unable to move, crying all the while for aid. With no coat on his back, he suffered from the severe cold and felt, besides the pain, fear of the consequences of long exposure. He continued to cry for help and finally the door of their house was opened. Carlotta stood framed in its small rectangular proscenium, her figure lighted by the vestibule lamp. She made no move. After a long silence, she delivered in histrionic tones these lines:

"How the mighty have fallen! The master is lying low. Now where is all your greatness?"

Wherewith she closed the door.

Fortunately, the doctor who had been due an hour earlier to administer medicine to allay Gene's Parkinson tremor was late. When he arrived, he heard Gene's cries from the path and hastened to his side. At a glance he could tell that the knee had been broken and nothing less than hospitalization could be of any help. He threw his own overcoat over Gene and went into the house to summon an ambulance from Salem. While telephoning it was apparent to him that he had two patients, not one, for Carlotta was in a state of hysteria.

When the ambulance arrived he had Gene placed on the stretcher and lifted into the vehicle. He persuaded Carlotta to accompany them to the hospital. Once there, his cursory diagnosis of a broken knee was confirmed by X-ray.

While the pictures were being taken Carlotta, her hysteria mounting, created a scene in the lobby of the hospital, screaming maledictions on Gene's head, insulting the doctors and nurses and threatening all and sundry with arrest and law suits or whatever else came into her disturbed mind. So great was the disturbance caused by her wild behavior that the police were called. They merely escorted her outside the building and appealed to her to calm down. Outdoors she continued her incoherent tirade and it reached such a peak of violence that the police decided to call a psychiatrist. He, at first ignorant of Carlotta's identity, saw the urgency of the situation and at once had her committed to a hospital for mental patients. The psychiatrist was the poet Merrill Moore.

That is how matters stood when I arrived by train from New York. Gene, in severe pain and trembling with nervous shock, his leg encased in a plaster cast that stretched from mid-thigh to ankle, lay on his hospital bed and pieced out the story for me haltingly and with desperate sadness. Little could be done for him now beyond attending to his needs, making him comfortable and trying to assure him that the doctors and the nurses of the hospital staff were eager to serve him with all the facilities at their command. Before I left he made me promise that I would come to him as often as possible.

Once a week thereafter I went to Salem from New York, by air rather than by train, because it was quicker and more convenient to travel by taxi from the Boston airport to Salem than to go by train to Boston, drive across the city, take another train to Salem and then be transported by taxi to the hospital.

Each visit brought more and more confirmation that, although Gene's knee was healing under the cast, his nervous condition was steadily becoming more aggravated. Consultation with Dr. Frederick B. Mayo and other physicians in Salem ended with their recommendation that the wisest course would be to take Gene to New York, where he would have his own physician and the best possible orthopedic and neurological care. When first told of the doctors' counsel, he vetoed the plan because he was gravely concerned about Carlotta. He had learned that she had taken steps to gain release from the institution to which she had been committed. Since she was not a voluntary patient and because she had been admitted in an emergency by a psychiatrist, she was within her rights to demand immediate dismissal. This was accomplished without any intervention on Gene's part and Carlotta left her hospital for parts unknown.

The doctors in Salem again urged upon Gene the wisdom and necessity of going to New York and he was finally persuaded to undertake the trip. Bill Aronberg, Lawrence Langner and I arranged ways and means of bringing about the transfer. We decided, with the doctors' consent, to engage a trained nurse as a traveling companion, take a room on the train to which he would be brought in a wheelchair with his physician in attendance and run the risk of his withstanding the journey to New York.

Aronberg, Langner and I met him at the Grand Central Station and with the aid of the nurse carried him to a waiting wheelchair. A limousine was in readiness to drive us to a Madison Avenue hotel where we were joined by Russell Crouse, a staunch old friend whose good sense and reliability in any crisis were always unfailing.

Within a few hours it became evident to the nurse and to us that a hotel room would not be adequate for his needs. The nurse had to return to Salem and we would have to engage three shifts of nurses to take her place. Then, too, sleeping quarters and food would have to be provided for them. Under these circumstances we agreed to telephone Doctors Hospital to arrange for a room and to call Dr. Fisk who was again to be in charge and would select an orthopedic specialist.

The nurse from Salem and our entire group attending, we accompanied Gene to Doctors Hospital where he was assigned a comfortable room overlooking the East River. He remained there for a month. X-rays showed that his knee was healing satisfactorily, but his general physical and nervous condition had undergone obvious deterioration. He was down to ninety-seven pounds.

Every day for four weeks we visited together for at least one hour, usually in the evening after work. His nights, he told me, were hideous, haunted by spectres and delusional terrors, asleep or awake. He was taking frequent doses of chloral hydrate at the time, both to reduce the Parkinson tremor and to induce sleep. Once, while I was with him, he sprang from the bed before I could grasp him and cowered in a far corner of the room nearest the door, crying out: "She's on the window sill. She's coming toward me. Please keep her away!" Whereupon he scraped the wall with his fingernails, trying vainly to get a finger hold so that he could climb the wall, cast and all, and escape whatever was pursuing him in his overwrought, phantom-ridden mind.

It was not entirely a sick fantasy that she was near. Upon her insistence and certainly within her legal rights, Carlotta was released from the sanitarium to which she had been committed by Dr. Moore and, after a brief delay, came to New York. There she engaged a room in Doctors Hospital underneath Gene's. Several times during my visits she telephoned him. Whenever she did so I waited in the hall until the conversation came to an end. It was all too manifest that she was regaining control.

Even in the face of Gene's imminent return to captivity, our group tried to make plans for an uncertain future. Bennett and Phyllis Cerf found and were about to sign a lease for a New York apartment for Gene to which he could move upon his dismissal from the hospital. This plan was vetoed and the option on the apartment was dropped. My wife and I had gained his half-consent to setting up an establishment in Princeton, New Jersey, where we would try to minister to his needs. Carlotta's appearance summarily disposed of this notion. Other friends generously suggested alternatives, to all of which he listened patiently but would not respond affirmatively or negatively. All of us soon began to realize that our good intentions only paved the way to nowhere.

As Gene grew a little stronger, he began to analyze or, more properly, to explain and rationalize his predicament. He realized, as we were beginning to do, that the tie that bound him to Carlotta was too firm to undo. Yet he was acutely aware that submission meant the final severance from all his old friends and repudiation of his own past. He realized that he would need constant care, would have to be fed and nursed and guarded. On that score alone he was unwilling to impose upon his friends. There was, on the other hand, the risk of other quarrels with Carlotta and perhaps other broken limbs. Consideration, too, had to be given to his Parkinson affliction; it had advanced to the point where he could not possibly live without close, moment-to-moment help.

Essential as this was, it cut a deep wound into his pride. After all, Carlotta had lived with him and it for almost a quarter of a century, and when she was not in a state of acute disturbance, she could be competent and devoted and even sacrificial in her imperious and managerial way. Hers was not a radiant future, he argued as much to convince himself as me, and she had relinquished a life of ease as a woman of conspicuous beauty in order to be at his side through all those years, for better or for worse. As the wife of a famous man (he smiled wanly at the use of the adjective), she had expected to be surrounded by all that wealth and recognition could bring. But, instead, the latter years had been bitter for both of them, and not only was he sick and unproductive, but so was she and hers was a peculiar sickness only he could understand and had to forgive. Together, they might help each other; apart there could only be even greater torture and then dissolution. And, finally, his chief article of faith was that doom had to be his companion to his last hour.

A pervasive theme in many of his plays was man's inescapable fate to suffer the anguish of humiliation on his way to defeat. Against suffering, man could only pit what little dignity he had in reserve. It was a pitifully weak weapon with which he must try, sometimes heroically and often self-deceptively, to reduce the overwhelming odds against him. Death alone brought a truce to the unresolved struggle.

Gene's illness, his tormented preoccupation with tragedy, even more personal than dramatical, his loss of friends, his moral and physical isolation, and his ultimate loneliness in his last love affair with disaster were all interwoven in the pattern of the unwritten tragedy of his life. The realization that his work was finished and could never be resumed was the last bitter indignity. It was impossible for him to hold a pencil in his hand. Desperately he tried to command its course along faltering lines over a sheet of paper; the pencil fell from his hand. Its falling was the final symbol and portent that the last curtain was coming down.

On 27 November 1953, the peace that had been denied Gene in life came to him in death. Not a single close friend was permitted to accompany him to his grave. Carlotta later told interviewers, "Gene wanted it that way, and I followed out his wishes to the letter."

About a year after Gene died, Saxe returned to his office one day to find an inscribed copy of *The View from Pompey's Head* by Hamilton Basso. From its opening pages, the novel produced in Saxe a shock of recognition. There, only thinly disguised as the story of novelist Garvin Wales and his wife Lucy, was the story of Gene and Carlotta, and there was the life-long editor-friend (Phillip Greene) betrayed by the perfidy of the wife of Garvin Wales. Where Gene was diagnosed as suffering from Parkinson's disease, Wales is portrayed as blind, walled in from the world by Lucy, just as Gene was shut away from everyone by Carlotta. Lucy was a professional beauty and a bit player on the stage; so was Carlotta. In his earlier years, Wales had gone to Mexico, as Gene had gone to Honduras.

Saxe had introduced Basso to the O'Neills in 1947. Soon after, Basso began interviewing Gene over a period of months, prior to writing the three-part profile of Gene which appeared in the *New Yorker* in 1948. Here is how Saxe reacted to the fictional account:

> Random House, Inc.
> 457 Madison Avenue
> New York 22, N.Y.
>
> 11 October 1954

Mr. Hamilton Basso
R.F.D. #2
Westport, Conn.

Dear Hamilton:
  The moment your book *The View from Pompey's Head* arrived I promised you and myself that I would write you my impressions of it as soon as I could finish reading it.
  It has been an emotional experience! I don't have to tell you how closely I identified myself with the tragic circumstances of Lucy's and Garvin's alliance in hatred and evil and weakness. Your portrait only faintly disguises the two we knew and who

wanted neither friendship, nor love, nor devotion, but only the mutual torment of their imbalanced love and hate.

But I realize that this is not the main theme of your novel. Where your heart lies is in recreating the social history of the town, and this you have done, not as a detached historian, but as a novelist of great sensibility and warmth and tolerance and perception. The past, even limited as it was to the fifteen years of Anson's absence, was quite immeasurable, and it was further complicated by the necessity of reconciling that past with the present and the flowing current of time. This you have carried off admirably, and, above all, honestly.

I realize too that the necessities of your purpose demanded that you place layer upon layer of personal history into the very anatomy of the town, and sometimes what concealed its heart was a thick covering of tissues through which you had to cut cautiously. And, too, I wish that there could have been another motivation for Garvin's cowardice and tragedy and guilt about his mother. I was surprised, as you intended me to be, when it is revealed that Anna Jones is part Negro. The surprise was no real revelation, nor was it quite plausible enough to explain the capture and destruction of a man like Garvin Wales. Yet, for the life of me, I can think of no other resolution of that terrible situation.

What impressed me the most, over and above your acute eyes and ear for every manifestation of local character and event, is the complete honesty of your particular view of Pompey's Head. It is seen with the eyes of affection and felt with the heart of a noble human being.

But that's the way you are and that's what I admire so deeply and enviously in you.

With all affection and devotion.

Saxe

P.S. Incidentally, you have, for the first time, given a picture of publishing that has, as the boys say, verisimilitude. Not an exaggeration or an extravagance anywhere, but that crazy world is described accurately and rationally. For that alone I am in your debt.

Far more tragic than any novel Gene might have written was the tragedy of his own life.

S. N. Behrman, Sinclair Lewis, and Others

What the whole tragic saga of the O'Neills did to Saxe can scarcely be expressed in words. Suffice it to say that it wounded him deeply. During this distressing period, Saxe had turned, when he could, to hard work as a refuge. One of the authors whose manuscripts, and friendships, helped Saxe in this time was the well-known playwright S. N. Behrman. As was so often the case with Saxe, author and editor in this instance became close friends, and Saxe was invited to share in Behrman's curiosity about many diverse people and subjects.

Saxe had worked with Behrman in 1944 on the manuscript for the play *Dunnigan's Daughter*, which required much rewriting by the author before it was eventually produced by the Theatre Guild in December of the following year. (Not long after that, it was made into a movie.) Saxe had written Behrman in April 1944, after having gone over an early draft of the play:

4 April 1944

Dear Sam:
    I am rushing in where angels ordinarily watch their steps. Yet I want to put down, as much for my sake as your own, the rather disorderly reactions I have had to your untitled and manifestly

unfinished play. It is underlining the obvious to say that in its present state the manuscript has not become crystallized, nor caught your intention (or even the conglomerate of intentions that are spread through it).

Ultimately, I know, you will bring a unity to all the loose elements you have gathered in these pages as working material. Read in that light, it is possible to make a few suggestions that may be of some use to you. Primary among these, it seems to me, is that you will have to decide whose play it should become. This decision will be almost like the cutting of a Gordian knot and will also resolve the question of the multiplicity of themes in the present version. When you determine whether it will be Miguel's play or Clay's or Jim's, you will then overcome the embarrassment of riches of themes. Just consider, you deal with academic freedom, the integrity of the artist, the irreconcilable conflict between fascism and democracy, misalliance and the family dilemma all in one play. These themes are represented by a succession of contretemps between Jim and Horace; Jim and Clay; Miguel and Clay; Clay and Ferne; Clay, Ferne, Waldo and Zelda, respectively. I am sure you will make one of these conflicts the foundation of your play, and the subsidiary ones its superstructure. That resolution found, I am convinced the present blurred outline will take on a clear architectural design.

All the foregoing is too general and also damn presumptuous. I promised you that I would be on the level and, having said this much by the way of generalization, I am morally committed to a bill of particulars. Perhaps my meaning and good intentions will be clarified by an act-by-act commentary. Here it is for whatever it may be worth to you.

ACT I. Jim and Zelda state a proposition. They are symbols in an equation, not human entities. The college professor who waves the banner of academic freedom is also a human being, and should be a little more than a flag planted at the opposite pole of reaction. Just consider what Shaw would have done with Jim and a kind of lesser Major Barbara of a Zelda! We are beyond the point where it establishes a liberal position and a crusading spirit to make a character a socialist, a mere antagonist to the power principle.

You stack the cards with Horace by making him a college president whose only existence is to focus the problem of academic freedom.

With the appearance of Miguel, the play has its first real manifestation of life, and you hold out the promise that he is going to dominate all subsequent developments. Beginning with page 25, in the proposal to exchange cliches, you are at your best. For underneath this bantering exchange, Miguel's essential gallantry and Ferne's groping towards some understanding of her predicament reveal what lies beneath the surfaces on which they are skimming.

There follows Waldo's explanation of his anomalous position, and the vitality goes out of the writing.

The rest of the act is expository, too, and made me want Miguel back on the scene.

ACT II. Act II employs a device I think you may have to abandon. More and more manuscripts are being written with the time element so arranged as to have the dramatic climax occur on the afternoon of December 7th. It is already a stencil. I can suggest no alternative, but I must point out the danger of your using a device that is becoming habitual with too many of the lesser writers.

Through all this act, I feel the need of a Shavian kind of brilliance in the writing. Otherwise we have merely the statement of action rather than the conflict of wills, points of view, temperaments, and prejudices. Of course, there is always your own special kind of sharp dialogue suggested. In the rewriting, I am sure it will be brought to a keener edge.

ACT III. What disappoints me in the final act is that Miguel, and all that he represents, tapers off into a more subsidiary character, and we get instead revolt against father and husband. It leaves me with the feeling that the act is no more than a notation to yourself of what you are going to do with it ultimately. The diffusion of themes is not resolved into a central theme, and that brings me back to what I said in the beginning, namely, that you have yet to find the core of the play. When you do, all the disparate elements will fall into place, and from the scattered themes you will select the essential theme.

God, but all the foregoing sounds captious, patronizing, and cheeky. And I want you above all people to understand that my motives in reading this draft were to be of some use to you. If what I have said so much as suggests a way of tackling the problem, it is worth the risk of having hurt you by my candor.

The hand of the writer is in everything you do. I always want that hand to be sure, and deft, and firm.

During the agonizing time of the O'Neill tragedy, Saxe had another Behrman manuscript to turn to, the biography of the famous art dealer Duveen. The book was eventually serialized in the New Yorker and was a great success.

Later, Saxe edited Behrman's autobiographical *The Worcester Account*, which was published in 1954, and following that his biography of Max Beerbohm, *Portrait of Max*, which was published in 1960. The letters written during the time the Beerbohm manuscript was being prepared add more to the picture of their close working relationship. In January 1954, from Rapallo, Italy, where he was interviewing Beerbohm, Behrman wrote expressing his pleasure at having received a letter from Saxe. He related Beerbohm's delight in Saxe's praise of the old man's wit and his own distress over Beerbohm's enfeebled and lonely life. Four years later, Saxe was writing Sam with his comments on the manuscript.

> Now, less than twenty-four hours after the arrival of the typescript, I must tell you that you are getting closer and closer in mood and selective detail to the impressionist portrait of Max both of us have in mind. Your own charm and unmistakable style are strikingly apparent on every one of the tentative forty-six pages, and the material is indeed rich if, until now, only suggested.
>
> I still feel very strongly that it cries for expansion. So far it only hints at its possibilities but I realize that once you put flesh on this skeleton, still a little disarticulated, it will begin to move and breathe and have a life of its own.
>
> It's no favor to you to make so generalized a statement. Unless I can particularize you won't be able to guess what I am driving at. So let me offer for whatever they are worth, page-by-page questions and suggestions, some sensible, some captious, to be accepted or vetoed, but at least a sort of agenda for our summit talks. To begin:
>
> Page 1. It seems to me that much more can be made of Max's and Herbert's[1] background by elaborating on Julius, Constantia, and Eliza,[2] more or less as you did with the forebears of Duveen.
>
> Also on this page, could there be a little expansion of Max's attitude toward the "theatrical columnists" and why he wouldn't deign to point his silver dagger at them?
>
> Page 2. Would it be possible to convey a little of the prevailing atmosphere in America, particularly in Chicago, when Tree put on *An Enemy of the People*. Here Max's attitude toward his brother's showmanship is clear enough, but what about Herbert

---

1. Sir Herbert Beerbohm Tree, Beerbohm's half brother.
2. These were, respectively, Beerbohm's father, his father's first wife, and his mother, Julius's second wife.

and the act he was putting on.

Page 3. Harry Paine's shot at Max suggests the reaction to "In Defense of Cosmetics," but do you give enough of the flavor of the essay itself to make the reader aware of what the shooting was all about?

Page 4. Would it be out of place to write in a sentence or two about *The Yellow Book*. It had quite a history. On this page you do give a little of the flavor of the essay, but I think it would profit by a few more comments almost in Max's own vein.[3]

Page 5. The references to Scott Fitzgerald and Ned Sheldon are dangling in midair. Unless you specify some of the similarities I'm afraid the comparison will be lost. And why not more about Aubrey Beardsley?

Page 6–7. The cracks at Pater are too good to miss. They make me want more. The gem-like flame should be blown on a little harder.

Page 7–9. There is a bite to the brief passage on the Prince of Wales.

Page 10–11. Watch repetition of "mimetic marvel" in first paragraph on tenth and fifth line from bottom on 11. The Le Gallienne episode is fine. Max's abstemious love for Cissi Loftus deserves more comment from you.

Page 13 et seq. We come to the problem of the Turner correspondence. It is essential to the book and we'll have to talk about ways and means of getting permission. Turner's pathetic attempts to write novels and Max's indulgence of them should give you a chance to extemporize in your own inimitable way about the folly of earnest but inept writers.

Can you make more of the courtship of Miss Conover? The reflections of fires come to an anticlimax on page 20.

What about the lifetime aversion for Rudyard Kipling? That's too good to miss.

Page 21. What *was* the solecism committed by Jefferson's hat? Merely that he kept it on his head?

---

3. The closing years of the nineteenth century saw a breaking away from the rigidity of Victorian conventionality and an acceptance of a realism and a freedom in writing rarely expressed in English literature of that time. In 1894 there appeared a periodical called *The Yellow Book*, edited by Henry Harland, with Aubrey Beardsley as art editor. The yellow color of its cover was inspired by Whistler's frequent use of that color in his paintings.

While the first issue shocked the sensibilities of most of the English public, there were many who were delighted with its contents, especially with Max Beerbohm's essay "In Defense of Cosmetics."

The story of how Herbert almost missed out on acquiring *Trilby* through Max's good sense in considering it rubbish is the sort of anecdotal material that adds immeasurably to the impressionist portrait. What follows on John Lane and J. G. Riswald is suggestive and the disdain Max has for success is revealing, as are all the accounts of the caricatures.

Can we use a little diminuendo of our own on "the Jewish friends of Edward's" (page 33)?

Page 34. I wonder whether the allusion to FDR and Cal Coolidge belongs here. I'll talk to you about that.

Page 35. Whatever you write about Turner is interesting and revealing. But without the letters it would all lose point. We must get those letters in.

What follows on Oscar Wilde and the Leversons is also of great interest. In fact, whenever you are anecdotal the whole portrait becomes more vivid. Note the Constance Collier story at the end.

Perhaps this is what I want to stress most: that you use anecdote as only you can, to portray Max and the people he knew and caricatured and loved and endured.

From all the foregoing do I make myself clear in the matter of the need for expansion and elaboration? You can afford greater length because the material is so richly suggestive and I'm willing to bet that your asides will match Max's any day. Don't hesitate to make them!

As I said in the beginning, this longish letter is only a memo, the agenda that can be amplified when we get together. It is a quick improvisation on a typewriter that is giving me trouble. Many of the letters get stuck and don't fall back into place and nothing could be worse for making what I want to say less halting than what I've said. But you can read in and between the lines, can forgive this goddamned b b bbbb (that letter is the worst offender) and me too!

All love

Alas! Saxe was never to see the finished book; it came off the press after his death.

Until 1920 Sinclair Lewis had been writing steadily, producing novels and stories without particular distinction. He then decided to write a novel based on his observation of the life and people of a midwestern town. This he did in *Main Street*, unsparing in his caustic treatment of the subject. It created a whirlpool of controversy, was widely read, and was translated into a dozen languages. Sinclair Lewis became a world figure almost overnight. In 1930 he was awarded the Nobel prize for literature, being the first United States citizen to be so honored.

Main Street was followed by other provocative books, *Babbitt*, *Arrowsmith*, *Elmer Gantry*, *Dodsworth*, and *Ann Vickers*, all published by Doubleday. His editor then was Harry Maule, a very fine man for whom Sinclair Lewis developed a real fondness. Then in 1940 Maule joined Random House and brought Sinclair Lewis with him. Saxe had known Sinclair at an earlier time, and now Lewis began to turn to Saxe in those moments of great despair in his writing and when other personal problems arose.

Sinclair told Saxe he wanted to write a novel that would center on a man who had given up a professorship in a midwestern college to engage in fund raising for noble causes, a man who felt that with his stentorian voice he could make a successful appeal, especially to the ladies, and who soon became involved with every kind of phony project. That man is portrayed in *Gideon Planish*. In his journal of November 22, 1942, Lewis wrote, "I'll be finished by the end of the week and in three weeks from day before yesterday, I'll be home in New York." He delivered the manuscript to Random House, and then began the work with Saxe to hammer it into final form. In his definitive biography of Lewis, Mark Schorer, who had access to Lewis's private papers, diaries, and correspondence, states:

> The matter of language is especially interesting at this time, because now he was making a considerable point of having to hear his prose. His editor at Random House was that man, famed among publishers and writers for his kindness, Saxe Commins; and Lewis now demanded that Commins read his manuscripts aloud to him. When his ear told him that something was not phrased properly, he would then change it.

Shortly before Christmas Saxe stopped by the Hotel Dorset to leave a copy of *Anna Karenina* for Lewis. On Christmas Day Lewis wrote a note to Saxe, which read: "Dear Saxe, I can't tell you how pleased I am to have *Anna Karenina*. What a gift that is! And how pleased and gratified I am that you should be saving my life by working on *Gideon*! The greatest of New Years to you. Ever, Sinclair Lewis."

Gideon Planish was published in April 1943. Even before Lewis had begun work on *Gideon*, the idea for another novel, set in Minnesota, had been on his mind. He had put the idea aside for a time, and then in May 1944, in Duluth, he returned to it. Soon the novel, *Cass Timberlane*, took shape. It was Lewis's nineteenth novel and told, with unflinching realism, of the marital problems of middle-aged Judge Timberlane and his young wife. When the manuscript was finished, Lewis brought it to New York. Then began the long sessions with Saxe. In the fall of 1945, *Cass Timberlane* was published.

Lewis established residence in an elegantly furnished apartment at 300 Central Park West. Despite the many friends he had in New York, he spent many lonely hours in his handsome quarters, and many were the times he would phone Saxe and urge him to come to him. They played chess, a game Lewis had only recently learned, and when Saxe would deliberately lose the game, Lewis would march up and down the room and gloatingly say to Saxe, "Who in hell told you you know anything about chess?"

In his youth Lewis had been much concerned about labor and social problems. More recently he concerned himself with the evil in racial discrimination, and while in Duluth he made it a point to seek out leaders in the black community and invite them into his home. He wanted their confidence and urged them to talk freely about their problems. He also did intensive research in the State Historical Library in Minneapolis and talked with ministers of black churches and with people in the Urban League. With this experience, he set about writing a new novel, *Kingsblood Royal*, which took shape quickly. In five weeks Lewis completed the first draft.

Then came another surge of restlessness. Lewis gave up his house in Duluth and bought a place in New England, a large estate just outside of Wiliamstown, Massachusetts. Having refurbished it to his satisfaction, he looked forward to the visits of his friends. Some came for short stays, others for longer ones, but when they left the ache of loneliness was still there. Poor Sinclair! What a tormented man he was! He moved from place to place, from house to house, but in none of them was there a corner that meant home to him.

In late September Saxe spent a week in Williamstown, working with Lewis on *Kingsblood Royal*. As before, the manuscript was gone over line by line. When it was done, Lewis followed Saxe to New York; the novel went to press and was brought out in May

1947. Lewis was of course elated when it was chosen as a Literary Guild selection.

Lewis's next novel, *The God Seeker*, was an outgrowth of his reading of religious tracts and of the history of Minnesota. In September 1948 he came to New York with his manuscript and had the usual long sessions with Saxe. Then in 1949 the book went to press.

October saw him in Italy, from where he sent Saxe a rare little urn with this note:

June 1949

Dear Saxe:

You the classicist, may like the fact that this humble little object from Italy is at least two thousand, three thousand years old. It's Etruscan pottery, a numbered piece from the Collection of Prince Pignatelli in Rome, excavated at his Castel Monterundi, broken up at his death. You are not to drink Coca-Cola from it.

Red

Coca-Cola was one of the many abhorrences Sinclair had, and he would swear every time he saw the sign flaunted in the streets and avenues of Europe.

During the summer he came back to America for a short stay, and the following September he sailed again for Europe. This time his brother joined him. They travelled a good deal; then the brother went off to England, and Sinclair decided to settle in a house in Florence. But wherever he went, he was hounded by the shadow of his loneliness. Once he was heard to cry out, "Oh, God, no man has ever been so miserable!"

This dejection precipitated his physical deterioration. He took to drinking as a means of escape, but that only helped to hasten his complete collapse. He died in a clinic in Rome on January 10, 1951, unknown to his doctors and nurses and surrounded by strangers— alone at death as he had been most of his life.

In the early 1950s Saxe was the editor for a series of science books for the general reader: *Basic Astronomy*, by Professor Peter Van de Kamp of Swarthmore; *Basic Biology*, by Professor G. Kasten Talmadge of Marquette; *Basic Psychiatry*, by Professor Edward Ames Strecker of Pennsylvania; and *Basic Psychology*, by Professor Leonard Carmichael of the Smithsonian Institution. Saxe always came to such projects with a fresh, inquiring mind, insisting that everything be explained clearly, and as a by-product extending his own education.

Out of another world came the books of John O'Hara. As a news reporter O'Hara had acquired all the vulgarisms of tabloid journalism, and his acute ear had caught all the nuances of colloquial speech. This served him well, for his best feature was his slick and adroit dialogue. His first novel, *Appointment in Samarra*, was a huge success, as were the books that followed: *Butterfield 8*, *Pal Joey*, and *Hellbox* (a collection of twenty stories). Then came *A Rage to Live*. A letter from O'Hara to Saxe, written on *New Yorker* stationery, was in the nature of a rebuke:

> I plan to come up to New York on Wednesday, for lunch with Terry Helburn, and after she has paid the reckoning I will bring some product to be retyped. By that time I think I will have reached just 500 pages of the original double spaced (I'm now seventeen pages short of that figure). Where you can help me is here: I am not sure where the first retyping job ended. I think it was at the top of page 385 of the original manuscript, but I may be wrong. So will you please look at what you have (the triple-spaced manuscript) and see what the last sentence is, and then telegraph me the wording of same. Naturally I don't want to lug the whole double-spaced manuscript up to New York.
>
> You'd better get that surgical glint out of your eye, because far from my doing any ruthless cutting on the final manuscript, there will be ruthful additions between now and the submitting of the printer's copy. You are in for some surprises when you see the final manuscript; extremely minor characters as of Book I, which you may think ought to go, will be popping up all through Book II. I don't suppose any of the critics will be alert enough to notice it, but in this book I have been influenced more by Jules Romains than by any other author. I am inclined to think he is the greatest novelist of our time. However, Harrisburg isn't Paris, and I am confining myself to one volume, you will be relieved to learn.
>
> Tell Bennett I complied with his suggestion that I have my picture taken in my new car. Belle took it, and if it turns out okay I'll probably have pictures when I see you Wednesday. But if he wants to run a cut in Trade Winds he is not to run a caption: "This is how Random House treats its authors." I had to write a

magazine piece to enable me to pay for the car, in spite of my strong hint that RH was going to be charming and give it to me as a bonus.

The title of my novel is *A Rage to Live.* I have tried it out on everybody from Rosemary Benet to Eric Hatch's mother, an enormous range, believe me. Several persons who didn't like it at first changed their minds days later. The best thing about it, or one of the best, as Rosemary pointed out, is the unusual juxtaposition of simple words. The best thing about it is how it, and the whole poem from which it comes, apply to my novel. And another best thing about it is that I like it. Actually, although my titles are usually pretty good, people don't buy books by titles as much as they do by the author's name. I know I do. I also know it's time for me to go to bed.

Hope to see you Wednesday.

Yours,
John

The title is from the *Moral Essays* of Alexander Pope.

When Saxe began reading the manuscript, he was taken aback by the obscenities in many passages. He called O'Hara's attention to this and urged him to cut them out, warning him that John S. Sumner, agent of the New York Society for the Suppression of Vice, was on the prowl and waging a vigorous campaign against off-color books. This so infuriated O'Hara, that he picked up a square piece of marble that Saxe used as a paperweight and hurled it at Saxe with an explosion of gutter language. Fortunately Saxe dodged in time. A few days later O'Hara dropped by Saxe's office, as though nothing had happened, leaving a gift of a gold pencil with a little note which read, "Still speaking, by God."

No doubt Saxe's warning to O'Hara would be considered ludicrous in this day and climate. But in fact O'Hara was obliged to absent himself from New York for a time to avoid arrest.

Though O'Hara and Saxe continued to work together for a while, there existed a mute uneasiness that ultimately caused a break, after which Saxe never touched O'Hara's books again. When he established residence in Princeton, O'Hara said to a newspaper reporter, "You see, I'm settling down a bit, but that is not to say that I do not have an occasional outburst."

There were, however, happier collaborations. Among the authors Saxe cherished was Ted (Theodore) Geisel, the nationally known author of children's books who goes by the name of Dr. Seuss. He and Saxe worked together from the time Random House began to publish such delightfully zany books as *Horton Hatches the Egg*, *The King's Stilts*, *If I Ran the Zoo*, *McElligot's Pool*, and *The Cat in the Hat*. In a letter to me, Ted said of Saxe, "He was probably the only editor I ever had who ever taught me anything. He did it with patience and understanding. I was terribly flattered by the attention he gave to my little books, when he was engaged in editing the much vaster books of William Faulkner."

Then there were some delightful times with Frank Sullivan, the writer and book reviewer. What a charming and witty man! During the Liveright days, Saxe had worked with Sullivan on a number of his books, including *Broccoli and Old Lace*. Several years after it was published, Russell Crouse told Sullivan that he and Howard Lindsay, following their triumph as playwrights of *Life With Father*, were about to try their hand as producers! Sullivan tells the story in a letter:

> I told him he and Howard were crazy, and he said, this play is about two crazy Brooklyn ladies. I asked him what the name of the play was and he said *Arsenic and Old Lace*. I said, Oh, yeah! Well, in that case, I'll thank you for two seats on the aisle for the opening, because you've swiped half the title of my *Broccoli and Old Lace*. I was being facetious but I think poor Russell was actually a bit embarrassed. The result was that Lindsay and Crouse let me have a share of the *Arsenic* play at, I think, around $580 and it returned me over $10,000 in dividends. I never hit the jackpot like that before or since.

Editing, Ghost Writing, and Longshoremen

One aspect of the literary life that Saxe tried to avoid as much as possible was cocktail parties, noisy affairs where new books are launched in an atmosphere of alcoholic euphoria. Shortly after we arrived at one party, Saxe took me off into a corner and whispered to me, "Let's go home." Just then an attractive woman carrying a highball came gliding toward him and asked, "Why are you in a corner? Are you a writer?" "No," was his monosyllabic reply. The lady persisted. "Then what do you do?" On impulse he answered, "I'm in the cleaning and repairing business." The lady immediately glided away, probably to ask her hostess, "How on earth did a guy like that get in here?"

Although Saxe had spoken in jest, he had told the essential truth about the work of an editor. Books are more a collaborative effort than the public realizes. Their quality, their impact on the reader, often depends on how well the writer's editor has done his job of "cleaning and repairing."

Saxe had once been described, in the *Saturday Review of Literature,* as an editor capable of "striking barren rock with his blue pencil and making champagne gush forth." The extensive revision and polishing that new manuscripts often required, however, though that alone would constitute a full-time job for almost anyone, were only a part of Saxe's work.

As director of the Modern Library for many years, Saxe had to read extensively to determine which titles should be added to that list. In addition, he found time to edit a good many works, both for the Modern Library and otherwise, and to write introductions and forewords for some of the works he edited, and for some that he did not, and even for one that was brought out by another publisher. He contributed, for example, introductions to *The Poems and Plays of Robert Browning* (1934), *The Complete Works and Letters of Charles Lamb* (1935), and *The Pensées and Provincial Letters of Blaise Pascal* (1941). He edited and provided a foreword for each of the two volumes in Scribner's Wilderness Edition of *The Plays of Eugene O'Neill* (1935), though the forewords were signed by Gene. Early in 1934 Gene had been requested to write the prefaces. He had declined, but had agreed to Donald Klopfer's suggestion that Saxe write a foreword for each volume, giving the facts about the plays, and that Gene sign the forewords as though they were his own. This plan was confirmed in an exchange of letters between Klopfer and Maxwell Perkins, who was then an editor for Scribner's. Saxe also wrote a statement about *Bound East for Cardiff*, the first of O'Neill's plays to be produced in a theater, and this was also signed by Gene. Another volume which Saxe edited and supplied with a foreword was the Armed Services edition of *Selected Plays of Eugene O'Neill* (1945). Among the works which Saxe edited and supplied with introductions were *The Selected Writings of Washington Irving* (1945), William Faulkner's *A Rose for Emily* (1945), *Selected Writings of Robert Louis Stevenson* (1947), *The Basic Writings of George Washington* (1948), and *The Tales of Guy de Maupassant* (1950). Saxe also served as coeditor with Robert W. Linscott for the four-volume *The World's Great Thinkers* (1948).

As if Saxe's calendar weren't crowded enough, he found time to give a series of lectures, "Editorial Practices and Principles of Book Publishing," at Columbia University during the academic years between 1947 and 1950. At the close of each term Saxe, instead of giving his students the usual exam, invited them to come to our apartment in New York for a party, which naturally included discussions about books and publishing.

I remember that at one of these evenings, in 1950, the following question was put to Saxe: "What is the public reading today?" Saxe replied by pointing to the world's upheaval following the war years.

It has revolutionized our way of thinking and given us a new set of values. Publishers can no longer get away with a list made up of escape books, inspirational tracts, and vicarious romances. The public's interest has been shifting to informative books, books that reflect the thoughts and spirit of a changing world. Eye witness accounts of events and interpretations by experts are in tremendous demand. Consider how avidly the public has been reading *Berlin Diary* and the books by John Gunther, Edgar Snow, and Louis Fisher. The world we live in is commanding everyone's attention. Obviously millions of people would rather have known the outcome of the Russian campaign than the solution to the fair heroine's dilemma on page three hundred and twenty.

The interest in the classics is phenomenal! And the explanation is not far to seek. Plato's *The Republic* has very special meaning for people of our time. Pascal's *Pensées* and the *Provincial Letters* are still among the greatest declarations of faith and in the finest tradition of controversial writing. The *Essays* of Montaigne and the philosophies of Bacon, Mill, Locke, Hume, Spinoza, and William James bring the light of reason into an otherwise unreasonable world.

Recently Random House published Machiavelli's *The Prince* and the *Discourses* in one volume. It had a remarkable sale. There is no mystery to that. In a world in which Machiavellian trickery in politics and international intrigue has proven, let us say, temporarily successful, the modern reader wants to go to the sources and learn what can be done about it.

It may seem that too much emphasis is being put on the classics. Nothing could be farther from my mind than to neglect topical books—the commentaries and interpretations of living history, the poetry, essays, short stories, books of the theater and the arts, the textbooks and manuals, and the really first rate books for children.

In pointing to the classics, I feel we cannot combat the evils of totalitarianism or give meaning to democracy unless we have an understanding of the forces that motivate both of them. And nowhere are those forces so perfectly revealed as in the classics.

Think of the extraordinary case of Aristotle! Last spring, Random House published a book called *The Basic Writings of Aristotle.* Then for the first time in 2,334 years his name appeared on the best seller list.

When *The Basic Writings of George Washington* was published, Saxe received a letter from a young associate editor at Macmillan, James A. Michener, telling him how impressed he was with the book. While at Macmillan, Michener had written his *Tales of the South Pacific*, which had won him the 1947 Pulitzer Prize. Not long after his letter to Saxe, Michener began work on his first novel, *The Fires of Spring*. When he had completed it, he again wrote to Saxe, offering him, as he put it, "cold turkey." Saxe's response was cordial, and their relationship began to thrive.

One Sunday Michener drove from Doylestown, Pennsylvania, to Princeton, where we rented a house for the summer. He arrived, after the two-hour drive, in time for breakfast, and the two men had a full day to work undisturbed. The book was eventually published in 1950 by Dymock of Sydney.

As yet Michener had not given up his position at Macmillan. He was in a quandary and deliberating whether he dare risk devoting himself to a full-time writing career. That he was a perceptive editor can be seen from the comments he made in a letter of June 2, 1947, on Saxe's introduction to the *Selected Writings of Robert Louis Stevenson*. The reversal of roles was complete, for now Saxe was the author.

> Your summaries which start on page xxiv are the best part of the essay for me. They are solid with thought and offer some good judgements. I was glad to see you stick your neck out on Stevenson's various types of writing. I agree with you on the essays (allay more than arouse); think you a little too hopeful on the novels; agree thoroughly on the short stories; and feel you don't quite do justice to *A Child's Garden of Verses*. I'm not an A. A. Milne fancier, and firmly believe that all the fairies at the bottoms of all gardens should be dealt with as Lady Peel proposes in her bloodthirsty ballad, and I'm not even very fond of the *Garden*, but I think it more substantial than your damning praise would infer. I found the travel books rather dull and cannot judge of the merit of your comments.
>
> The total effect of your essay is strong. Your writing certainly shows the marks of a consolidated mind in charge of what's going on down on the typewriter keys. I like it as a style and should think most readers would share in this judgment. Sometimes your use of big words engulfed a struggling sentence, but usually your wedding of word and movement was most felicitous.
>
> Your portrait of Stevenson was quite fresh, and very much of this age. I think you did the man a service; but the true idolator would, I am sure, think you had written some of your passages with tongue in cheek. I thought you identified the myth rather

nicely (I would have enjoyed a fuller treatment) and you gave some clue as to the nature of the real man. (Again, I'd have liked more development of the last paragraph on page vii.) A rather different man came through your sentences than the one I had heard of in all parts of Scotland, and strangely enough it was a more universal man—more French and American and Samoan— than the reedy figure they remember in Edinburgh and the University circles.

Mrs. Osbourne was a real surprise to me. I rather hoped that you might mention the parallel case of Rudyard Kipling, whose American wife was certainly a vibrant experience for him during his American days, at least. In fact, your entire coverage of Stevenson in this country might have been lengthened and still met my taste.

Finally, I think I may have found two small mistakes. In the recent obituaries of Lloyd Osbourne (who astonished me by being alive as late as two weeks ago) it is said that he drew the map of Treasure Island, that he brought it to the flagging Stevenson, and that in a real sense he inspired and perhaps motivated the story. I'm not sure that you say Stevenson drew the map (I can't find the place) but I did get the idea that you inferred it.

On page xxi your love of a rounded sentence tricks you into a slight geographical slip. ". . . in the forest of Upolu on the island of Samoa" has little geographical meaning, for Upolu is itself the island and there is no island of Samoa. It's a group of islands, foully torn into two governments. Upolu, second biggest and most important island, along with Savaii, the biggest, are governed by New Zealand. Tutuila, quite small in comparison, is, of course, governed by our navy.

As for the inclusions, *The Beach of Falesa* is alone worth the book. I never even knew it had been written.

Saxe convinced Michener that his was a real and natural gift and that he must pursue his career as a writer. Michener did give up his post at Macmillan and came to Random House as an author. By this time Saxe was convinced that he himself was primarily an editor and only coincidentally a writer. In an address many years later, in May 1958, before the Nassau Club in Princeton, Saxe described his life as a ghost writer. In many ways, his ghost writing was not so far removed from his work as an editor.

No doubt you have heard many speeches which begin "I stand before you . . ." This time, strange to say, it is not I who face you but an apparition. Lest you be frightened, let me assure you that my real self—whatever that may be—is sufficiently identifiable to have Mr. Zarker cash checks for me at the bank or have Mrs. Yeoman extend credit for liquor. I pay my taxes, carry my own driver's license, and have a nodding acquaintance with many members of the Nassau Club and the Police Department.

That other self—the one I have kept concealed in shame until now—has had a strange life of its own, and, contritely, I am today revealing its ghastly sins. That self was a ghost and was representative of other ghosts, living and dead, who moved about in terror, afraid of discovery and exposure. But what is really unique about this ghost is that he himself was afraid, scared out of his wits, as the saying goes, and the men he haunted were not.

Let me confess, I have been a particular kind of ghost, one who possesses and then becomes possessed, who takes over for a little while a man's ego and then is unceremoniously thrown out. My great fear in that life now past was that I would be discovered, exposed, and punished for being a ghost who writes—a ghost writer!

How did I become a ghost writer, a being of countless sins, and then, so to speak, become a ghost emeritus?

The answer is simple—hunger! An emptiness of the belly and a gnawing of the mind, a gnawing whetted by a desire to write, a love for words, an insatiable curiosity about what other people think, and a passion for anonymity. All these combined to bring about my damnation.

As with all sins, the beginnings were small, English compositions for classmates with too large an allowance and too little inclination to study; letters for girls over signatures of young men incapable of giving form to their desires and dreams. In those days I liked to think of myself as a Cyrano de Bergerac with a not-too-prominent nose.

I helped to write a textbook on psychology, prepared a brochure on the therapeutic resources of Mother Nature, sermons for a minister, and briefs for a lawyer. I became a scientist, explorer, healer, athlete, mystic, detective, and lover, all by one remove. Out of this torrent of words came just enough to pay the rent of my attic apartment. I was then hiding behind a whole census of pseudonyms. To see those names in print enlarged the world I was populating with my shamelessly procreative brain.

When the balance of rejection slips outweighed acceptances I sought out my literary agent. All I knew then about agents was that they dwelt on the periphery of the literary world, bargaining with its griefs and privy to its secrets. They mated hunger of the ego with hunger of the stomach and brought forth from this unholy union men who craved to express themselves, but couldn't, and their ghosts. They fattened on both.

It wasn't necessary to tell the agent why I had come. He riffled through some large cards and said, as if he were a fortuneteller reading them, that the outlook was dark. Then he pulled one from the stack and said, "Here's something you might possibly do."

He mentioned the name of a famous motion picture actress, an aging woman who still played young parts, a woman who was able to look, on the screen, as immature as she pretended to be. I knew her face, her gestures, her wide and pleading eyes, as did every American at that time.

"The idea is for you to explain how it is possible to act these young parts convincingly," the agent said. "I haven't the slightest notion how the old bag does it. Neither has she. Do it in twenty-five hundred words and bring it to me by nine o'clock tonight. You know, the innocent touch. Purity is the pitch. It will pay five dollars."

I walked out of the agent's office carrying an envelope with photographs of the actress. I went to my room and spread the glossy pictures on my bed.

There remained five hours for twenty-five hundred words, five hundred words an hour—long words, short words, articles, prepositions, connectives, and even the vertical pronoun, that thinnest of letters that sometimes seems to carry so much weight—they all counted at one-fifth of a cent each. One by one they were frightening, yet, once set down, they added up and the total did not seem staggering.

I scanned the photographs. The actress had been beautiful at one time, but now she was a long way past her first blossoming. What made her play children's roles? How could she—or I, for that matter—know what it means to be a child? How did it feel to be a woman of middle age playing the part of a young girl?

How did it feel, for that matter, to be a man of middle age playing the part of a young man? I was a young man; I knew how that felt. For a long time I considered the problem of being a woman. Getting nowhere, I shaved, thinking it might help if I were smoothfaced.

At six o'clock I sat down at the typewriter, trembling and sweating lest I fail in my effort to make—well, to possess—the actress. I searched for a word, for a beginning. I pondered stealing something from Shakespeare or Milton or Balzac or

Tolstoy. In despair I put my head on the typewriter and let the
cold metal press into my forehead. At seven o'clock I roused
myself. I had to write something. Under the name of the actress I
began to type. "There is only one sort of woman who never
grows old, and that is the woman who is in love. All my life I
have been in love—with people, with places, with trees and birds
and weather and music and the soft wash of tides against beaches
when the moon is low." More garbage of the same kind came out
of my typewriter.

At nine o'clock I went to the agent's office and handed him a
manuscript of twenty-five hundred words. He read it, reached
into his pocket, and handed me a five dollar bill.

"Not bad," he said. "Let me know when you need more work."

Two months later I saw my article in a national woman's
magazine. I found out how much the actress was paid for her
confession. The price was $750. The agent, then, received
seventy-five dollars, the customary 10 percent. Of this, I, the
author, was given five dollars.

Since the night I received five dollars for possessing a middle-
aged actress, I began to eat well and could pay my rent
promptly. I was still sane and more solvent than I had ever been,
though now and then, like any businessman, I made a deal that
had to be written off as a loss. There was, for instance, the case
of the Doctor of Philosophy. He needed only his written thesis to
fulfill the requirements for his degree and a job in a midwestern
university. His notes on "The Narrative Correlations in Chaucer
and Boccaccio" were a chaos. There would be $500 dollars in it
for me if I could bring those notes into order and provide
forty-five thousand words, impressively documented and sprayed
with citations and footnotes. I went to work with a will made
strong by years of hunger and lustful at the thought of scholarship. The public library was my university and its attendants
were my faculty advisers. Painstakingly I ground out the dissertation, embellishing it with so many learned references and
parenthetical analogues that I came to believe myself an aca-
demician who ultimately would be immortalized in a footnote.

The thesis was finished, submitted, and accepted; my em-
ployer was granted the right to wear the hood of his fellowship.
When I asked for my fee, he laughed at me. "Try and collect," he
said. He taunted me into suing him. I consulted a lawyer friend, a
man for whom I had once written a brief. He said, "Not a
chance. You haven't a leg to stand on. You'd be coming into
court with dirty hands. You're a party to a fraud. Forget it."

Well, if I could stir up in my witch's cauldron a potion that had been swallowed by learned examiners of candidates in philosophy, why could I not concoct a book? That would be more like real writing. I might even get enough money from it to buy back my own identity.

I let my agent know that I might be induced to possess an "author," one who had an interesting story to tell but not the skill to tell it. . . .

He was an adventurer, an extrovert with an itching foot. He had been around the world a half-dozen times, hunted everything from heiresses to tigers, flew over the Himalayas, walked on the floor of the sea, was awakened one morning to find a cobra curled up on his pillow, and had lost part of an ear to a certain Asiatic young lady who resented his decision to leave town without her. Except for the mutilated ear, he was a perfect physical specimen. He was utterly without fear. I shuddered as I listened to his tales. I loathe snakes. I am afraid of women. I have never been close to a wild animal or discharged a gun except at a Broadway shooting gallery. His was the sort of book I longed to write. I took the job.

I was fascinated by what I heard; I shivered as I sat down to write chapters describing nights in the jungle. Things that creep, things that crawl, things that fly quickly, things that are damp and soft and slimy are not for me. I am a city boy. I had nightmares after writing about the cobra. I screamed and leaped up, feeling the stab of the snake's fangs in my wrist as I rolled off the bed. But on paper I willed the reptile to glide away.

The publisher was delighted with the manuscript. The author was pleased and amused. "You make me sound like quite a hero," he said. "Most of the time I really wasn't in danger, if you figure the odds." I told him that I had injected my own fear into the book for the reader's sake. How could I explain to him or to anyone else that even a ghost can be afraid of his own shadow?

The success of the adventure book lifted me into the first bracket of ghost writers. That category was occupied by those who supplied statesmanship for politicians and philosophy for financiers and industrialists. No man, I discovered, was honest enough to refuse to wear my talent as his own. Honesty, I found, is generally confined to concrete things. What is abstract seems to be in public domain and is anyone's to take. I shuddered now as I realized the implications of this simple fact—that a man will steal another's mind and never think of it as theft.

No matter how we of the dark brotherhood of ghosts question our own ethics, we are quick to recognize many fine distinctions of rank. We look with envy on those superior spirits who influence and mold the mass mind. We have a sacred awe for the men of our anonymous guild who are called up to take possession of national or world leaders and guide them subtly toward our own utopian dream of the commonwealth of man.

The opportunity to prompt a notable figure on the world stage, to mount to exalted heights of ghosthood, came from an unexpected source. An attaché of a foreign nation summoned me to his embassy in Washington for an interview. The punctilious career man spoke with an Oxford accent and with the prudence of an intermediary of an intermediary. He made no agreements or commitments; he felt his way with caution, looked ahead, and kept many roads open for retreat.

His "principal," as he called him, was an ex-premier, honored by his own government and people with the highest offices and rewards which were in their power to grant. He was a man, I was assured, whose work and influence could no longer be contained within the boundaries of his own nation; he now had to make himself felt on a global scale. What he needed was a sympathetic presentation to the American people, who were not yet sufficiently aware of his greatness.

What could serve that purpose better than a glowing biography by a statesman of this free land, an American risen from humble beginnings to serve his people in their Congress? Incidentally this servant of a free land would profit by a new reputation in the honorable field of letters, and, besides, he was up for reelection in the fall.

The plan was flawless. All I had to do was write a book about a man of whom I knew absolutely nothing and sign it with the name of a politician I had never met. There was, I was told, an advantage in beginning without any prejudice toward the subject or the author.

The congressman, my author, fell into the general category of a client. He meant no more to me than the famous actresses, scholars, narcotics addicts, adventurers, or others whose alter egos I once had been. It was the prospect of entering the arena of world affairs that stirred my imagination.

The attaché placed at my disposal a library of press cuttings in many languages. The career of my distant subject was recorded in volume after volume of proceedings. The archives of his attainments were complete and unabridged. His mistakes had been carefully edited. Nowhere could I find in this anthology of praise a line of dissenting opinion. I arranged this staggering mass of material and blocked out a general outline of the book. It was to begin with childhood and end with an apotheosis of the hero as a sponsor of a program for a multilateral government of the sovereign states of the world, a plan which anticipated the United Nations by many years. It was a daring, revolutionary idea. This alone made me think I was serving a good and necessary cause.

With the nimble curiosity of my kind, I began to search afield for obscure facts about my world benefactor. I wanted to discover how his life became dedicated to the brotherhood of man. I was dismayed to find that in his youth he had faced the charge of rape, that in his early manhood he had violated the trust of his best friend, and that as a public official he had betrayed the people to whom he owed his position. Still, I rationalized, no man is perfect. A critical biography would only defeat the higher purposes the book was to serve—the political unity of man.

I disposed of the statutory crime as a youthful folly. I wrote a stirring tribute to the best friend who had been betrayed. Over the act of apostasy against his own people I brushed a heavy varnish of explanation, so that it was made to seem that our hero was more of a John the Beloved than a Judas Iscariot.

The book was published. It was given front page reviews; it inspired editorial writers to discussions of the "new world policy." One prophet among the critics declared that the book foreshadowed the coming of "the responsible world citizen." The author-politician, who saw his work for the first time in its bound form, was hailed as a "creative statesman." He autographed hundreds of copies. He went abroad, and my subject, the ex-premier, awarded him the ribbon of the highest order of the land.

At last my spectral life had been crowned. This was my greatest success. I had attained the top rung of my Jacob's ladder. I was a ghost of ghosts, a shade at the height of shadow.

There was nothing more for me to achieve in the world where I had lived through other men and other men had come to life through me. Now I was ready for the great fulfillment, the realization of myself. Now I could admit my own identity; now I could speak for my personal convictions; now I could write my own book. I had money in the bank; I had experience in a hundred styles and a thousand plots. I could now fashion my own masterpiece.

I gathered material. I made notes. I blocked out chapters. I sat down at my typewriter and prepared to begin.

Then I began to look for the person I was to represent in the book I was about to write. I searched through the jungle of my mind for myself.

I was not there!

I was a ghost, an apparition composed of the memories of the men and women I had possessed, whose minds I had been for a little while, whose beings I had stalked and trapped and cunningly snared in prose.

What I had been was lost and gone, dissipated and scattered through the people I had seized upon and impersonated. In each I had left a part of me. Now nothing of me was left. I had given myself away!

Now I was really afraid, for I no longer knew who I was.

I got up from the typewriter and telephoned a literary agent. "I have an excellent idea for a book," I said. "Do you know somebody who would like to be its author?"

Budd Schulberg, who lived in Bucks County, Pennsylvania, in the late forties, often drove to Princeton for Saxe's counsel on both his writings and his personal affairs. The two had first met in 1933, when Budd turned up at Random House with a couple of stories about a sleezy Broadway character named Sammy Glick. Saxe perceived in these stories a basis for a novel and urged Budd to develop the idea. Sammy was without doubt reprehensible and utterly devoid of any scruples. He ran from one shady situation to another. Then he ran off to Hollywood and got involved in the life there. Budd did write the novel, which, of course, was *What Makes Sammy Run?* and in it he excoriates this objectionable specimen and the environment in which he finds himself. The novel is a vitriolic indictment of an ugly side of American life. It became a best seller and started Budd's successful career as a writer.

One day in 1953 Budd came to Princeton to tell Saxe he wanted to write a novel about the corrupt, gangster-ridden New York waterfront, where violence was a regular part of the longshoreman's life. Budd intended to expose the thuggery of the bosses who mercilessly exploited the stevedores. The announcement led to a series of weekend discussions. As Budd talked, Saxe sat there carefully taking notes. These sessions not only took up most of Saturday but often spilled over into Sunday. I often wondered whether Schulberg realized what a drain all this was on Saxe's strength, after he had put in a demanding week at his office.

When Budd had finished his first draft of *On the Waterfront*, Saxe urged him to revise and polish it as soon as possible so that the manuscript could go to the printers at an early date. Meanwhile, movie rights for the novel were sold.

At Random House, Bennett Cerf and Donald Klopfer, on learning this, were more eager than ever that the book should appear simultaneously with the movie's first showing. But Budd was not to be found. He had gone off somewhere out of reach of telephone or telegram. Finally, after much searching, Saxe caught up with him in Florida and brought him back to Princeton.

For days they worked together, and Saxe did not let Schulberg out of his sight until the manuscript was ready for the printers. This required more than a simple transformation. Schulberg himself later, in a letter written March 28, 1956, contrasted a movie script with a book manuscript.

A film script is a funny animal. It is a sort of live skeleton. As soon as you begin to flesh it up too much it is way over-length.... One odd thing about a movie is that people accept things that would never pass in a novel. In the *Waterfront* film play, you may remember, I originally wrote some scenes showing the priest mulling over what has happened on the docks, and coming around to his decision to do something about it. Both Spiegel and Kazan objected that this took too much footage—Kazan assured me it would work simply for the priest to show up on the waterfront already committed to his new mission. I must admit that in the picture this did seem to work, at least no one objected, not a single critic asked how the priest was converted to this new interpretation of his religious responsibility so quickly. It may have something to do with the techniques of the Dissolve and Fade-Out. When you dissolve through to a new scene, it only takes a few seconds, but the audience seems to accept the fact that much may have happened in between. It is an interesting phenomenon. It is as if this twentieth century audience has trained itself to respond to a new technological art form. Somehow they are able to fill in the gaps themselves.

At last the book was completed. The proofs arrived and they had to be carefully checked, particularly for the authenticity of the waterfront jargon, and it was important that it be done without delay. Too much time had already been lost. To the dismay of Random House, the movie was on its way to being launched, far in advance of the book's publication.

To speed matters, Saxe thought it best to call in the longshoreman who had helped Budd when he was searching for reliable information about the waterfront. If any questions should arise about conditions around the docks or the jargon spoken there, surely the longshoreman could supply the answers.

One morning Saxe phoned from his office to say that he was bringing Budd home with him. "Hold your breath," he added, "the longshoreman is coming, too!" Then he went on to explain, "The disturbances as well as the curiosity at the office were too much. At home, with the longshoreman there, the work to be done on the proofs can be dispatched in no time."

I was a bit bewildered, to say the least. Throughout the day I kept wondering what the longshoreman could be like. Surely he was a man of brawn. His shoulders would be broad, each capable of supporting a weighty trunk.

When the three men arrived, Budd said, by way of introduction, "Here is Brownie." I looked for a moment and was speechless. Brownie was not even of average height! His face—that poor face—looked as though it had been bashed in a dozen times. His flattened nose bore no resemblance to what it might have been. His eyes did not set right, no doubt due to the buffeting they had suffered.

I said, "How do you do, Mr. Brown."

"Aw," came a quick reply, "cut it out. Just call me Brownie."

While Budd and Saxe were hanging up their coats, Brownie stood near the entrance to the living room, gave it a long look, and burst out, "Jesus Christ, some joint!" Budd took Brownie's bag and put it in the bedroom assigned to him, while I tried to make conversation with our guest. Dinner was ready to be served and soon we were seated at the table. After asking whether I had done the cooking myself, Brownie allowed as how he was a pretty good cook himself.

"My mother had nine kids, and I was the oldest of the lot. Somebody had to give her a hand. Them was the war days, and they handed out ration tickets. Ration tickets!" Brownie laughed scornfully. "This is what I did with 'em." He grabbed his napkin and made the motion of tearing it to shreds. He repeated, "Ration tickets! What would a bunch of hungry people be doing with ration tickets?"

"How else," I asked, "could you manage to feed such a large family?"

"Aw, lady, you don't know the first thing about it. I work on the waterfront, see, and I learn. Them crates that comes in day after day, full of all kinds of grub. Do you know, there's hundreds of crates of beef coming from Argentina? With so much beef around, would I be letting my family walk around with empty bellies? I just helped myself to a side of beef now and then!"

I exclaimed, "A side of beef! But, Brownie, how could you get away with a side of beef!"

"Lady," said Brownie, "come on down to the waterfront sometime and I'll be showing you a little Catholic church not far away. When it comes to hiding things, you can't beat the confessional."

After dinner the men went into the study and set to work, while I went into Brownie's room to turn back the covers of his bed. To my amazement, I saw the most exquisite pajamas and robe on the bed. The label read "Sulka." "Why," I thought, "I couldn't possibly afford such magnificent clothes for Saxe!" The toilet articles, equally elegant, had beautifully shaped black bone handles and were lying on a rolled-out, dark green brocaded case. All waiting to serve the well-groomed man! It wasn't hard for me to guess where they came from.

It was past midnight, and we had all turned in, when I heard a tip-toeing down the hall. Thinking that Budd or Brownie was in need of something, I quickly slipped into a robe and stepped into the hall. There I saw Brownie fishing into the pocket of his coat which was hanging in the hall closet.

"Brownie, are you all right?"

"Yeah, lady, this is what I want," and with that he showed me a little leather case, somewhat larger than a key case. When he opened it, there rested a string of rosary beads on a colored lithograph of the Madonna. All Brownie said was, "I can't get to sleep without it. I always put it under my pillow."

The next morning as the men set to work again, they soon discovered that the last ten pages of the proofs were missing. Saxe phoned his office and was told that they were on his desk. Brownie was sent into New York to fetch them. He was put on the train at about eleven in the morning. Allowing for delays and what not,

Brownie should have been back by six, or in time for dinner. Dinnertime came, but no Brownie; Saxe and Budd were frantic. They phoned everywhere trying to track him down. No luck!

About 10 o'clock in the evening a taxi drew up in front of the house, and I saw the driver helping a staggering Brownie to the door. He greeted me with, "Hi, lady! I missed you."

Trying to be helpful, I handed him a glass of milk. He took one sip and spit it out.

"Jesus, lady, I ain't had a taste of this here stuff since I was weaned!"

Saxe and Budd, with grins on their faces, stood in the kitchen doorway watching this performance.

The following morning found the men on the final sheets of the proofs. I stole off to the piano to work on an arrangement by Respighi of a lovely sixteenth-century lute piece. Ever so lightly came the footsteps of Brownie, who seated himself at the farthest end of the room. At a pause in the playing, I turned to Brownie and asked him if he liked the music. He came toward me and gently put his hand on top of my head, saying, "And sure, lady, Mother Mary couldn't play any better than that!"

The checking of the proofs was finished, and now Budd and Brownie were packing to leave. When they got into the car and were moving out of the driveway, Brownie stuck his head out of the window and shouted, "I'll be sending you French underwear!"

A week or so later, the waterfront priest called Saxe at the office. "I don't know what's happened to Brownie," he said, "he told me he wants to learn to play the piano."

Adlai Stevenson, W. H. Auden, and Other Writers

8

When President Harry S. Truman announced that he would not seek reelection in 1952, his staff and the leaders of the Democratic party were dismayed. No pressure on their part could persuade him to revoke his decision, and so the search began for a Democratic candidate for the presidency. The search ended at the Democratic National Convention with the nomination of Adlai Stevenson. Stevenson had been elected governor of Illinois by the largest majority any candidate had ever received in that state's history. He had distinguished himself as governor, in his many services in the federal government, in the State Department, and as representative to the General Assembly of the United Nations.

Stevenson waged an impressive campaign. His superb eloquence, his clarity of thought, his nimble wit, his forthright appeal to common sense were unique in political platform oratory. As quickly as possible his speeches were assembled during the campaign for nationwide distribution, with John Steinbeck writing a fine foreword.

In spite of Stevenson's political defeat, his stature as a statesman and man of impressive intellect remained undiminished. The moral effect of his speeches was such that many people felt they were of historic value and should be given permanent form in a book. Saxe was asked to work with Governor Stevenson on the project. On December 28, 1952, Saxe was driven to LaGuardia Airport by our son Eugene and our son-in-law William R. Bennett. He arrived in Springfield late that night, and on the next morning he was warmly greeted by Stevenson at the governor's mansion. The two men set to work. They worked fifteen hours a day, stopping only for some talk, luncheon, or tea. During a stay of only a few days Saxe completed his editorial work on thirty-four speeches.

Four days after Saxe's return to New York, the manuscript went to the printer. The governor was given the galleys just before he left for a brief vacation in Barbados, where he would make such revisions as were necessary and write the introduction. Shortly afterward he left for a two-month tour of the world. When the book came off the press on April 13, Saxe immediately airmailed a copy to the governor, then in Malaya. His acknowledgment came: "You'll forgive me if I don't read it. I shall be forever grateful to you for your help which alone made it possible."

On June 16, 1954, of the following year, Princeton University bestowed an honorary degree on Governor Stevenson. After the ceremony he visited our home for a warm reunion with Saxe, and on the following day Saxe took him to meet Professor Einstein, an old friend and neighbor. Saxe jotted down some notes of that meeting. Stevenson asked, "Can you, Professor Einstein, apply a mathematical law of probability to a prediction of the development of world conflict?" This launched Einstein into a brilliant and humane exposition of his views on the problems of world peace. When taking his leave, Stevenson said, "I also want to thank you for endorsing my candidacy during the campaign." Professor Einstein answered, "Do you know why I came out for you? Because I had still less confidence in the other one." Stevenson laughed uproariously.

If the publication of Stevenson's speeches was remarkably fast, the publication of the *Introduction to Aristotle*, edited by Richard McKeon of the University of Chicago, was remarkably slow and laborious. In the summer of 1940 McKeon was writing to Saxe about finishing the job. He had time, as well, to question Saxe's familiarity with Plato:

> Your boasts about the complete and unabridged Plato [Jowett's *The Dialogues of Plato*, published by Random House in 1937] caught me by surprise, particularly when you add that you

think you're safe from sniping "because of the omission of even questionable works." You have a complete Jowett, possibly, but not a complete Plato. I haven't looked into your edition but here are a few snipes. I usually start my classes in Plato by reading the seventh Epistle: almost all scholars think it is genuine, some think all thirteen letters are authentic; but I don't remember that Jowett got around to translating them. As I recall, Jowett translated a few of the doubtful and spurious dialogues so you probably have the Menexenus and the Hippias Minor. Some scholars think the Epinomis is genuine; do you have it? And to run through the doubtful titles that come to my mind, check up on the Cleitophon, the Hippias Major, the two Alcibiades, Hipparchus, the Lovers, Theages, Minos ... but you get the idea. I think I could make as good a case for the 2,300 page Aristotle.

Saxe did not allow the case to rest:

Let me make myself clear about my previous reference to our complete and unabridged Plato. I should have been more explicit and said the complete and unabridged Dialogues of Plato. One can't be too careful with a scholar. In view of our title, and because of the limitation in the number of pages placed upon us, we had no other recourse than to omit the Epistles. And then, too, as far as we know, the translations of these letters were not Jowett's. If you will look in Volume Two, pages 715 and 775, you will find the Lesser Hippias and the Menexenus.

By the end of October the first batch of proofs had arrived, and the professor was starting to put in the running heads.

As I remember, the form we agreed upon was the repetition on both the left- and the right-hand pages of title, book, and chapter. It would run, say, *Metaphysics*, Book I, Chapter 12. Am I correct in remembering that "Book" and "Chapter" were to be repeated in each instance? The other point has to do with the titles themselves. As I recall, we agreed finally that the English titles were to be put in the main position and the Latin titles in parentheses. In the proof the older arrangement is followed: that is, the titles are in Latin and the English translation is in the parentheses. Do you want the running heads in English or in Latin, that is, *Categories* or *Categoriae*? One aspect of the problem is that I changed the style of reference in the Introduction and made all the references to the works under their English titles. There seem to me to be three possibilities: (1) to change the titles as they appear at present at the head of each treatise to an English form; (2) to leave the titles as they stand but put the running heads in English; or (3) to put the running heads in Latin and then either change the footnotes to Latin or let them stand as they are. Any one of these is agreeable to me, although I should incline to consistent use of the English in important places. Let me know which you prefer.

I have not yet received notice that the manuscript of the Introduction has arrived. I trust that before you receive this you will have the manuscript and I will have your letter to that effect.

I am sending under separate cover glossy print photographs of the two Aristotle prints that I mentioned. Let me know if they seem satisfactory to you. The remainder of the Introduction will be in the mail within twenty-four hours; it had to be rewritten two or three times to be reduced to intelligibility, which it has now, I hope, achieved. How are you standing up under the strain?

The answer was immediate:

I am all for rendering the running heads in English with the book and chapter numbers repeated on each page, right and left. We might abbreviate "Chapter" to "Chap." Thus we would have *Politics*, Book I, Chap. 8. This is in accordance with your number (2) suggestion. I think it's best to leave the heads at the beginning of each section in the Latin, and the English rendering in italic parens below, as we originally planned. This arrangement will not necessitate any changes in the footnotes.

For God's sake, how long is your Introduction going to run? The first 131 pages, which I acknowledged the other day, are almost ready to go to the printer now. I still find that it takes a distance runner's wind to manage some of your longer sentences. No doubt the proofs will show us where we can overcome a few of these involved sentences.

I will continue to write you as your material comes in and as I send stuff off to you. Please don't keep me too long with the proofs.

McKeon wrote back to Saxe.

I am returning herewith the proof for the introductory material for the *Introduction to Aristotle*. To begin with, the statement on the title page seems to me too abbreviated and cryptic: "Edited with General and Particular Introductions" is intelligible only after you have a look at the table of contents. I recommend, therefore, that that be changed to a slightly longer description (which should be set up in smaller type than that used at present) to run as follows: "Edited, with a General introduction and Introductions to the Particular Works." That does not add much to the length, and it is, I think, considerably more intelligible.

I have a similar suggestion for the simplification of the contents. I don't like the emphasis which falls on the omissions in the present form, and I don't like the necessary multiplication of parentheses. The form I should recommend would, therefore, change the setup as follows. Instead of "Physica (Physics) Book II (Books I and III–VIII omitted)," why not have it "Physica (Physics) the Second of the Eight Books"? Then Metaphysics would be "Metaphysica (Metaphysics) the First and Twelfth of the Fourteen Books," and finally, Politics would run "Politica (Politics) the First and Third of the Eight Books." That would make it possible to change the form of the four works that are included complete by dropping the parentheses around the word "complete." Thus, for logic you would have "Analytica Posteriora (Posterior Analytics) *complete*." I think that this would improve the appearance of the contents without altering our accomplishments of the ideal of giving specific information about the contents and omissions of the books.

The letter ended, "The front material and the proofs look fine, and I think it will be a handsome book.'" It was also a successful book, as Saxe told his students, but it took exactly six years from the day McKeon wrote that "the first batch of proofs has arrived" to the letter returning the last of the proofs.

Saxe had a very good relationship with Henry Steele Commager of Columbia. The title for Commager's *America in Perspective*, which Saxe edited, was suggested by Saxe after "As Others See Us" had been turned down by Commager as too hackneyed, and after Random House had rejected "The American Character: As Seen through Foreign Eyes."

As the book was about to be published, Commager wrote Saxe about another proposal, which he thought might be welcome in theory but "rejected in fact."

I've mentioned it before, Lester Ward. I wish you would take a chance—a long range affair—on a one-volume selection from Lester Ward. It could go eventually into your Modern Library, or into your Living Classics. There is little knowledge of him and less interest in him but one of the satisfactions of—shall I say scholarship—and of publishing is to rediscover someone important or some important book and be responsible for recreating him. I'd like RH to see it that way and take Ward on as public service, as it were—hoping that in the end he would pay his way as others who have been neglected (Veblen for example) have paid their way in the end. I'm giving a long chapter to him in my new book on the American Mind in the twentieth century, and I think he is about due for a revival. If you give the word I will start in making the selections.

Saxe replied:

I am afraid I won't get very far with the Lester Ward project. Either you and I belong to an obsolete generation or all the others around here are too young to know the facts of life, but Lester Ward might just as well be a pseudonym for Henry Steele Commager so far as they are concerned. Against this kind of opposition, we won't go very far. Let me try to do some of my insidious propaganda around here and see whether the idea will grow into a sprout at least.

The selection was eventually published—by another house. So was a volume of Commager's children's stories, which had been rejected by Random House. The professor quoted some "typical reviews" to amuse Saxe.

"This magnificent book," says the Tampa *Herald,* "is unquestionably the greatest classic in children's literature since *Little Women.*"

"Commager combines the best qualities of Mark Twain, Louisa May Alcott, Arthur Ransome, and the Grimm Brothers." (Phoenix, Arizona, *Gazette*).

"Only Commager could write a book like this and only children would read it." (Kalamazoo, Michigan, *Clarion-Times*).

In the fall of 1947 Saxe had before him a new manuscript by Robinson Jeffers, consisting of a long narrative poem, *The Double Axe,* and twenty-seven short poems, all written during World War II. The collection was to be Jeffers's fourteenth book of verse. In it Jeffers advocated complete political isolation. He saw American participation in World War I as a grave mistake and our entry into World War II as even more disastrous. He maintained that we had not been forced into World War II but that our national leaders had misled us.

It is obvious from his memo to Bennett Cerf that Saxe found the manuscript upsetting.

13 October 1947

To: Bennett Cerf
From: Saxe Commins

Robinson Jeffers's new manuscript, *The Double Axe*, raises questions of policy that must be considered with the utmost care. That the tone and purport of the poems themselves indicate a bitter malevolence toward man in nature, a kind of dying howl of pessimism into a black sky in the presence of death, is the poet's view and can be argued endlessly for its validity. Agree or disagree with him in his central argument that mankind is not important in the universe and is the only blemish in nature, no one can deny that Jeffers has earned the right to deliver his last dicta on man, no matter how sophomoric some of them may be.

It is on other counts, however, that his pessimism must be examined (1) for the impression it will leave of his tight and narrow thinking as a Cassandra-like prophet, and (2) for our tolerating angry and irresponsible statements about America and more particularly about Roosevelt. The first makes him an out-and-out champion of isolationism, and the second a wildly prejudiced slanderer.

In a rather loosely thought-out preface, Jeffers's second sentence runs: "it had long been evident that our government was promoting war—not with threats, like the Germans, but with suggestion and pressure and personal promises—and would take part in it." This is the opening statement of the theme that torments him through the poems, long and short: America has been committed by its leaders—notably Roosevelt—to an insane power dream.

Hoult Gore, the dead soldier whose ghost returns to haunt and torture his mother, declares on page 26:

He [Roosevelt] had already duped us
Deep into war, he'd fooled us into doing everything
Except declare it and send armies abroad: but if we were
   blooded,
Then we'd be mad. Germany wouldn't attack

Although we sank her boats and supplied her enemies:
He needled the touchy Japs and they did his business for him.
And don't for God's sake,
Pretend that we had to fight while we still had friends
In Europe: what do we want of Europe?

(Bear in mind that Hoult is Jeffers's mouthpiece)

Pages 28–29

Be sorry for the decent and loyal people of America
Caught by their own loyalty, fouled, gouged and bled
To feed the vanity of a paralytic and make trick fortunes
For swindlers and collaborators.

Again page 47

Destruction's bride. "Curious," he said, "the power-mad vanity
Of one paralytic politician—"

Roosevelt and Tojo are linked on page 51, and without preference.

Page 57

                              . . . beseech God
Forgive America, the brutal meddler and senseless destroyer;
    forgive the old seamed and stinking blood-guilt of England.

Page 91

                              . . . Human antics, human antics:
Or Roosevelt's if he really believed the enormous phrases
He buttered his bloody work with, while Churchill grinned

Among the shorter poems, there is "Fantasy" (page 122)

On that great day the boys will hang
Hitler and Roosevelt in one tree,
Painlessly, in effigy,
To take their rank in history;
Roosevelt, Hitler and Guy Fawkes
Hanged above the garden walks,
While the happy children cheer,
Without hate, without fear,
And now men plot a new war.

Page 125 (dated December 1941)

The war that we have carefully for years provoked

For his position on isolationism—Page 126

> You knew also that your own country, though ocean-guarded,
>   nothing to gain, by its destined fools
> Would be lugged in.

Page 129 "Wilson in Hell" (dated 1942)

> Wilson accuses Roosevelt of "having too much murder on
>   your hands"
> Calls him liar and conniver and by his presence [Roosevelt's]
>   makes heaven a hell for Wilson.

Page 135 "Historical Choice." Here is the explicit statement for isolationism.

> . . . we were misguided
> By fear and fraud and a great tricky leader's orotund
>   cajoleries
> To meddle in the fever-dreams of decaying Europe. We could
>   have forced peace, even when France fell; we chose
> To take sides and feed war.

Page 136 "Teheran." (Teheran is seen as a plot by "attendants on a world's agony")

> . . . there will be Russia
> And America; earth-power and air-power; earth is the
>   breeder—
> but what was poor hopeful ambitious Germany
> Doing in this squeeze!

(Shocking to see Jeffers weep for the Fascists)

Page 137 "What Odd Expedients." (The repetition of phrase is most damning to Jeffers)

> The crackpot dreams of Jeanne d'Arc and Hitler; the cripple's-
>   vanity of Roosevelt . . .

Page 139 "An Ordinary Newscaster." (Again the obstinate isolationist speaks)

> We are not an ignoble people, but rather generous; but
>   having been tricked
> A step at a time, cajoled, scared, sneaked into war; a decent
>   inexpert people betrayed by men
> Whom it thought it could trust: our whole attitude
> Stinks of that ditch.

Page 142 "So Many Blood Lakes." (Again)

But we were tricked

Page 143 "The Neutrals"

> I praise thee Ireland...
> And high Switzerland ... and Sweden ... these three hold
>   all but all
> That's left of the honor of Europe.
>   I would praise also
> Argentina, for being too proud to bay with the pack,
> But her case is a little clouded.

(Peron should be pleased!)

Page 150 "War-Guilt Trials." (Tribute to Ezra Pound and a slap at us!)

Page 151 "Moments of Glory." (So that Truman should not feel neglected, he comes in for a slap on the wrist)

> Consider little Truman,
> That innocent man sailing home from Potsdam—rejoicing,
>   running about the ship, telling all and sundry
> That the awful power that feeds the life of the stars has been
>   tricked down
> Into the common stews and shambles.

––––––––––––

In all charity, I can only explain this melancholy book as proof of early senility. What the provocation for all these maledictions in our time and the insane hatred of Roosevelt, I can't guess. Well, we've marveled at Jeffers's brooding hatreds before, but they were disguised in horses and hawks and incestuous relationships. Now he personifies his bitterness in Roosevelt and in the whole human race.

> "The human race is bound to defile ... whatever they can reach or name; they'd shit on the morning star if they could reach." Page 59

I don't see how we can do anything else but protest to Jeffers about the Roosevelt and isolationism passages that are manifestly obnoxious. If we can't make him see reason, we'll have to take a strong position on principle. If he does take out the objectionable passages, we will then have a book obscurantist enough to please the dwindling Jeffers following. This book has made me *dwindle!*

Two days later, Saxe was writing to the poet himself, setting down his misgivings about Jeffers's politics but not mentioning a word about his poetry. In saying he was writing on his own responsibility, Saxe was primarily trying to protect Random House from any accusation that it was frightened of unpopular opinions; yet he was also motivated by a desire to protect the poet.

15 October 1947

Mr. Robinson Jeffers
Tor House
Carmel, California

Dear Robin:
    During all these years—and it is now over twenty—I have been writing to Una, knowing, of course, that you would realize that my letters were meant equally for you. Always I must have made it plain enough how meaningful and important every word you wrote has been to me. Ever since *Roan Stallion*, and in book after book in which I was so honored to have a hand, mine was a labor of love.
    And now, before anyone else has had a chance to see the manuscript of *The Double Axe*, I made a lunge for it, as a matter of earned right. Once again I was made to feel your elemental force and could only wonder at your endless resources in creating images and symbols of overwhelming power. Hoult, as the spokesman of the young dead in war, is indeed a daring and frightening conception, and his brutality grows out of the brutality on which he was nurtured.
    But I am disturbed and terribly worried, and that's why I can do no less than be completely candid about my misgivings. I want to put them down here without even mentioning the matter to Bennett, or anyone else, and I do so entirely on my own responsibility, counting on you to understand my motives. I refer, of course, to the frequent, damning references to President Roosevelt. Manifestly he cannot defend himself, and on that score there arises the question of fairness and good taste. But what is worse, in my opinion, is the conviction that these bitter charges will feed the prejudices of the wrong people, especially those, with the worst motives in the world, who have tried so

hard and so vindictively to discredit him. It is startling indeed to find that time after time you lash out at his memory, as if the need to do so had become almost obsessive. On page 26 indirectly; on page 29—"to feed the vanity of a paralytic"—on pages 91, 122, 125, 126, 129, 135, 137 (and here for the second time you used the phrase "the cripple's-vanity of Roosevelt"). And so on, page after page, to the end.

Frankly, I cannot make myself understand it. This may be because I do not share your bitterness toward Roosevelt and his historic role; nor do I believe, as you reiterate so frequently, that this country was drawn into the carnage by fools and treacherous men or that a better destiny would await us if we had isolated ourselves from the rest of the world.

As I said, I am writing this letter on my own responsibility, and with the hope, for the sake of your book and the effect it will have, that you can temper these references before we think of beginning composition. Please understand that this is in no way, and I can't make this too emphatic, an attempt to intrude upon your rights as a free artist. It is meant to be the friendliest of suggestions, made with the hope that you can be persuaded to my strongly personal view. I would hate, above everything else, to have you, of all people, linked with the most reactionary elements in America. That would be unthinkable!

Please give this your most serious thought, and write me privately about your own feelings, as you would to an old friend.

Always,
Saxe Commins

4 December 1947

Mr. Robinson Jeffers
Tor House
Carmel, Calif.

Dear Robin:

I keep wondering why there has been no word from you on *The Double Axe*. Our Spring catalogue is being prepared now, but I cannot make an announcement in it until I hear from you. May I have word soon as to when the revised manuscript will be coming my way?

I can tell by the difficulties my wife and daughter have had in getting seats for *Medea* that it is a tremendous hit. On your account I am happy indeed. Who deserves such a success more than you?

Best,
Saxe Commins

12 February 1948

Mr. Robinson Jeffers
Tor House - Route 1, Box 36
Carmel, California

Dear Robin:

At long last I have been able to go over the script of *The Double Axe*. I noticed, of course, all the changes you have made and in almost every instance they are immense improvements. There are two, however, which give rise to misgivings on my part. I refer to page 25, where you changed the line

To feed the vanity of a paralytic and make trick fortunes

to

To feed the power-hunger of a paralyzed man and make trick
    fortunes.

This is hardly a change at all. Would you consent to a further revision to make it read

To feed the power-hungry and make trick fortunes.

I do wish I could persuade you to take out the word "little" describing Truman on page 136. To me it seems that the adjective, referring to size, is as gratuitous an insult as if you described a man by a physical defect, as "boneless hunchback Steinmetz." It would be hitting below the belt in that instance. As it is, your poem, without the adjective, is contemptuous enough.

Otherwise I can make no specific recommendations for changes, although in general I still disagree—and vehemently— with some of your interpretations of recent world and political events and the causes underlying them. But that is a matter of opinion and consequently open to debate. Certainly I can't subscribe to your apologia for Peron, when you say on page 132, "I would praise also Argentina, for being too proud to bay with the pack," nor your defense of isolationism in "Historical Choice" and in "Fourth Act."

I cannot subscribe to the mildness with which you chasten

Hitler (Cf. page 101) and with the scourging remark with which
you flay England and America, and their war leaders. Because
these are matters of opinion and you hold yours so firmly, there
is a moral obligation to present them in your terms and on your
responsibility.

Lest there be any misapprehension about the difference of
views between us, it occurred to me to write a publisher's note to
appear on the flap of the jacket and also in the front matter of the
book as a statement of our position. Here it is as I have written it
for that purpose. Tell me candidly how you feel about it. At best
it is an honest statement of my viewpoint and at worst it will
seem to underline certain passages which otherwise might even
go unnoticed. Since both of us are responsible for our convictions and must stand by them, why not have them out in
the open?

A Publisher's Note

The Double Axe and Other Poems is the fourteenth book of
verse by Robinson Jeffers published under the Random House
imprint. During an association of fifteen years, marked by
mutual confidence and accord, the issuance of each new volume
has added strength to the close relationship of author and
publisher. In all fairness to that constantly interdependent
relationship and in complete candor, Random House feels
compelled to go on record with its disagreement over some of the
political views pronounced by the poet in this volume. Acutely
aware of the writer's freedom to express his convictions boldly
and forthrightly and of the publisher's function to obtain for him
the widest possible hearing, whether there is agreement in
principle and detail or not, it is of the utmost importance that
difference of views should be wide open on both sides. Time
alone is the court of last resort in the case of ideas on trial.

Best to Una and you,
Saxe Commins

P.S. By the way, you did not provide a dedication. Did you want
one? To whom?

Tor House   Carmel, California
Route 1, Box 36

19 February 1948

Dear Saxe:

(1) If you insist, let the verse read "To feed the power-hunger
of a politician"—instead of "paralyzed man." And I hope you

will always protest when Caesar's epilepsy is mentioned. Or Dostoevski's—though it influenced his genius, just as Roosevelt's paralysis influenced, and to some extent excuses, his character. This is my reason for speaking of it.

(2) As to "little Truman"—the adjective cannot possibly refer to physical size, since Truman is a bigger man than either Churchill (except the fat) or Hitler. But you will admit that he is "little" in a historical sense (and also "innocent") compared to either of them. However—to show you what a good fellow I am—write "Harry," if it really matters to you, instead of "little."

(3) As to other things, I'm sorry we don't agree completely. And I do agree that Hitler deserves worse then he gets—but you know the whole world is full of people cursing Hitler.

(4) As to the suggested "Publisher's Note"—it will certainly make every reader think of politics rather than poetry, and is therefore deplorable. But put it in, by all means, if it is a matter of conscience. I shall probably in that case have to add a short paragraph to my own "Note," saying that any political judgments in the book are not primary but part of the background, the moral climate of the time as I see it; and perhaps ending with a sentence from Shaw's preface to *Heartbreak House*—I quote badly, from memory—"Only a man who has lived attentively through a general war, not as a member of the military but as a civilian, *and kept his head,* can understand the bitterness . . ."

(5) No—I didn't think of any dedication.

Thanks for your clear and fair letter. And for your not complaining about the dirty manuscript—I didn't have time or energy to type it over again. It was a joy to see you recently; and I hope to repeat the pleasure if we go to Ireland this spring, as appears likely.

Yours—
Robinson Jeffers

24 February 1948

Dear Robin:

First of all, let me tell you how much I appreciate the friendliness of your letter. It is heartening to know that mere differences of opinion need not affect a relationship tried by the years. If only the same tolerance could exist where other differences of view separate whole peoples. All moralizing aside, I can only say that I was made happy by your letter.

The changes have been incorporated; the Publisher's Note will

appear and I await your addition of a short paragraph to your
own "Note." If it comes before we get into galleys, you will see it
in proof; otherwise it will be added to the galleys themselves.
Please prepare it as soon as you can so that your statement will
get as prominent a place in the Note as you want it to have.

I look forward to seeing you this spring. Best to you and Una.

Yours,
Saxe Commins

March 2, 1948

Dear Saxe:

Will you please substitute the enclosed page for the "Note"
that I think is page 1 of the manuscript?—As you see, it is
practically the same thing, except one paragraph added in
response to your "Publisher's Note." And since there are now
three paragraphs I call it "Preface"!

Best wishes,
Robin

Preface

The first part of *The Double Axe* was written during the war
and finished a year before the war ended, and it bears the scars;
but the poem is not primarily concerned with that grim folly. Its
burden, as of some previous work of mine, is to present a certain
philosophical attitude, which might be called Inhumanism, a
shifting of emphasis and significance from man to not-man; the
rejection of human solipsism and recognition of the transhuman
magnificence. It seems it is time that our race began to think as
an adult does, rather than like an egocentric baby or insane
person. This matter of thought and feeling is neither
misanthropic nor pessimistic, though two or three people have
said so and may again. It involves no falsehoods, and is a means
of maintaining sanity in slippery times; it has objective truth and
human value. It offers a reasonable detachment as a rule of
conduct, instead of love, hate, and envy. It neutralizes
fanaticism and wild hopes; but it provides magnificence for the
religious instinct, and satisfies our need to admire greatness and
rejoice in beauty.

The shorter poems that tail the book are expressions, in their
different ways, of the same attitude. A few of them have been
printed previously; three in *Poetry Magazine*, one in the
University of Kansas Review, two in the *Saturday Review of
Literature*; several in some recent anthologies.

As to the Publisher's Note that introduces this volume, let me say that it is here with my cheerful consent, and represents a quite normal difference of opinion. But I believe that history (though not popular history) will eventually take sides with me in these matters. Surely it is clear even now that the whole world would be better off if America had refrained from intervention in the European war of 1914; I think it will become equally clear that our intervention in the Second World War has been—even terribly—worse in effect. And this intervention was not forced but intentional; we were making war, in fact though not in name, long before Pearl Harbor. But it is futile at present to argue these matters. And they are not particularly important, so far as this book is concerned; they are only the background, or moral climate, of its thought and action.

R.J.

4 March 1948

Dear Robin:
Many thanks for sending me the new Preface. I am really happy that you have stated your position so clearly and precisely. Even though we differ, it is certainly reasonable that our opinions should be stated forthrightly. It will be interesting to watch the reaction of a jury of readers.
Best to you and Una.

Yours,
Saxe Commins

Of another genre entirely is the poetry of Dr. William Carlos Williams, another of Saxe's authors. He had been a practicing physician in Rutherford, New Jersey, since 1909, and in the ensuing years wrote more than twenty distinguished books of verse. He also wrote critical essays on a wide variety of subjects, including the poetry of T. S. Eliot, Dylan Thomas, Karl Shapiro, Ezra Pound, e.e. cummings, Carl Sandburg, and a number of others. In the Foreword to his autobiography, he said of himself, "As a writer, I have been a physician, and as a physician a writer. Five minutes, ten minutes can always be found. I have my typewriter in my office desk. All I needed to do was to pull up the leaf to which it was fastened and I was ready to go. I work at top speed. If a patient came in at the door while I was in the middle of a sentence, bang would go the machine—I was a physician!"

A collection of Dr. Williams's short stories, *Make Light of It*, was published by Random House in 1950, and the *Autobiography of William Carlos Williams* in 1951. *The Build Up*, his fourth novel, was published in 1952, and both *The Desert Music and Other Poems* and *Selected Essays* in 1954. After he reached his seventy-first year, he wrote *Journey to Love*, which was published in 1955. Saxe worked most congenially with Dr. Williams on all these books.

The year 1953, during the early days of the Eisenhower administration, was the beginning of a most trying period in our nation's history. From Wisconsin came a Republican senator named Joseph McCarthy who charged that the State Department was riddled with Communists and Communist sympathizers. At first his charges were dismissed, but that did not deter McCarthy. He grew more arrogant and slashed out in every direction, stopping at nothing to defame anyone who dared challenge him. He attacked such men as Dean Acheson, George C. Marshall, and J. Robert Oppenheimer. In most instances his accusations were unsupported by proof or relevant evidence. His inquisitorial technique would have won applause from the G.P.U. in Russia and the Gestapo in Germany.

When McCarthy launched a series of attacks on James Wechsler of the *New York Post*, Wechsler took up the fight. With clarity and a seasoned analysis, Wechsler wrote of this battle and of this black page in our nation's political history. The manuscript needed to be scrupulously reviewed before going to the printers. It was August 23 and Random House was pressing for an early fall publication. To expedite matters Saxe suggested that Wechsler come to Princeton for a day.

A relentless heat wave enveloped our whole area, yet the two men sat there with sweat on their faces, hard at work. When Wechsler left that evening, I heard Saxe say, "Don't worry, Jimmy, I'll take care of the rest when I get to the office in the morning." Saxe put rubber bands around some notes he had made and put them in his brief case. He sat for a while, not saying a word. Lord, how tired he looked!

I urged him to turn in early, even though it was too hot to sleep. He prepared for the night, while I stayed in the living room listening to some music. About ten o'clock I tiptoed into the bedroom and Saxe seemed to be sleeping. About an hour later I heard him call. His voice sounded strange. I ran to him and he gasped, "I can't breathe. I have a pain in my chest."

Alarmed, I ran to the telephone and called the hospital.

At the hospital I watched as Saxe was wheeled into a room, transferred to a bed, and immediately enclosed in an oxygen tent. Every effort was being made to arrest further damage to Saxe's heart.

Our children arrived in early morning. While standing watch, we suddenly noticed a change of color in Saxe's face. A miracle had happened. Soon Saxe opened his eyes and began to notice the figures standing near the bed.

News of Saxe's illness spread quickly. The first visitor was Don Klopfer. Bennett's calls and letters were constant, and the members of Random House were magnificent in their loving concern. Then began an avalanche of telegrams, cablegrams, letters, and phone calls. Flowers filled Saxe's room day after day. Attached to one bouquet was a message from Professor Albert Einstein, in German.

So haben Sie den Teufel gebraucht,
um Ihnen etwas Ruhe zu bringen.
Herzliche Wünsche,

Ihr A. Einstein
25, VIII

("Well, it needed the devil
to get you to rest a bit.
Heartfelt wishes,

Yours, A. Einstein
25, VIII")

And there was a telegram from Bill Faulkner.

Glad to hear it. Begged you last spring to rest and let joint
explode. Maybe you will now. Love to Dorothy.

Bill
Oxford, Miss., Aug. 29, 1952

Keeping Saxe quiet was not the easiest task in the world. Dr.
Rampona had to reprimand Saxe once or twice because he tried to
get out of bed. We tried all sorts of diversions during those long
weeks. Yet this enforced rest did help to bring strength back to
Saxe. In the first week in October Saxe came home.

Soon I began to notice those restless signs and hear the familiar
refrain, "What a useless life I am living! There is so much work to
be done." I talked with Dr. Rampona about this, and he advised
that Saxe be given a manuscript to do, if I would see to it that he
worked on it only an hour or two a day.

I relayed the word to Don Klopfer, who sent Saxe, of all things,
Etienne Gilson's *The History of Christian Philosophy in the Middle
Ages*, with a little note that read: "This should keep you busy for a
long, long time."

I was stunned at the sight of the manuscript—700 typed pages
and about 400 pages of notes. My God! This would be a Herculean
task! I asked Saxe, "Can't this magnum opus wait until you have
fully regained your strength?" Then by way of trying to dissuade
him from tackling it at once, I asked, "What do you know about
medieval Christian philosophy?" Saxe looked at me and quietly
replied, "I'm learning."

Right after the new year, on January 4, Saxe returned to his
office and plunged into a pile of work that had accumulated during
his absence. He had already finished editing the first draft of *A
Fable* while still at home, a period during which Bill Faulkner
stayed with us for some weeks. Now the galleys were beginning to
come in, and on January 8 Saxe brought home 118 of them.

Saxe was back at the old pace; it worried me not a little. And
when I pleaded with him to let up a bit, all he said was, "I will, I
will."

8 Elmsley Place, Toronto 5. Ont. Canada.
December 27, 1954

Dear Mr Saxe Commins

I thank you for sending me the review written by Miss Virginia Kirkus. I did not know that there were professional pre-reviewers. America will never finish to surprise me! Anyway, Miss Kirkus did a very good job. I only think she slightly overstressed the Catholic/Protestant angle. Protestants will find practically no controversy after page 20, and even before, it is less controversy than honesty in stating one's own position.

Everybody is delighted with the book and I can assure you that, without a single exception, all those that received it are singing your praises. As to the content, it will take readers more time to form an opinion about it.

Thanks also for your good wishes. Please accept mine in return, and rest assured of my sincere and constant gratitude. I am realizing more and more clearly that, without you, the book would not exist.

Sincerely
Et. Gilson

PS. I am paying the invoices as they come. So far, I have only received five invoices, but more books have come.

Letter to Saxe from Etienne Gilson, December 27, 1954, concerning Gilson's *History of Christian Philosophy in the Middle Ages*

In the daily treadmill of an editor's routine, he always hopes that in the pile of manuscripts confronting him he will uncover a nugget of gold, worthy of refinement and coining. Alas, he is obliged to reject most of the writing that comes to him, not without regret, knowing well how much zeal and toil and hope the writer has put into his work.

For those whose manuscripts have been accepted, it is only the first step. After a careful rereading of the work, the editor may find that certain sections need to be condensed, that some paragraphs and even chapters may be in need of cutting and rewriting. When this is suggested to the author, he winces at the mere thought of such surgery. Then patiently the editor tries to point out that the manuscript will not suffer but rather benefit by omissions and changes.

Saxe's experience with the manuscript of Ernest Gruening's *Alaska* illustrates how overwhelming this task of editor-counselor can be. As governor of Alaska for fourteen years (1939 to 1953), Gruening was qualified by political background and experience to tell the fascinating story of that immense territory. The amount of material Governor Gruening had accumulated was staggering and was certain to bog him down. "In its present condition," Saxe said, "it reads like a *Congressional Record*. It needs clearing in an orderly fashion. To suggest what should be done could hardly be possible by correspondence."

Lugging the voluminous script along, he went to Washington, D.C., early in January 1954 to spend a day with Governor Gruening, who was living in retirement there. From the outset, to Saxe's dismay, the governor was absolutely averse to any cuts or revisions whatsoever! Marshaling his arguments, Saxe pointed out the many repetitions, the long-winded polemics, the pages and pages of footnotes that should be moved to the end of the text. All to no avail! Though disturbed by the governor's obstinacy, Saxe, who did not give up easily, came away hoping that Gruening would consider his suggestions. It could be a fine book, Saxe felt, but at the moment it was too involved, too detailed, too long. He urged the governor to stress the three highly dramatic episodes that mark Alaska's history: the discovery, the purchase by the United States, and the Klondike gold rush.

In the months that followed, Saxe was in constant touch with Governor Gruening. There was considerable shunting back and forth of messages suggesting certain deletions, shifting of passages, and placement of notes. At last the book was in galley proof—and the Governor insisted on adding five indispensable items: three charts on fishing production and two isothermal maps. I do not know what Governor Gruening's reaction was when the book was published, but I do know that the praise of the reviewers was unanimous. To quote but a few lines:

"In spite of the strong political emphasis, this work is unsurpassed as a local history." *Foreign Affairs*, April 1955.

"A beautifully organized book which covers the political and economic development of Alaska down through 1954." San Francisco *Chronicle*, January 1955.

"Not for thirty years has any book on Alaska appeared that can compare with this meaty, vigorously written volume." *U.S. Quarterly Book Review*, March 1955.

It was not only Saxe's physical state of health that was taxing. He was also deeply worried about the trend publishing was taking. To his way of thinking, publishing was becoming a high-pressure business with the emphasis on large volume, quick turnover, and sure profit, and with less and less concern for editorial quality. There was at this time much concern about the decline of fiction. Saxe as editor, Malcolm Cowley as critic, and John Hersey the novelist were asked to present their views at a meeting of the International Association of Poets, Playwrights, Editors, Essayists, and Novelists (informally called P.E.N.). The discussion was lively and provoked many opinions. In the main, it was agreed that the swift changes in literary taste and in popularity of subject matter conferred little permanence upon the average book and that the market was being flooded with books of transient value.

Yet, though all that was as true then as it is today, that same year (1955) Random House published W. H. Auden's *The Shield of Achilles*, hardly a book aimed at the fickle taste of the mass market. Saxe managed to forget the sad state of publishing, at least for the moment, in his enthusiastic reaction to Auden's collection of twenty-eight poems.

"I must read Auden again and again," Saxe vowed in his notes. "This is at first glance a demoniacally gifted, strangely allusive, witty, brilliant, and tantalizingly suggestive collection of poems in three sections—almost in the manner of three movements of a symphonic suite. The first (Bucolics), a group of *Pastorals*. The second (In Light and Shade), a wayward, occasional and capricious part, a kind of *Scherzo*; and the third and final sequence (Horae Canonicae) is profound and sometimes self-mocking in its religious devotion." Saxe went on to say, "Auden is undoubtedly the most gifted of living poets, flawless when he wants to be and only faltering over his own prodigious virtuosity. One does not remember his poems: one is impressed, overawed and a little dumbfounded by them. After all the layers are peeled, there remains a core of solid idea and purpose." *The Shield of Achilles* won the National Book Award for poetry; the following year, Auden was appointed to the Poetry Chair at Oxford University in England.

Saxe had worked on earlier books of Auden's published by Random House. A modest man (he once asked Saxe to "tell Marie Melrose in the Shipping Department that my name is not William"), Wystan was also a poet with very definite ideas, not only about what was in his poems but about how those poems should be printed. "About the chapter headings" in *For the Time Being*, he wrote Saxe in June 1944, "my opinion is unchanged. It isn't that I don't realize that, as such things go, the fount is well designed. It's a matter of principle. You would never think of using such a fount for, say, 'The Embryology of the Elasmobranch Liver,' so why use it for poetry? I feel very strongly that 'aesthetic' books should not be put in a special class. The fact that literature in this country is taught almost exclusively by women causes enough trouble as it is, and nothing should be done to make matters worse. I do hope very much that you will see your way to using something more straightforward."

Saxe complied.

Three months later Auden had some suggestions and changes for his *Collected Poetry*.

> Enclosed is a postscript to add to the preface, and two more poems . . .
> Oh yes, by the way, there is a correction I want to make in "In War Time," the second poem in the book ("Abruptly mounting her ramshackle wheel"). In the last line, for

> *Be somewhere else. Ourselves, for instance, here, tonight*

read

> *Be somewhere else, yet trust that we have chosen right.*

Could you make the change for me?

P.S. The title of this volume has become, unintentionally, a misnomer. Publication was originally planned for last April, so as to precede the appearance of *For the Time Being*, but the paper shortage made this impossible.

P.S. If you are doing a second edition of *For the Time Being*, and it is possible, could you scotch a misprint on page 128, line 3 where "looked" should be "locked."

This time Saxe complied with the changes but put up a fight about the title.

19 September 1944

Mr. Wystan Auden
16 Oberlin Avenue
Swarthmore, Pa.

Dear Wystan:

I hasten to answer your letter. First of all, the two new poems "A Healthy Spot" and "Few and Simple," have been placed in their proper order. The first between "The Creatures" and "Pur," and the second between "The Exiles" and "Canzone." I am assuming that these are new poems and consequently have marked them with an asterisk in the table of contents. If they are not, please let me know so that I can erase this distinguishing mark.

The correction has been made for the last line of "At a Party in War Time" to read: "Be somewhere else, yet trust that we have chosen right."

I have ordered, just in time, the correction on page 128, line 3, of *For the Time Being* to make "looked" read "locked."

I come now to the question of the postscript to the preface. I hope you don't mind my saying that I consider it inadvisable. The reader will say, naturally, that since this volume postdates *For the Time Being*, why shouldn't some of the latter be included? To call attention to the title as a "misnomer," when we have had plenty of time to correct it, would be a grave error. We can blame many things on the paper shortage, but we shouldn't make it seem that it covers our omissions. Perhaps we can include excerpts from *For the Time Being* and a *Christmas Oratorio* as Part VIII to follow the sonnet sequence *In Time of War*. Please let me have your decision and your instructions on all these matters at once, since I am ready to begin composition.

I think it would be equitable all around if I split the author's

alteration bill in half, and let us assume $46.38 and you $46.47.
This means a reduction of $13.41 from your bill and makes a
division of charges equal all around. What do you think?

There followed an exchange of letters over several months. On
September 20, Auden was hoping "that the printers will be able to
decipher my fist which, even in its Sunday Best, is not easy for a
generation brought up on the typewriter." He goes on to say, "I'm
afraid you can't include any of *For the Time Being* in the new
volume, which is not a selection, but the definitive collection of all I
wish to preserve prior to the former. That's one reason why I titled
it as *Poems 1928–1942* (or 43). The question came up last April
about the difficulty of publishing a *Collected Poems* after a new
book, and you seemed to think it all right, but it seemed only fair to
say something about this in the preface, if we are going to adopt the
second title."

21 September 1944

Dear Wystan:
    I still think that the use of dates in the title is inadvisable.
Nothing makes a book more antiquated after a season or so than
the appearance on the title page of a definite year. And it is my
hope that your *Collected Poems* will go on selling for a very long
time.
    Why not consider the title simply as *The Collected Poems of
W. H. Auden* and leave out all mention of dates? The word
"collected" itself suggests selection and elimination and warrants
the exclusion of certain long or short poems on the grounds that
they were deliberately omitted because of the architecture of the
entire book.
    My preference is to let the book stand on the title as suggested,
since it will speak for itself as the very best representation of the
poems selected by you. There is a great deal of time before the
book actually goes to press to have a change of heart on this
matter of title. Let's both of us think it over and suspend our
decision until something better comes along.

All best,
Saxe Commins

On November 7, 1944, when the book was further along, Auden
wrote to Saxe:

Thank you for your letter and the suggested cover material. My own feeling is strongly against having any quotes as, apart from the embarrassment I feel in reading them (I feel the same when I read anyone else's blurbs), I don't believe they affect the sales of poetry, after one's third book anyway. They may have some effect when quoted in newspaper ads, I think, but as jackets, no.

What I should like is simply:

"This volume contains all that Mr. Auden wishes to preserve of the poetry he has written so far."

i.e. The Garbo note
I hope you'll agree.

Two months later, Auden wrote again:

I sent the proofs back to you on today by hand. I hope they arrived safely.

I take it you are looking after the dedication page (which has a four line epigraph on it) and that there will be pages between the various sections.

As to title, I want *Poems 1928-1945*. The word "collected" suggests finality which, I hope anyway, is incorrect.

And Saxe replied:

22 January 1945

Dear Wystan:

I hasten to assure you that the proofs arrived. Please don't worry about the dedication page or the half title, which are all set together and sent as separate proofs.

I hope I can dissuade you from the new title you suggest. All our catalogues and advertising and jacket are set with *The Collected Poems*. My objection to the new title is that it takes no time at all to date the volume. *Collected Poems* certainly need not mean complete, and we have many instances of poets collecting a sort of retrospective exhibition of their works under the title of *Collected Poems*. I hope you see it our way.

Perhaps we will see each other over the weekend.

Yours,
Saxe Commins

Auden lost, but was not convinced. "Dear Saxe," he wrote on the book's publication, "I've seen some copies of the *Collected Poems* which, bar the title, look very nice I think. Thank you. If there is a reprinting, could you make the following corrections . . . "

When Random House published *The Age of Anxiety* two years later, Wystan wrote to congratulate Saxe, and in his unassuming way he asked: "If there should be a second printing would you let me know as I have some little alterations I would like to make in the text." Saxe was enthusiastic.

19 June 1947

Mr. Wystan Auden
Cherry Grove
via Sayville, L.I.

Dear Wystan:
    I needn't tell you how delighted I am that you like the book. I wanted this one, above all others, to please you.
    By all means send in whatever revisions you consider necessary, and I'll do them at once so that we shall lose no time in printing if we require a second edition. Merely identify the page and line numbers, giving me the wording as it is and the wording as it should be. I'll take care of the rest.
    Have a marvelous summer.

Best,
Saxe Commins

Auden's response to this encouragement was the occasion for a letter a month later from Saxe.

Dear Wystan:
    I certainly was staggered by the number of plate corrections which came this morning. As you know, this is a rather expensive operation. It means cutting the line out of the plate in each instance, re-setting it, and electro-plating and welding it into place. The cost per line is about $2, which means that the total will run to somewhere around $100. If, under these circumstances, you still want it done, I'll go ahead and we'll make the charge to your royalty account.

Of the number of memories I myself have of Auden, one that stands out vividly is of a New Year's party that Saxe and I attended at Auden's St. Mark's Place apartment. Even the stairs in that old brownstone had seen better days, and the apartment was wonderfully disheveled. We toasted the New Year with cracked coffee cups. But none of that mattered because there was an atmosphere created by his books and beautiful drawings which dispelled the sense of disarray. What was most delightful was the formal card of invitation with a gentle reminder in very small print at the bottom: "Carriage at two."

And of course with Auden there was always the conversation. Saxe put it this way: "It is an intellectual feast to chat with Auden. His mind dances. We talked of Mozart and Stendahl, a natural pair. He is going to do a documentary film of Mozart that should be extraordinary. We talked a little about his *New Yorker* piece on Tolstoy, about his father, T. S. Eliot, and whatever occurred to us."

Actually, Auden was only too willing to pay for his alterations. Better perfect poetry than whole coffee cups.

W. H. Auden's fellow poet and friend, Stephen Spender, was equally meticulous about proofing his work, but in one instance slightly absentminded: "I return now the proofs of *The Edge of Being*. You will see that I have been through them with very great care. You will see also that wherever I thought my corrections might at all confuse the printer, I have attached a typewritten corrected version of the poem . . ."

Eight days later (February 20, 1949) Spender wrote:

Dear Mr. Commins, dear Saxe, I mean,
    This is posthaste.
    I have discovered one misprint, if it is not too late to alter this.
    In the first poem, the first line of the third stanza should read:

    O, thou O, beyond silence

Not, as I have typed it:

    O, thou, O, beyond silence.

An extra comma got in by mistake—unless the copy you have is correct, but I don't think so, to judge from my carbons. I hope it's not too late to change this.

Saxe replied:

    As soon as your note of February 20 came to me, I communicated with the printer about that misplaced comma. In the galleys themselves, the line read:

    O, thou O, beyond silence

The only place the comma appeared was in your attached type-script. I simply deleted the comma there and all is as you want it.

Earlier, Stephen Spender had very much wanted Random House to publish both his autobiography and his poetry. However, the author with a long established reputation is fought over, in contrast to the beginning writer, who has to fight for his chance.

Spender wrote Saxe from Mrs. Frieda Lawrence's place in Taos.

18 September 1948

Dear Mr. Commins:

Miss Kellman has passed on to me your urgent message about the book of poems. The position is that at present I am working on the book called *Autobiography and Truth* which I very much want Random House to publish, so I had put aside the poems for the moment. However, if it is very urgent, please cable me, and I shall let you have the poems by the end of October. I am sorry not to have let you have the poems before.

I have written 350 pages of *Autobiography and Truth*, which will altogether be about 500 pages long, and which I hope to have ready by November 15. I have no contract with RH for this book, because of my difficult arrangements with Reynal and Hitchcock, but I very much want to offer it to you.

The position is as follows. When Frank Taylor was at R and H, I made a generally binding contract with him, on his account for personal reasons. Since I have been in America I have lunched in New York with members of R and H, and they have told me they would like me to keep it. It was a very friendly discussion, but only verbal. Harold Matson[1] and I have also discussed these various contracts, and what we agreed in principle was that I should simply deal with each book as it came along. The important thing was to write my books, and then I could do my best to fulfill my various contracts.

Why I am anxious that you should have this book is that it goes with my *Collected Poems* almost as a commentary. In fact, it is complementary to both of them.

I am sending a copy of this letter to Matson. What I suggest is that I should write to R and H and say that I particularly want you to have this one prose book of mine for the reasons I have stated. But I now intend to do almost nothing but write books, including two novels. I could perhaps offer them the novels.

To return to the subject of the poems. Will you cable me if you urgently want these as soon as possible, even if it means putting aside the autobiography. Incidentally, the autobiography is far and away the most ambitious thing I have done, and is quite unlike other autobiographies. It is general essays covering a) politics, b) literature, c) belief, d) love, and e) childhood (in that order), prefaced by a general essay on the "Problem of Self-Revelation in Our Time." It is very elaborately worked out and upsets the whole time sequence conventions of autobiography.

I am sending a copy of this to Matson. Please let me know what you want about the poems, and your general feelings about *Autobiography and Truth*.

Sincerely,
Stephen Spender

The situation was a complicated one, as Saxe's letters of October 7 and October 18 make clear.

7 October 1948

Mr. Stephen Spender
c/o Mrs. Frieda Lawrence
El Prado
Taos, New Mexico

Dear Stephen Spender:

You must be wondering why there was no immediate response to your letter of September 18. First of all, I had to communicate with Harold Matson to confer about procedure with him. When he received his copy of your letter to me he immediately got in touch with Harcourt Brace & Company. They, in turn, put him off because of the absence from the country of Mr. Eugene Reynal. When he finally did return, Mr. Matson acting as your agent was able to arrange a meeting, the result of which no doubt has been reported to you by Mr. Matson himself.

My own knowledge of the Harcourt Brace position is this: that they are adamant in holding you to the existing contract for your autobiography. Perhaps they have written you to tell you of their position, and in that case this is no revelation to you.

You understand, of course, that we are powerless to change the minds of Harcourt Brace. No doubt Mr. Matson, deferring to your wishes, tried to do so, but apparently to no avail.

Under all these circumstances it seems to me that the only thing we can now do is to proceed with our original plans and issue the two volumes of poetry under the Random House imprint. If you remember, we had hoped to have the first

manuscript this fall, and we have in fact scheduled the first
volume of verse for early spring publication. Is there a chance
that the manuscript will be ready soon?

I need not tell you that I am genuinely sorry that an obstacle
stands in the way of our doing the autobiography. You certainly
can count on us to do our utmost for the new book of poems.

Cordially,
Saxe Commins

18 October 1948

Dear Stephen Spender:

In order that there might be no misunderstanding in
connection with the publication of your autobiography, we
asked Mr. Don Congdon of Matson's office (to whom I had sent
a copy of my letter of October 7 to you) to send me, in turn, a
copy of what he had written to you.

Bob Haas tells me that its contents checks with his understanding of his telephone conversation with Congdon, excepting
that it was never clear to him that Reynal had indicated so
definitely that—if you were "adamant" in deciding to leave
Reynal & Hitchcock—they would release you on payment by us
of $750.

On the contrary, it was Bob's interpretation that the entire
emphasis was put on Reynal's unwillingness to drop the option,
and consequently (although certainly Congdon mentioned the
$750) Bob looked upon this simply as one more complication in
an already complicated picture. In the circumstances, he did not
wish to press another house to do something they were evidently
so very reluctant to do. And, although I say it with genuine
regret, this position is the one to which I think it wisest for us to
adhere at this time.

Cordially,
Saxe Commins

Spender was not to get his way. "I quite understand the
position," he wrote. "I would have liked Random House to have
the autobiography, as I feel it is my most important work, and I
wanted you to publish my serious work. However, I see that this
cannot be so, and now I shall try to arrange that Harcourt Brace
and Random House divide everything between them." This was not
complete defeat, for *The Edge of Being* was published by Random
House in early spring, as Saxe had planned.

In the fall of 1949, Saxe did succeed in fulfilling a request from Stephen Spender. Owing to Senator Joseph McCarthy's anti-Communist witch-hunt, Spender was experiencing some difficulty in getting permission to enter the United States. As his editor, Saxe cabled the attorney general and then wrote to Spender himself: "Personally, I feel a sense of outrage that any question should arise about your admission to the United States. If that decision is unfavorable, I wish you would tell me how far we may go in organizing some sort of dignified but effective protest. I would do nothing along these lines without consulting you."

This was another instance of the suspicion and distrust which McCarthy's wild accusations were breeding in this country. McCarthy had almost managed to convince Americans that the way to fight communism was to build a fortress of fear and conformity. Of course, since this English poet was a liberal who often expressed his views, he could only be a spy or at any rate a bad influence. But on November 11, Stephen Spender wrote to thank Saxe and to announce: "As you will see, I am here, in New York."

From *Guadalcanal Diary* to *Lillian Russell*

It is always gratifying to an editor like Saxe when a good book makes money. *Guadalcanal Diary*, published by Random House in 1943, was one of these. It became a Book of the Month Club selection; film rights were sold to Twentieth Century Fox; and it was featured in a *Life* magazine story.

Richard Tregaskis, the author, was a World War II correspondent who in 1942 had landed on Guadalcanal with the first detachment of marines and had stayed with them for about three months. He later suffered a head injury when a piece of shrapnel penetrated his helmet. Fortunately, a skilled surgeon performed a miracle and saved him. When he returned to the United States for a short rest, he brought with him his Guadalcanal diary. After reviewing the manuscript, Random House accepted it without hesitation.

Though still very shaky after his hospitalization, Tregaskis came to Saxe's office, where they went over every detail of the manuscript. One morning the author suddenly slumped in his chair. He was unconscious. Saxe, very much alarmed, called for help and tried to get an ambulance, but there were none to be had. So Saxe decided to get Tregaskis to the hospital by taxi. Saxe and his helpers managed to get Tregaskis into the taxi, where he was braced against Saxe. But Tregaskis was over six feet tall. His legs were so long they stuck outside the cab door. The driver didn't like that one bit, for fear Tregaskis's legs would be sideswiped by a passing car.

When Tregaskis was wheeled into the emergency room at Mount Sinai Hospital, it was discovered that his collapse had not been due to his head injury but to a lack of insulin. A diabetic, he had run out of his supply.

After a brief stay in the hospital, Tregaskis was able to resume his sessions with Saxe, and soon the book was sent off to the printers.

Another book that was sold to the movies—this one for a fabulous sum—was Irwin Shaw's *Lucy Crown*. Before Hecht-Lancaster Productions bought the film rights, however, many years of hard work went into the manuscript. In 1955 Shaw wrote to Saxe as follows:

> On the novel, I've had a terrible struggle. I've written about five hundred pages, and just this week I decided to put it away for a while again, because it wasn't shaping up to my satisfaction. It's a different kind of thing from anything I've ever done, and I've attacked it from six different angles and it still doesn't seem to work for me. Nobody else has read what I've done, and I'm not sure whether it's just fatigue on my part that makes me look at it with a jaundiced eye or whether it's really no good at all. If I had finished it by the end of the summer, we'd have come home [from Europe] this autumn—but I hate to come home after all this time without a book. Especially since a part of the book is laid in Europe and I don't want to move away from the scene before I'm finished with it. You know what would be wonderful—if good old Random House put you on a plane overnight to Europe and you came and stayed with us—(it would do you a world of good, even if the book didn't meet with your approval)—and we could whack away at what's right and what's wrong with the novel. What's kept happening to me the last few months is that ideas for another book have kept intruding on my consciousness, a book that seems much better and more attractive than the one I'm working on—much more in line with the way I feel about life at the moment—and holding me back from finishing the work in progress.
>
> I'd send you the manuscript of the book, except that it's in bits and pieces, with unfinished sections and developments left out,

and the main lines not yet securely in place, so that it would be too hard to judge. It would take long hard hours, face-to-face, to clear it up even just enough to judge it.

Incidentally, if Switzerland is too far and there were other things that you had to do in Paris or London or Rome, I could of course meet you there. It would be an invaluable service to me. I don't want to go back just yet to New York because I'm afraid it would unsettle me for months and I might never get back to the necessary mood to finish this book. Also, I have a vague notion at the back of my head for a book in the future, which will depend upon my coming back to the States after a long absence, an unbroken absence, and my first, uncluttered reactions to everything at home. A visit in between would cloud that, I'm afraid.

If you can't make the trip, I guess I'll just have to struggle through it myself. What I might do is start the new book—(it should be short, comparatively, between 70,000 and 100,000 words)—and go as deep into it as my first burst will take me—and then take another long look at the unfinished novel. I've never written two novels at a time, but there's always a beginning for everything. As I grow older, I find myself more dissatisfied with my work as it comes out in first draft, with a much greater tendency for revisions after long periods of absence from it. The last short story I sold to the *New Yorker* was two years (count them—two years) in the writing. I must have spent four months of actual writing on it, with characters and scenes and themes going in and out like people in a revolving door. However, I think in that case, it turned out to be worth it.

While, so far, my time in Europe has not produced much in a quantitative sense, I have a feeling that it is all ripening within me, just about now, and will be an invaluable mine of experience for the future.

There was no trip to Europe for Saxe. Shaw was a professional and he completed the manuscript alone. In his notes Saxe summarized his impressions of the novel:

> It combines something of Candida and Nora in *The Doll's House* with the extension into the consequences of an affair with a latter-day Marchbanks and the closing of the door on what seems to be an insecure marriage. Skillfully written, sharply observed and set down, with the adroitness of a practiced short story writer, this novel of a woman's declaration of independence and what follows thereafter will not stir up a flame of

enthusiasm; partly it lacks the violence expected of Shaw and partly it restates a theme that is now none too new.

It is no startling departure for a woman to declare herself free of a marriage that denies her whatever she happens to desire. What is original is what she makes of herself. This Shaw is trying to do sometimes convincingly, sometimes slickly, sometimes passionately. Some of the writing, as his observations, is extraordinary. Must wait until we get together in a few weeks for further discussion.

When Shaw arrived from Europe, he and Saxe had a long session, going over the notes Saxe had made. "Irwin was amenable and gracious and altogether pleasant to work with," Saxe wrote. "He is, I believe, a victim of his great facility. He does everything too easily and never under the duress of doubt. If it's a story one wants, a paragraph, a phrase or a word, it flows from the top of his mind. This indicates he relies on talent and he has a super-abundance of that. It is as if he were improvising all the time, unconsciously, spontaneously, and effortlessly."

There was much cutting, adding, and changing. Finally all the revisions were made and the book, now bearing the title *Lucy Crown*, was published on March 30, 1956. Shaw wrote to Saxe:

> This is a letter of thanks for everything you've done for me on *Lucy Crown*, and on the other books in the past. As you know, from a financial point of view, at least, *Lucy Crown* has already been enormously successful. This is doubly gratifying because I had so much trouble with it and gave it up completely on two different occasions, and in giving it up, was ready to write off years of work as useless and unproductive. Even Marian, my wife, advised me to jettison it while I was struggling with it and hating it. If it hadn't been for you, and your faith in the book and in my ability to make something of it, I would never have finished it. And then your help, especially in seeing what could be done with the extra chapters that I had cut out, brought the book to whatever level of excellence it finally reached. There it is—in black and white. As you know, I am a lonely man at the typewriter. I don't talk much about a book before I attack it and I fight my way through it more or less alone. It is only when I am at the end of my rope that I look for affirmation. Well, you gave it to me, and more, and we have a big fat book to show for it. I hope it finally does you proud.
>
> I'll be thinking of you on March 30, and I'll be thinking of you when I sit down to start my new book this fall.

God, it's been twenty years that we've been working together!
They certainly haven't been bad, have they?

But there were painful moments, too. Saxe believed himself a
realist who knew when a book was beyond saving. Another
publisher asked him to look at the manuscript of a writer who
through the years had developed a rather precious but loyal
following. After a detailed analysis of what he felt the story was
about, Saxe railed against the author's "irresponsibility to the
reader."

I can name no editor, living or dead, who could accomplish
the miracle of transforming the author's private introspections
and loose ramblings into an attention-compelling novel. Editors
read manuscripts to the bitter end; purchasers of books are not
compelled to do so.

Please believe me when I say that if there is anything I could
possibly do to salvage this manuscript, this is the very place I
would be explicit about it and give you, at great length, what
might be done, chapter and verse. But, unfortunately, I am
convinced that this novel is beyond repair.

It may well be that my own prejudices got in the way of
understanding what is, to the author, a private kind of symbol-
ism to the whole thing. There may be meaning within meanings
that my intelligence cannot grasp; there may be a code to a
comprehension of those meanings that the author is holding in
reserve. But even with it, I would demand a kind of structural
unity and some sort of architectural plan. That lacking, I am
helpless. This is not to say that the structure must be rigid and
formal; but it is to say emphatically that it must command
interest, no matter what liberties are taken with form. *The Flying
Swans* forfeits interest and therein lies its fatal weakness.

All the foregoing is much harsher than I want to be—or than I
really am, for I am not a son of a bitch, the evidence to the
contrary notwithstanding. Particularly am I unhappy that this
had to be Padraic Colum's work, since I have long had an
affection for him, though remote, and would do anything, except
to be dishonest about a manuscript, to show my respect for him
by way of helping him. But I am stymied by the nature of his
novel and the manner in which he has executed it.

I beg of you not to show this long and wordy letter to him. It
must be a highly privileged communication between you and
me—and possibly your editorial staff. Padraic Colum is an old

man who has made some genuine contributions to the world of letters. Who am I to hurt him?

Many years before writing this report, Saxe did perform a miracle of sorts for a writer not to be compared in any way with the author referred to above. Actually, it is a question whether he was a writer at all, although an earlier book had been published with his name on it. Bennett Cerf, learning that a movie about Lillian Russell was to be released, had drawn up a contract with Parker Morrell to produce a biography of the star and had paid him an advance. Saxe was sent to Pennsylvania where the self-styled author was living with his heiress bride and presumably working on the book. Saxe, in his diary, recounts what he found.

Note:
This journal was begun after my first week in Bryn Mawr, where I was sent on April 15, 1940, on an assignment that specified my work to be the "whipping into shape" of a book to be entitled *Lillian Russell: The Era of Plush,* by Parker Morrell. The manuscript would, presumably, be in first draft upon my arrival. To facilitate matters for the author, Random House had engaged a research man, Schlanger by name, who had worked for eight weeks at the New York Public Library, gathering data from the newspaper files of the period from 1880 to 1922. The author, it was assumed, had devoted that time to the arrangement of the material and to the writing of a rough version of the book.

Prior to my departure from New York, my knowledge of the subject was limited to the bare fact that there had been an American actress, ample in bosom and pink in complexion, named Lillian Russell. On the train to Bryn Mawr, I expressed to myself my conception of the job and confessed my ignorance of its details by saying, "My task will be to gild the lily," adding that the phrase itself was good enough to use somewhere in the manuscript. That was all I was prepared to contribute at the time.

To my great consternation, I discovered on my arrival at Bryn Mawr that not only had not one word of the text been written, but no outline had been made, nor had a general table of contents been considered. The material sent by Schlanger had not even been segregated! Most of it, it is true, had been digested by the author during the two months that it was in his possession. He knew the dates of birth, marriages, death, and the general order of La Russell's stage appearances.

It became immediately apparent that the book needed, first of
all, some kind of organization. Accordingly, the first day was
given over to the formulation of a plan, a general division into
chapters, twenty-two in number (subsequently reduced to
twenty), and the working out of a schedule aimed at achieving a
75,000-word script by May 1. A blurb was also written on that
day.

By Sunday April 21, six chapters were completed, and I
returned to New York with them, so that they could be submitted for approval by Bennett Cerf for content and style. When
I left Bryn Mawr, the author promised to devote the two days of
my absence to the arrangement of more material and to the
actual writing of two chapters, even if in the rough. He pledged
that I would find on my return at least thirty pages of typescript.
My misgivings about his ability to keep his word were based
upon his performance during the first five working days. However, I had to hope that he would do his stint; otherwise it would
be almost impossible to complete our task before the all-too-near
deadline.

At any rate, my two days in New York permitted me to get a
little sleep.

Tuesday April 23.

Left New York at 1 PM in terror lest nothing had been done
during my absence. Arrived and met by Madeleine [Mrs. Parker
Morrell]. . . .

Nothing at all had been accomplished over weekend. Maestro
asleep. Dug into *Diamond Jim* to make abstract for chapter ten.

M awake at 6:30 PM—most contrite, pleading sickness, dizzy
spells. . . . Dinner in gloom.

Retire to organize book. No use trying to write under the
circumstances. Best to know where we can possibly go from
here. M pitiful in helplessness, storms against wife, himself, life.
Swears he'll find "groove" and be able to "give" at least thirty
pages per night, if I undertake to do chapters on Diamond Jim
and Weber and Fields. At that rate we can finish next Thursday
night, right under the wire. He is encouraged. We lay out new
arrangement of chapters and outline four chapters for him to do,
point by point, episode by episode, and key everything to his
sources. Holy vows are made to keep to program. I am saviour,
etc. Go to sleep at one, exhausted.

Wednesday April 24.

Arose 7:30 to find M at work downstairs, far behind stint
outlined for him. My program for day is to make something of

what he has perpetrated during the night. For most part it is verbatim transcriptions out of books used for source material or stuff Schlanger has sent. From 8:30 AM to 9:30 PM I sit at typewriter and manage, one way or another, to complete chapters seven, eight, nine, a total of thirty-eight typewritten pages.

M awakes at 7:30 PM and comes down, full of contrition and good resolution. Tonight he'll make up for lost time; it's not too late; the trouble was that he was sick; that he cannot change his style, etc., etc.

We go upstairs again to outline a stint for the night. He has had nine hours of sleep and now has no excuse.

I retire early, exhausted, hoping for the best in the morning. Have taken sleeping draught and hope to fall off soon.

Thursday April 25.

When I awoke at 7:30, I find note attached to mirror. It's no use. The chief this time had dizzy spells all night and could do nothing. But, whistling in the dark, he still has faith in his ability to hit the "groove." He goes to bed. After breakfast I abstract enough for the Diamond Jim chapter and begin to write while the stenographer types out the three chapters I did yesterday.

Wife takes me for a walk to complain bitterly about failures, misalliance, etc. I am mute. Return to my stint and finish chapter just before dinner time. M has awakened and is very glum. Large box of flowers from W. Winchell lifts his spirits. . . . We go to General Wayne Restaurant for dinner and a gloomy silence persists. . . . I will not mention the book again. Only a miracle can save it. It is beyond any help he can give it. He is psychotic, unstable, imbecilic. He simply cannot do his job.

Returned from dinner, I added an insert—Lillian at the races—to chapter ten and deliberately stayed out of sight, writing this record, so that he could write.

Tomorrow's schedule calls for me to write at least 3,000 words on Weber and Fields. That will be the last writing I shall do. The author will then have eleven out of the twenty two chapters. Eleven must be done between now (Thursday 12 PM) and Tuesday next. It is a physical and psychological impossibility. I wonder what inkling the office can have of all this. Do they take it for granted that I can perform miracles under these conditions? Or don't they care one half as much as I do? To me it is an agony of the spirit, a revolting, abhorrent job and I am humiliated beyond my ability to express it. But it is also a challenge to my skills, and I would like to triumph over it before Grobian collapses altogether into a driveling idiot. God, I'm home and heartsick!

Time to retire. Pray that some copy will emerge tomorrow. If none does we are sunk, and I suppose I'll be blamed for it.

Friday April 26.

Managed to get seven hours' sleep and awoke to find M at his desk, staring vacantly into space and shaking his head in imbecilic fashion, while repeating over and over again, "It didn't go. It didn't go. I'm sick. I'm not licked yet." A glance at his desk showed that he had merely sat all night looking blankly at Schlanger's material. There were some sheets on chapter eleven—"Hope Springs Eternal"—which he had done yesterday. All of which I must re-do today, instead of getting at the Weber and Fields chapter as planned. There were also a few pages, copied out from Schlanger and other sources, for "Repentance at Leisure," chapter twelve. That, too, I am supposed to complete today. How, only God knows. That leaves us ten chapters to finish by Tuesday night, less one, Weber and Fields, which I have promised to write. It is utterly impossible to complete the program especially since M cannot write a line.

Sample page [proof] came from Herbert [at Random House], but it makes the situation here all the more a mockery. Bennett's letter shows his good will, but it also shows he can have no realization of what is going on here. Nor can he be expected to know. What good would it do if he did know? In the end he will feel that the book could be better here or there—if ever a book there will be—and not realize what it has cost me in anguish and compromise and humiliation. But I ought to be realist enough to know that even such a sickening job puts me to a test, and I must not allow myself to give it any subtle meanings. It's a job to be done, and that's all.

Friday 12 Noon.

Have just finished re-write of "Hope Springs Eternal"—chapter eleven—and the stenographer is typing it. M is asleep and he leaves me to the task of making chapter twelve out of a mess of hieroglyphic notes. God knows what it will turn out to be.

Friday 3 PM

Wrote Bennett what he will be sure to take as a hysterical outburst, but at least it was a factual statement of conditions here. I failed to tell him, as I intended, about the sprinklings throughout the book of verbatim sections from *Diamond Jim* [written by Morrell]—not in "It's Fun to Be a Sucker," however, which at least is paraphrased [, but] in other books. Now I am convinced that *Diamond Jim* has large sections lifted word for word from other sources. At this juncture, with the desperate need for copy, I can't stop to examine every word too closely and track it down to its origin.

Friday 5 PM

M has just arisen from the long sleep and has gone over what I have written today and has expressed complete satisfaction, as if he could know its merit or lack of it. He must produce, in the rough, about twenty five pages a day until Tuesday night. He bravely assures me he can do it. I have very grave doubts. At any rate, he understands that I must take the nine o'clock train for New York on Wednesday morning, whatever he has done or failed to do by then. That was an ultimatum.

Friday 10:30 PM

I have reached page 18 of chapter twelve. It must be finished before I turn in, although I am exhausted after thirteen hours at the typewriter. M has only four pages to show for the day. Yet he says he will get more done tonight. I don't believe it. He is talking of "blowing," saying things that indicate he has suicidal ideas, and I am very uncomfortable, to say the least, besides being damned tired and nervous. I predict that by tomorrow morning he will have nothing for me to work on, and still there will be ten chapters to go.

Friday Midnight.

Chapter twelve is finished—"Repentance at Leisure"—for better or worse, after fifteen hours at the typewriter. In itself it runs about forty-five hundred words, each one dragged out of virtually nonexistent material. That, plus what I had done on chapter eleven this morning, constitutes my day's work. M still has only four pages to show for his efforts today, but he will work until 2 AM, since he didn't get up until four this afternoon. Again I predict he will have nothing for me when I wake up Saturday morning. We shall see.

I have taken another sleeping draught, and it is making my heart hop, skip, and jump in my chest. Oh, nuts!

Saturday April 27. 8 AM

At breakfast. My prophecy came true. Again he folded up completely. Again excuses. Again promises. What in Christ's name can be done now? I, too, am tired. I have done six chapters since Wednesday, and there hasn't been a word from him except what he has painstakingly copied out of books. He simply cannot write or think or plan. He is a complete imbecile. The note I found under my door says that he still hopes a night's rest will fix him up. He has slept eight to ten hours daily. He asks me not to be too discouraged. Whose book is this?

Saturday 10:30 AM

M is still asleep while I am trying to find a way to break into the Weber and Fields Chapter. A long talk with Madeleine helps not at all; it simply reveals that this is an old story. She advises me to pack up and go home. Nothing can salvage the wreck, she insists. She knows her man. . . . She tells me how he fails in everything he undertakes, how she provides the money so that he can live and keep up the myth that he is a writer, how day after day, he sits upstairs copying paragraphs out of books and never has anything to show for it. . . .

Saturday 12 Noon.

I have been trying unsuccessfully to get a lead for the Weber and Fields chapter. I can't concentrate, so angry have I become. M has just come downstairs. Either he gets twenty five pages written today or I pack up and go home tomorrow, Sunday, and tell the whole truth to Random House. I made it very plain that he would have to return the advance and we would insist upon it. He whined and begged and pleaded for one more chance. He has gone upstairs to try again. The odds are overwhelming that I'll be on my way home tomorrow, thank God.

Saturday 2:30 PM

A rather sheepish author descended from upstairs at lunch time. There was a long and uncomfortable silence. Finally I broke it by saying, "Well?" The reply was, "Do you want the truth?" "Of course," I said. "The truth is that I have been asleep for the last two hours. What am I to do? I am punchy. I am sick. Maybe if I get more sleep, I'll be all right." I agreed he was sick, and told him again that it was unfortunate, but it did not help our problem. Again I reminded him that his responsibility was to meet the deadline. I would do everything in my power to help. He admitted I had done far more than my share, and then burst out that it was all hopeless. I tried to encourage him and pleaded that he go back to his room, while I worked downstairs on the Weber and Fields chapter. If at the end of the day he could do nothing, I would go home tonight and report all the facts to the office. Again I pointed out that he would have to repay the advance and the money we've laid out for Schlanger. Thereupon he went upstairs to try again. I know nothing will come of it. Meanwhile I must peck away at Weber and Fields. The whole damned thing is becoming a comedy.

Saturday 6 PM

This time the author came downstairs with two pages of his chapter instead of—not in addition to—the four he had previously written. It is hopeless. I proposed an idea to him, and he is thinking about it in retirement, viz., that I finish the Weber and Fields Chapter and take back what I have done this week to New York on Sunday, show it to Cerf and let him decide what should be done next. The author is naive enough to believe that if Cerf gives him a two-day extension, he will be able to complete the script himself. He is clutching at another straw, and this time the straw is C's pity on him, the overworked author, who hasn't written a word for a week—that is, a word that was worth preserving. He is mentally bankrupt, if that is possible when a man has no mentality to begin with.

Saturday 11:30 PM

Time to quit. Weber and Fields chapter almost finished. Managed, in spite of everything to get down three thousand words. The author has done nothing. He is still sitting at his desk with the same sheet of paper he had this afternoon in the typewriter.

Dinner was a ghastly affair. Madeleine tried to make conversation and was violently squelched. She is very angry and has left the house in a huff. This has got to end. I am at my rope's end. Maybe sleep will come quickly tonight. There isn't a chance of going any farther with the book. Certainly twenty-four to twenty-five thousand words since Wednesday represents enough work on my part to clear my conscience. Why do I let myself in for such humiliating affairs? When will I ever learn to say no? The whole thing is taking on a nightmarish quality and I may wake up in New York. Even this silly thought-by-thought account on these sheets will read like the memory of a bad dream.

Sunday April 28. 11 AM

Oh, my prophetic soul! He did not write a word last night. He went to bed a little after midnight and slept until after 9. Now

Madeleine comes down and tells me he is asleep again on the couch in his workroom! This is getting to be like a Weber and Fields burlesque! I must go back to New York today. I am approaching the end of the chapter. As soon as I finish, I shall pack up and go home.

Sunday 1:00 PM

The Weber and Fields Chapter is finished. It runs sixteen pages. That is all. I can't do any more.

The author has summoned a doctor, and he is due any minute. I am convinced the doctor will comfort him in the belief that he is sick, and thus he will have the best of all rationalizations for having quit cold on me. The only reason for sending for the doctor is to save face. He is malingering like a petulant baby.

Sunday 3:00 PM

The doctor has left. There is nothing the matter with the patient. He has been advised to stop taking those sleeping potions because their effect is accumulative. He needs exercise, regular hours, etc. There is no reason why he can't work. Now M pleads for one more chance. He wants me to get an extension from Bennett until a week from Monday, which will be May 6, and then he will bring in the balance. I am positive he can't do it. But that's up to Bennett now. The conditions under which I am to leave for New York on the five o'clock train are that I take what I have written so far back with me, show it to BAC and try to persuade Bennett to give him until May 6 to produce another one hundred-odd pages. Bennett is to telephone him Monday morning and come to terms with him. So happy am I at the prospect of getting away in a couple of hours that I was hypocrite enough to say that I thought M could do it. I certainly cannot recommend that we set the first one hundred seventy pages I am bringing back because I am positive M won't write twenty pages in that time.

Sunday 5:30 PM

I'm on the train! It's over so far as I am concerned, and I have nothing to reproach myself with—not even after reading over these scribbled pages. At least I have a record of the silly, neurotic things that happened from Tuesday to Sunday. And there are ninety-seven typewritten pages to show for all those hours at the machine!

[After a two-day interval in New York]

Tuesday April 30. 3:00 PM

Arrived at 11. Met Madeleine at North Philadelphia Station. M awake and waiting for me. Began at once to lay out remaining chapters, outlining them point by point. Here is our schedule as of this minute, with number of pages for each chapter and assignment of writing:

	Writer	Pages	To be finished
14 The Way of All Flesh	SC	25	Tues. night
15 The School for Scandal	PM	22	Tues. night
16 The Lost Chord	PM	25	Wed. night
17 Reunion in Variety	SC	25	Wed. night
18 It's Never Too Late	PM & SC	17	Thurs. night
19 Mama's Daughter	PM & SC	12	Fri. night
20 The Plush Fades	PM & SC	10	Sat. night
		136	

Sunday for editing
Train for home Sunday 5 PM

Holy vows that this schedule will be kept, sound wonderful at this stage. We'll see. At any rate, I'll have the work as outlined above—Sunday 5 PM—or else!

Wednesday May 1. 1:00 AM

There is a glimmer of hope for this damned manuscript. After working from three o'clock until five minutes ago—ten hours—on "The Way of All Flesh," I have completed twenty closely-typed pages, a total of 6,000 words, the greatest demonstration of logorrhea in my experience. I only hope it does not smell too offensively. Yet, strange to say, it reads with ease, goes from point to point in natural transitions and—fills space! Twenty-six thousand words to go by Saturday midnight. That is a frightening number!

My hopes are raised by the fact that M has gotten a few pages written on "The School for Scandal." Even if he falls behind the above schedule, the rate at which it is pouring out of me will make up for his lapses.

The nightmarish feeling is passing. Maybe because I am so stimulated by the long and intense concentration and cannot sleep. I am not tired, in spite of the fact that I had only five hours last night, dreading what was to come today. But 6,000 words in nine hours *is* a help.

I still reproach myself for being so tongue-tied in explaining my position in this matter. They couldn't and wouldn't see beyond the practical necessity of finishing the job. How could I expect them to feel the emotional state I had gotten into? And why was I silly enough to feel hurt because Bennett had no interest in my record of last week's purgatory? Well, that's past. Another 6,000 words by tomorrow night and the bastion will fall. Rhetoric! Nuts!

Wednesday 2:00 AM

It's no use. I can't fall asleep. Overstimulation and too many cigarettes. What fear and doubt and timidity can do to a guy! Yesterday the outlook was hopeless. Maybe because I was on the verge of mental and physical collapse. All for dear old Rah Rah! Now sleepless and with 6,000 words on paper I feel confident that the whole thing will be finished on Sunday and will be promptly forgotten. I will ask myself why I get into such states and will laugh it off—I hope.

Wednesday 3:00 AM

No sleep. The damned thing is getting me. I must watch out.

Wednesday 9:00 AM

It must have been 4 AM when finally I fell asleep. Up at 7:30 nonetheless, and now at 9 AM, chapter thirteen—"The Way of All Flesh"—is finished. Nobody in the house has begun to stir yet. If I can get fourteen hours in today without collapsing I may be over the ridge. Today is crucial. We'll see.

Wednesday Noon.

Fifteen hundred words into "Reunion in Variety" as a starter. Just went upstairs to see M, and not a single word has been added to what he tried to do yesterday. The same sheet is on the same line in his typewriter. He has sat all night and morning reading what I wrote yesterday, and he had the effrontery to say it is not quite up to *our* standard, but we might get by with it. I am furious and too mad and tired and nervous and depressed to argue the point. I simply must go on grinding out 6,000 words each day, regardless of what he says or thinks, until Sunday, and then smuggle the script out of here. If only I don't fall asleep at the machine today . . .

Wednesday 4:30 PM

I was interrupted to examine what M had done on "The School for Scandal." It is awful, besides being illiterate. Twelve pages of stuff badly copied out of stupid sources, it still has to go. I took out most of the cliches, fixed the solecisms, rephrased it here and there, and let it go. This will be his writing, the very first he has done in ten days. Jesus, the irony of this horrible business!

Wednesday 8:30 PM

About three-quarters finished with "Reunion in Variety" and will try to pound a few more pages out of my weary brain before I quit for the night. Even so I have done more today than M has accomplished from Sunday night until this minute. Yet he says, "Now I feel that I've got this book licked!" When I went upstairs, he was staring vacantly at his typewriter and seemed a little embarrassed at being interrupted in his empty reverie. At supper the same ghastly silence.... And it is to keep alive his myth that he is a writer that I undergo these tortures. That's nonsense. The real and only reason is to get finished somehow on Sunday night, deliver the script to Random House, and be comparatively free again. It's a job to be finished, and, as Don Klopfer said, it has no relation whatever to the question of integrity. But that is how one's life is squandered. I, too, once believed in my own myth!

Wednesday Midnight.

Finished chapter—"Reunion in Variety"—about 5,000 to 5,500 words. Exhausted, but sleepless. M, still in the middle of his first chapter, busily copies out squibs from his sources and other books. To hell with it! Now is no time to stand on scruples. According to schedule, he should have finished his chapter Tuesday night. Here it is Wednesday midnight and he is still in the middle. I'll have to finish it tomorrow.

Tonight he again brought up the point that this will be more my book than his. It was no hypocrisy to deny this, because by no stretch of the imagination can this kind of book be considered mine. It's a penalty, a sentence, an expiation, a penance— anything but my book, it must be understood. I must sleep tonight, else I'll collapse. Fifteen hours at the typewriter. What a life!

Thursday May 2. 1:30 AM

Still no sleep. Have taken a sleeping potion, but it's useless. Quite calm, but I can't stop my heart from bouncing against the walls of my chest, all bad shots that don't hit hard enough and come off at a bad angle for the return.

M still working, and getting nowhere. What goes on? What does he do all the time? All sitzfleish, and nothing comes of it.

Thursday 9:00 AM

It must have been three o'clock when I fell asleep. Awake, as usual, at 7:30. Cannot find what M has done last night. Apparently he has hidden it, so that he can show it to me when he wakes up around noon and then explain why he has fallen so far behind. The only thing to do now is to plunge into chapter eighteen—"It's Never Too Late"—otherwise we are sunk. I must do at least 5,000 words today. Feeling very jittery and have developed uncontrollable tremor of the hands.

Thursday 11:00 AM

M arose 10:30 and sheepishly admitted that he had not finished his stint. It should have been completed, according to our schedule, on Tuesday night. And here it is Thursday. It's lucky that I am ahead of my program and can work today on "It's Never Too Late," which was assigned to M on Tuesday with the understanding that he have it ready by tonight, Thursday. I plan to finish it before I go to bed. I have a start of three pages at this moment of writing. I've got Lily married for the fourth time.

Thursday 2:30 PM

Had to stop work on "It's Never Too Late" to finish off M's chapter, "School for Scandal." That, at least, is out of the way. Now he begins on "The Lost Chord," which, by schedule, should have been finished last night. But I'm ahead, and that helps.

Amusing, incidentally, how I've counted to thirteen the number of times he has suggested the use of the word "effulgent" when I have hesitated for a word. Whether the sense called for it or not, he tries to get it in somehow. That or "lush." But "lush" only runs to ten or eleven. In the script neither word appears more than once or twice, and I must consider that one of my major accomplishments during these weeks.

Thursday 6:00 PM

I am incapable of feeling furious any more. Having finished about two-thirds of my chapter—"It's Never Too Late"—I went upstairs, and there I was calmly told, "I think I have an idea for a new lead to my chapter." That means that he has done nothing today on the chapter that should have been finished, by our reasonable schedule, on Wednesday night. It isn't even started! I see where I shall have to do that one tomorrow, too. Of the seven chapters we had to write when I came on Tuesday, he has done one, with help, and I have completed three. Of the remaining three, I shall probably have to do two, thus making the score for the week 5 to 2, with a few assists to add to the five and subtract from the two. And I'm not even angry any more. Just goddamned tired and in an agony of nervous jitters.

Thursday 9:30 PM

Coming to the end of "It's Never Too Late." Another page or so and it will be finished. M has not yet started his chapter, but he promises he will work until four in the morning. Lot of good that will do. Just now he said something that staggered me, although I should have expected it. He had been reading over my chapter—"Reunion in Variety"—and had made a few pencilled notes, adding a connective instead of a comma, a qualifier where the noun carried itself, and so on. About ten picayune marks in the whole chapter, eight of which I'll throw out. I made the remark that I often like to let the punctuation mark do the work of a connective. He did not know what I meant, I am sure, but he said he made the changes to have the chapter conform to the style of *his* writing in the first six chapters! As I might have guessed, he has by now convinced himself that he has written the first six chapters all by himself. Next week, it will be the first twelve, and in a month, all the twenty. His style! Good God, does he think this is *his* style? Or mine, for that matter? It's a collection of 75,000 words put down to get finished and out of here. Nothing else!

Thursday 10:30 PM

Just finished "It's Never Too Late." If only I sleep tonight . . .

Friday May 3. 9:00 AM

Finally got some sleep, thanks to two shots. Woke up to learn that M has been working all night, according to his note, but still he has not finished the chapter that was scheduled for Wednesday—and today is Friday. That means there are only two days left. How, in Christ's name, are we going to finish at this rate? I simply cannot speed up. So far I have done three chapters, 16,000 words since Tuesday. If I do 4,000 today, we still have a chance.

Friday 10:00 AM

Have just read what M has written since Tuesday—about one-half a chapter, all of which must be done over again. It consists entirely of synopsization of three plays—*Barbara's*

Millions, The Butterfly, and *Wildfire*—all very badly done and obviously space fillers. The man has no shame. One would think he'd be embarrassed to let me see this tripe after he had worked on it for three days. I'll try to fix it up somehow, and finish the chapter today. One way or another I must get out of here. The whole point, and I must not forget it for a moment, is that these chapters must be finished on Sunday. Pride and sensibilities and principles and dignity and even regard for craftsmanship must be subordinated to the one purpose of departing on Sunday with a completed script. If I can restrain myself from bursting out with a hysterical denunciation of everything in this place, I shall accomplish a victory over myself. The manuscript will leave here with me on Sunday! A pounding headache is slowing me up. But, somehow, I'll pump out the quota of words today.

Friday 6:00 PM

Have just finished his chapter—"The Lost Chord." Of all the outrages! I have done in a half day more than he has accomplished since Tuesday.

Friday 10:00 PM

No entry tonight. Sick. Strangest goddamned sensation of being drunk and about to fall over. Knees weak, and everything is going around. It must be the dope I took to fall asleep last night. Well, anyhow, the chapter is finished. And now there are only two more to go—short ones. The doctor prescribed a hot bath and some silly nerve pills. Madeleine, alarmed, called him up. It's all nonsense.

Saturday May 4. 10:00 AM

The medicine did it. Slept ten hours. Awoke to find M still over the typewriter with exactly three pages written, and not a word on them intelligible. He had solemnly promised he would have fifteen pages of chapter nineteen—"Mama's Daughter"— ready for me. Today, according to schedule, should have seen us finished, with tomorrow for last minute revisions. Now everything is thrown out of gear. To save the mess, I have insisted upon his going to bed, while I try to hack out fifteen pages on "Mama's Daughter." If he sleeps until 6 PM and stays out of sight, I may be able to do it. Then tonight, we may be able to write the concluding chapter and thus fulfill the schedule in spite of hell, high water, and the author himself. It can be done yet. Perhaps it would be easier if my head would stop throbbing and I could vomit up all my nausea and sickness of heart.

Saturday 3:00 PM

Out for a walk for the first time in days with M. He is having an acute attack of conscience, wants to tear up contract with Random House, wants to tell Bennett all, wants to share all profits with me 50-50, doesn't want his name on the book, is a "mediocrity," a failure, a louse, never was a writer, never would be, etc. All very disconcerting and embarrassing for me. The lame response, to placate him. "You'd do as much for me, if the situation were reversed," brings assurances he'd go to hell for me. The guy is suffering, now that we are in sight of the end. My job is to put it all on a practical basis: viz., we have twenty four pages to go. Let's get them done. That's all there is to it. Will Sunday 5 PM never come?

Saturday 6:00 PM

Have just finished chapter nineteen—"Mama's Daughter"—thirteen pages, about thirty-two hundred words. It went faster than I thought it would. Then, too, I wasn't disturbed. M has been sitting upstairs—believe it or not—for all these hours with a sheet in his typewriter which had these words—and these words only—typed on it:

"The Great War brought many changes to America."

Not another syllable has he written. But what difference does it make? There is one more chapter to write and then I can go home.

As an aside, I want to put down my sense of shame over and my pride in a phrase or two in this manuscript that gets itself written in spite of me. Here and there the goddamned thing comes alive and I try to explain it by the fact that it is easier to let a decent impulse find expression than to crush it. Besides, it adds to the wordage. Right now we have reached page 289. That means about 73,000 words. Another twelve pages will bring down the curtain. *Gott sei dank.*

Saturday Midnight.

Hurrah! The book is finished. The last word was written at 11:25 tonight. It's over! Thirty two thousand words in five days, an average of sixty five hundred words a day. I have never seen a more crestfallen author in my life. On our walk just now, he wept all the way, saying that the book was mine, that he had failed, that he hates himself and wishes he had never seen the book, Random House or me. He begs permission to make a few verbal changes. He cries that he has failed and could not write a word, which is true.

Now my great fear is that in his present psychotic state he may tear up the manuscript as an act of revenge for his failure. He has taken it to his room to read. I pray he doesn't have that aberration tonight. *I've got to get that script out of here!* I'm scared out of my wits.

Sunday May 5. 6:15 AM

Have been waiting for hours for daylight to come. At 3:00 AM, M was still up, poring over the manuscript. He heard me tossing around and offered to get me a glass of hot milk. We talked for a while. He apologized profusely for all he had said earlier in the night and added: "The book has unity. How you did it, I don't know. It was awful to blow on you like that." More tears, more promises to share royalties and tell the whole story to everybody. I said, "Forget it." Which is exactly what I ought to do. . . .

Sunday 8:30 AM

The manuscript is intact. M is asleep. All is well. Not a wink of sleep all night. I'll make up for it in New York.

Sunday 11:00 AM

Stenographer here to type out last twenty four pages which were written yesterday. As soon as she finishes, I can go home. Maybe by three o'clock.

Sunday 3:12 PM

On the train at last. It is all over. The script is in my suitcase. In the words of the last line of the book:*

"The last curtain had fallen in silence."

No more.

*Subsequently I added a paragraph following this sentence because two readers thought the story ended too abruptly.

In reality, the curtain did not fall in silence. Ralph Thompson wrote in his review in the *New York Times*, "Mr. Morrell . . . seems to have Lillian herself so nearly right that neither she nor her Mama, were they still alive, could very well approve. The rest of us should, whether we saw the English Ballad Singer in the flesh or have recently seen Alice Faye going through the appropriate motions on the screen." In conclusion, the *Times* felt that the author told his story "with skill and amiable malice, and at least, so it seems to one who arrived too late to know much about it—catches the spirit of the gold-plated bicycle days." Stewart Holbrook reviewed the book in the Sunday *Herald-Tribune*, ending with the paragraph, "I enjoyed the book thoroughly. It is as much a story of the time as it is of Miss Russell, a time seemingly as far in the past as that of Helen of Troy.... The format lends added nostalgic charm to this narrative of America's best-known woman to date." Lewis Gannett was not as enthusiastic, but he did point out how admirably "synchronized" were the movie and the book, and he devoted more space to *Lillian Russell* than did the other reviewers.

Mr. Morrell, writes Saxe, "was guest of honor at a party given by the publishers. He was urbane, self-assured, and theatrically modest—a successful author precisely as envisioned by Hollywood. Some members of the party had copies of his book and asked if he would autograph them. As he wrote his name, I turned away and began to moan and mutter, just as he had done when I had brought the manuscript to his bedside."

10 Four More of Saxe's Authors

Like all editors, Saxe had his failures. These were of different sorts. In the case of the Columbia professor Maurice Valency, Saxe was voted down by others at Random House. Here is the manuscript report for Professor Valency's *The Third Heaven*. Conscious of the manuscript's limited appeal in 1957, Saxe might have had better success today.

10 June 1957

To: DSK
From: SC
Subject: *The Third Heaven* by Maurice Valency

One of the least commercial manuscripts to come my way in a long time is one of the best in content, in style, and in scholarship. It undertakes to study the formative stages of the lyric tradition and the evolution of the changes in attitudes toward love, beginning with the eleventh century and the troubadours, with a backward glance at the Greek and Roman and Patristic poets, and culminating with Dante's *Vita Nuova*.

The author provides the title *The Third Heaven*, an allusion to the third of the seven arts, Rhetoric, the heaven of Venus, according to Dante in the *Convivio*. This title fails to suggest the substance and the spirit of this wise and witty and penetrating book on the tender passion as revealed by "the sweetest of sciences." It would be far more accurate and suggestive to paraphrase Erasmus and call the work *In Praise of Love*. Certainly it is a history and a critical evaluation of the changing expressions of the adoration of women by the poets of Provence and Italy.

How amatory patterns change, and with them the role of women, is developed with the utmost good sense in the analysis of the poetry that made women the symbols of their century, their place and their culture. They become indeed in this study projections of the poet's record of their society and their time. They are idealized and idolized; they are the images of desires, both sacred and profane. Their appeal is both physical and metaphysical and the rewards they offer range from an embrace with the corporeal reality to a passion for the divine.

Maurice Valency, who adapted the play *The Madwoman of Chaillot*, is a professor of comparative literature at Columbia. Manifestly his study of the poetry of the troubadours and Dante and Petrarch is his major scholarly interest and *The Third Heaven* embodies his vast fund of knowledge and his unfailing critical insight. His book is a delight for the scholar and for a handful of laymen who, if they are not excited by Renaissance poets are interested in love. There can be no question of the merit of his manuscript.

The only question that concerns us is whether we want to undertake a book of true scholarship on a subject remote from topical interest and have on our list a book that will bring prestige if not profit.

This must be decided by a second or third reading by members of our staff or outside experts who can confirm or refute my enthusiasm for this book. I am quite certain that if we do not publish it, another publisher will. We are the first to see it.

Ultimately, Saxe had to send the bad news to the professor.

You will have to believe me when I tell you that I did my utmost to persuade my colleagues to undertake publication of *The Third Heaven*. My report on your manuscript reflected my unreserved enthusiasm for your work, which to me is a wise and penetrating study, rich in content, in style and in scholarship, and eminently deserving publication.

Unfortunately, I was outvoted on the grounds that a study of the formative stages of the lyric tradition in Provence and Italy seemed—but not to me—too esoteric for trade exploitation.

Everyone else seemed to think that yours is a work that belongs more properly under the imprint of a university press.

My own belief is that it would dignify the list of Oxford University Press, and I strongly urge you to submit it to them. In fact, I would like to be the advocate of your manuscript with that house.

It would be a pleasure to me to talk with you about your book, not that I would have any valuable suggestions to make, but I could then convey how deeply impressed I have been and how enthusiastically I recommend it. Can a meeting be arranged?

May I put forward a suggestion about the title? Reference to the third heaven does not occur until page 306, and only then do we learn that, according to Dante's *Convivio*, it is the heaven of Venus. It occurred to me that a paraphrase of Erasmus would describe the book more familiarly. What do you think of *In Praise of Love*? Please consider this alternative title.

I can't tell you how sorry I am that the decision went against you—and me.

"My contacts with editors thus far have not been memorable," Professor Valency replied. "Now you have changed all that, and I am grateful not only for your enormous kindness, but also for this pleasant reminder that there are still some nice people in this naughty world."

Saxe had been ill when the next letter arrived from Columbia.

> 22 November 1957
> 410 Riverside Drive
> New York, N.Y.

Dear Saxe Commins:

I'm much relieved to hear that your illness is not as grave as I was led to expect. The hushed and mysterious tone in which your secretary informed me that you weren't well made me feel far worse—believe it or not—than any bad news from Oxford. I want to thank you, too, for the consideration which prompts your note at a time when, by all the rules, you should be thinking only of yourself.

The Oxford Delegates sent me back my manuscript together with a letter which didn't add up to anything, except that their readers didn't wholeheartedly recommend it to them. Apparently these readers disagreed in everything except this conclusion. One of them thought, it appears, that this book would not make an appropriate text for a beginner in Provencal poetry, and he objected to the sociological and psychological implications. The other apparently wanted more said about the Arab background. Neither seemed to me to be very much on the ball.

I was afraid that might happen at Clarendon. Scholars in this field are apt to be terribly narrow and specialized in their views—that was one reason why I wrote this book. But of course difficulties of this sort are to be anticipated, and I anticipated them. I've now sent the manuscript to Knopf, with whose Mrs. I have a slight acquaintance. I don't have any hope for it there, and I would have consulted you first, but I couldn't very well trouble you with this sort of question when you weren't well. I thought I might try Princeton next, or perhaps Macmillan, and I'd be terribly grateful for any advice you can give me if and when you feel up to it. I think it's not a bad book, and I'll certainly see that it gets around.

In the meantime, please get well as soon as you decently can. You have indeed made a devoted friend and one who counts heavily on spending many a pleasant hour with you in the not too distant future.

Yours sincerely,
Maurice Valency

Professor Valency wrote to me after Saxe's death. "My own acquaintance with Saxe was much too brief, cut short as it was by his illness. But I shall always remember him. *The Third Heaven*, incidentally, had its title changed to *In Praise of Love*, according to his suggestion, and was eventually published by Macmillan. But as a result of his sending the manuscript to Oxford, I have since gone over to Oxford."

A new author, Walter Van Tilburg Clark, was introduced to us in 1939 with his first novel, *The Ox-Bow Incident*, a terse and compelling story of a lynching bee in a Western cattle town in 1855. It was hailed as a masterpiece. During the writing of his next novel, *The City of Trembling Leaves* (published in 1940), he was on the teaching staff of the Department of English and Drama at Cazenovia Central School, in Cazenovia, New York. Whenever he had a free weekend, he would come to our apartment in New York, where he and Saxe could work undisturbed. One came to recognize the fine sensibilities of the man and his keen awareness of the beauty in music and the other arts.

After he had written *The Track of the Cat* and *The Watchful Gods and Other Stories*, which contains his famous story "Hook, the Hawk," there came a lull in his output. Saxe was worried, for he felt that Clark had established a distinguished place for himself in American literature.

Then in 1954, when Clark came to visit us in Princeton, he unburdened himself. It was evident that he had become deeply concerned with problems of conscience and moral obligation. He wrote, he told us, pages and pages, but the sheets ended up in the fireplace. His fear was that what he was writing was not faithful to his literary ideals.

If Clark's writing impasse was caused by his high standards and self-doubts, it was worsened by his sense of obligation to his students. As he put it in a letter to Saxe while he was teaching at San Francisco State, "I keep writing, first paragraphs and first chapters, but they keep dying under the insidious pressures of the cirical self at my elbow, and the more decent demands of student manuscripts and the lapses of time and breaks of continuity they bring about." He goes on to call the division between teaching and writing an expensive one, but worthwhile.

As for the books he'd already produced, Clark wrote Saxe in 1956 that he felt *The City of Trembling Leaves* was in some important ways his "best book to date, despite various narrow-gauge Freudian misreadings and urban misunderstandings." "With *The Track of the Cat*," he went on in the same letter, "I've received even more inquiries about it and all in the same vein—is there any unabridged edition available? I'm convinced, for practical as well as personal reasons, that we were wrong to put out an abridged one. It is my somewhat more than guess that if the *Cat* were available in full in paperback it would go at least as well as *Ox-Bow*."

Saxe arranged for a reprinting of *The Watchful Gods*, but today only the *Ox-Bow* is in print, and the film adaptation can still be seen.

Saxe came to know Edgar Snow when Snow's *Red Star over China* was submitted to Random House for publication in 1936. So enthusiastic was Saxe with Edgar's amazing narrative of his life in China, that he contacted Edgar at once.

Edgar was the first Westerner to write or even know about the Chinese Communist movement in the 1930s. He had won the confidence of Mao Tse-tung and had spent months with him in the remote mountains of China. He had also established intimate relationships with Chou En-lai and his associates that were never forgotten by them. Edgar tells of his walking across the hilly terrain of Shensi, south of the Great Wall, and coming upon a forlorn little village, where he encountered parts of a straggling army that had just concluded the historic 6,000-mile "Long March" from southern China to Shensi.

In subsequent books, *The Battle for Asia, People on Our Side, The Pattern of Soviet Power,* and *Stalin Must Have Peace,* on all of which Edgar and Saxe worked closely together, Edgar tells of his talks with Gandhi, Nehru, Chiang Kai-shek, Mme. Sun Yat-sen, King Ibn Sa'ud, Roosevelt, Churchill, Stalin, Truman, and many, many simple people everywhere who suffered and made extraordinary sacrifices in World War II.

As early as 1951 Edgar had begun to reflect on his own personal history, casting a backward glance at his youth in Kansas City, Missouri, and those impulsive years of wanderlust that led him to China, Manchuria, India, and Russia. Yet perhaps because he had so much to tell, an experienced journalist like Snow found it very difficult to talk about himself. The first draft of his autobiography was a disappointment to Saxe. In a memo, Saxe gives some indication of how much effort he had already put into the book.

What I had feared most has happened with Edgar Snow. His many postponements in delivering the manuscript indicated a great uncertainty in his own mind about the nature of his book, his point of view and his method of recording his experiences. Long ago, by dint of a great deal of prodding, I saw a few sample chapters and was dismayed by their lack of organization, their diffuseness and their carelessness. These were sent back to him with many notes containing suggestions for radical revision. At a luncheon, about a year or so ago, we went over those notes and Ed took these chapters with him, promising to work over them and bring the manuscript into some kind of order. After another long absence, during which I pestered him with notes asking him for a promise of delivery of manuscript so that we could set a pub date, he finally sent in a larger fragment of his proposed book.

Saxe went into some detail, recognizing that Snow himself was dissatisfied with the work, since he had promised "to supply the missing sections later." As a friend as well as an editor, Saxe was concerned, because "it would do Snow a great disservice to publish it as it was, even if it were polished up."

Finally it became clear that the two men would have to have some long sessions. Edgar came to us for days at a time. Those were days of intense, hard work. The entire book had to be reshaped. Saxe and Edgar went over every chapter line by line. Even the title gave trouble. The first draft had taken a mere two years. It was four years after he had written his report on this draft that Saxe felt the book was publishable, and *Journey to the Beginning* at last appeared in 1958. A generous man, Edgar was grateful and wrote to Donald Klopfer that he could not have managed without Saxe's help, then as in the past.

Before merging with Random House, Robert Haas and Harrison Smith, Inc., had published the stories of Isak Dinesen, who in real life was the Danish writer, the Baroness Karen Blixen. When she came to Random House, Bob Haas continued to be her publisher. In 1944, during the occupation of the baroness's homeland by the Nazis, a novel, *Ways of Retribution*, written ostensibly by Pierre Andrézel, had been published and widely read. To the German censors it had seemed an old-fashioned novel, a bit hair-raising, but harmless enough. It is a disguised tale, beginning in an atmosphere of charm and beauty, then suddenly catapulting into a world of horror and danger. Certainly the story could be read as a symbolic condemnation of the evil forces let loose by Hitler in World War II.

When, early in 1946, the baroness sent a translation of her book to Haas, she insisted that the real identity of the author be kept secret. This despite the fact that Bob urged her to change her mind. "The name of Isak Dinesen," he wrote her, "is now so well known in the United States that were we allowed to use it, the chances are one hundred to one that considerably larger sales could be obtained." The baroness had to be told this, for during the war, communication between her American publishers and herself had been for all practical purposes nonexistent. In fact, *Winter's Tales* had gone to press here without some of the last-minute changes she had added to the British edition. Now Bob Haas conferred with Saxe and then wrote to an author, who was not easily persuaded.

20 February 1946

Dear Baroness Blixen:

   The translation, as I wrote you recently, arrived last week and I read it immediately. I have also had a reading by one of the best judges in our organization. We were both delighted with the story, and I think that the way you have created an authentic Jane Austen atmosphere is a real *tour de force*. As a matter of fact, up to the time of the death of the Pennhallows I was literally on the edge of my chair. In one of your earlier letters, however, you asked me to give you my frank and unvarnished opinion of how the book stood up. At the risk of rushing in where angels fear to tread, then, I feel I must make the comment that the last few chapters dealing with the romance of the two girls and concluding in a happy ending were just a bit anticlimactic. Of course we may be quite wrong about this, and very possibly this section was deliberately written to fit in as an appropriate part of the whole canvas. However, it seemed to us that had those chapters been telescoped and not quite so much emphasis been given to what happened after the deaths, the books might have been more of an integral whole. I don't know—I simply submit this for what it might be worth. But should you think that there is any validity in the comment, we would be delighted to undertake the necessary editorial work to bring this about. It would be almost altogether a matter of cutting, and for this reason I think you would not have to fear that it would be clumsily done.

   There is another point in connection with the above, and that is the movies. You yourself suggested, in your letter of 13 September 1945, that you felt there was a chance to have the book filmed. I thoroughly agree with you on this. It seems to me to be just the kind of story that a director like Hitchcock might want; but from our experience here I am strongly of the opinion that it would stand a much better chance were the suggested changes to be initiated. But, of course, this is a matter for you and you alone to decide.

   While on the subject of comments, may I ask again whether you would consider letting us publish the book under your name rather than under the name of Pierre Andrézel? I brought up this question once before, and the only reason I raise it again is that I imagine you are interested in sales just as we are. Here again I hesitate to press a matter which I know lies otherwise in your mind, but I think it only right to point out to you that we could double the distribution of your book were your name attached to it.

We have had correspondence back and forth about the title and I would like to present, now that I have read the book, a new suggestion: *The Innocent Avengers.* It seems to me that it describes the main characters accurately and that at the same time there is an intriguing idea in the juxtaposition of these two almost irreconcilable words. I do hope that it will strike your fancy. *The Angelic Avengers,* as the book is being titled in English, doesn't strike me as quite as good. For some reason which I find it hard to put into words but which I feel strongly, "innocent" is an interesting word and "angelic" not quite so interesting. What do you think?

When Charles Robbins first told me about this book he gave me to understand that there were a number of implications in it which did not meet the eye. I think I appreciate what he meant—in a confessedly somewhat vague way—but may I say that they seem to me to be so oversubtle that it would be inappropriate to refer to them in any advertising campaign or in any publicity progaganda. Don't you agree? . . .

The baroness was reasonable but adamant.

Thank you for your kind letter of February 20. I have had my operation done and am back in my own house. But I am still feeling terribly weak, and I am afraid that this letter will be rather confused and incoherent. But I should like to answer your letter at once, and I hope that you will be able in any case to gather the sense of it.

I am extremely pleased that you like my book, and I hope that we shall manage to get some fun out of it.

As to the romance of the two girls, and the happy ending of the novel, being a bit anti-climactic, I feel that you may be altogether right, but somehow I rather prefer the book to end in this way. It is not meant to be an orthodox crime novel, where the whole plot finishes with the discovery or punishment of the murderer. I see it more as a kind of "hold-all," where romance, crime, and idyll are all blended. And it also seems to me that the long introduction before Mr. Pennhallow makes his entrance on the stage does somehow require to be weighed up by some kind of conclusion after he has disappeared. So, all things considered, I think I shall leave the book as it is.

With regard to the movies, it would certainly give me the very greatest pleasure to have the book filmed, and I should of course like to give it every chance here too. But I am under the

impression that the movies, when filming a book, do not
absolutely feel it their duty to follow the plot page by page, and
they might easily shorten the last chapters, if it so suited them. I
should not of course like these chapters, after the death of the
Pennhallows, to be omitted, but they might certainly be condensed to a few scenes.

As to the "implications" in the book, I entirely agree with you
that it would be inappropriate to refer to them in any advertising
campaign. They hang together with the situation here in
Denmark at the time when the book was published, when the
German censorship was at its most severe, and also with Winston
Churchill's little joke about the Danes, when he referred to us as
"the Gangster's canary birds." It might possibly be mentioned in
an advertising campaign that the book had been published in
Denmark at such a time.

In the Danish edition, I wanted the page and line of Zosine's
remark: "You serious people must not be too hard on human
beings for what they choose to amuse themselves with, when
they are shut up as in a prison, and are not even allowed to say
that they're prisoners. If I do not soon get a little bit of fun, I shall
die!" (English typescript, page 120, the four last lines) to be given
on the title page of the book, but even that my publishers dared
not quote. I should like this page and line to be given on the front
page of the American edition, if you think the people would
understand.

Now I come to the point of your letter, by far the most
important to me, and for the sake of which I am really pulling
myself together to write to you today. It is the question of my
anonymity. I wish I was feeling stronger, for I want to oppose
you here with all my force! Also, I should wish that my brain
was a bit clearer, so as to put forth my arguments better, but
even if I do not succeed here, I trust that I shall make you realize
that this is a matter on which I cannot be moved. In fact, the very
reasons which you produce in order to make me give up the name
of Pierre Andrézel are those on account of which I shall never
consent to let the book be published under my own name.
You will understand what great delight it gives me to be told that
my name has become one almost to conjure with in the American
market. But the more it is so, the greater care I will take of that
name, the more I shall feel my artistic responsibility, and the call
of *noblesse oblige.* You tell me that as far as you know, I am the
only author who "till now has written just three books, all of
which were Book of the Month Club selections." I do not want to
give my name as an author to a book which cannot possibly

come into consideration for such a selection. (Or even if, *par impossible*, the Book of the Month Club should consider this book, I would refuse to have it selected, and would rather withdraw the manuscript altogether, than have it placed in this way with my other books!)

I have already in Denmark found some difficulty in making my publishers see the point of my anonymity, and of the existence of Pierre Andrézel. It is rather a difficult thing to explain, when the idea is not grasped immediately and so to say by intuition. It is not a deceit, it is a mask! People may be allowed to guess the real name of the person behind the mask, but they must fall in with the spirit of the game, and must never address him by this name. You may hint as much as you like at the identity of Isak Dinesen and Pierre Andrézel, but you must never let out that I had admitted to the identity. You might tell that in 1944 a book was published in Denmark under the name of Pierre Andrézel, and gave rise to a long discussion as to its authorship.—and I might even give you here, for your own amusement, some cutting from the newspapers—but I would rather not have the book published at all than I would have it published under the name of Isak Dinesen or Karen Blixen! Kings, princes, and other elevated personages at times, when travelling, and when in want of a bit of fun, make use of an incognito, and their surroundings agree to respect.

The book was published as *The Angelic Avengers* by Pierre Andrézel. When the Book of the Month Club wanted it, the baroness's first reaction was to turn down the offer. Only after she was guaranteed that the author named on the title page would be Pierre Andrézel did she cable her permission.

Ten years later, in August of 1956, Saxe jotted down in his notebook, "Bob Haas has just returned from his vacation in Europe and has accumulated a number of stories by Isak Dinesen which he turned over to me with the idea of making two books of them. My job is to disentangle the mess they are in and turn in a report within a few days." This is how his diary continues for the next few days:

10 August 1956.

By way of getting started, I read the longest of the stories, "The Caryatides," an unmistakable Dinesen performance, mingling reality and witchcraft against her own kind of Gothic background. By orthodox standards it is not a good story; as an evocation of a mood and the communication of a brooding tragedy-laden atmosphere, it is inimitable. The individual sentences, twisted and inverted and carelessly punctuated would never pass the scrutiny of a grammarian, but the total effect is quite startling.

11 August 1956.

Taking advantage of the glittering sun, outdoors at work on the Blixen manuscript and made order of the scramble of stories. These stories are indeed remarkable, even when they are banal in theme, as in "The Cardinal's Third Story," wherein the Amazon lady finally kisses the foot of the statue of St. Peter after a young man had done so and left lingering spirochetes. She contracts the disease. But Dinesen has the power to create an atmosphere suspended between the natural and the supernatural. Her resourcefulness of plot and her Gothic atmosphere make of her one of the great storytellers. There hovers over her stories, a sense of mystery, foreboding, and tension. She evokes a mood and sustains it.

12 August 1956.

Back at work on the terrace in the blazing sunlight and completed the reading of the stories—three, which were not listed. Typed out my report. It runs to four pages single space.

13 August 1956

In New York and submitted my report on the Dinesen stories and that meant a protracted conference. We arrived at an agreement with what is to be done. Bob Haas then dictated a letter to the Baroness.

A good manuscript report must consider questions of detail and yet convey the overall impression of the book. Here is what Saxe wrote about the two collections of Isak Dinesen tales.

12 August 1956

To: RKH
From: SC
Subject: Two New Collections of Short Stories by Isak Dinesen

The eleven stories planned for the volume at present called *Last Tales* are in three categories, one of which gives the source, the novel *Albondocani*, and the other two are descriptive: "Gothic Tales" and "New Winter's Tales." Their titles are as follows:

The Cardinal's First Tale ⎫
The Cloak   ⎪
Night-Walk   ⎬ From the novel
Of Secret Thoughts and of Heaven   *Albondocani*
The Cardinal's Third Tale   ⎪
The Blank Page   ⎪
Tales of Two Old Gentlemen ⎭

The Caryatides ⎫ "Gothic Tales"
Echoes   ⎭

A Country Tale   ⎫
Copenhagen Season   ⎬ "New Winter's Tales"
Converse at Night in Copenhagen ⎭

Of these eleven tales we have six in our possession:
The Cardinal's First Tale
The Cardinal's Third Tale
The Blank Page
The Caryatides
A Country Tale
Converse at Night in Copenhagen

This means the following tales are still to come from Baroness Blixen:
The Cloak
Night-Walk
Of Secret Thoughts and of Heaven
Echoes
Copenhagen Season

The word count of the stories in *Last Tales* which are now at hand runs to approximately sixty thousand. On the assumption that the missing five will be of average length, the entire collection for this volume should come to between ninety and one hundred thousand words. An analysis of the stories now in our possession will be made later in this report.

The second manuscript, under the title *Anecdotes of Destiny*, calls for seven tales, of which three are in our possession...

The word count on the three stories in *Anecdotes of Destiny* which have come to us totals close to twenty thousand. The missing tales will have to be considerably longer if we are to make a second book comparable in length to the others by Baroness Blixen already published by us. The ideal length is around eighty thousand to ninety thousand, and we come well within those figures for *Last Tales*, but from present indications *Anecdotes of Destiny* may be half or a little more than that.

The stories themselves, with some qualifications, are simply marvelous. They are pervaded with a mood, part real and part mystical and always compelling, of a uniquely original mind and a sure, deft hand. They are, for the most part, fairy tales and certainly parables told with a somber earnestness and always with a haunting atmosphere of the tragic.

"The Cardinal's First Tale" is a magnificent story in which one never knows until near the end which of the twins the cardinal really is, since he is both artist and priest. The tale he tells to the nonpenitent lady is his own and is yet a universal experience of ambivalence. His apostrophe to the "story" as an art form and as a symbol of life is masterly. As in all her stories, Dinesen here maintains a delicate equilibrium between the natural and the supernatural, yet she never does anything to disturb the atmosphere in which her tale is unfolded. (In order to overcome the objection you raised on page 11 about summoning the sponsors in three days, I recommend that we omit the three words "within three days" and have the passage read: "And in order to prove the worth of his princely word he had the baptism of his sons take place in the chapel. The elder of the boys was christened Atanasio...").

"The Cardinal's Third Tale." Here comes my first reservation. But for the unfortunate ending of this tale, it would compare favorably with all the others. After drawing a wonderful portrait of an utterly indomitable woman, huge in stature and adamant in her skepticism, especially in all her encounters with the humble priest Father, Baroness Blixen lapses into a banality. In the end the Amazonian Lady Flora contracts syphilis after kissing the foot of the statue of St. Peter just after a peasant had planted the spirochetes on the marble foot of the saint by touching it with his lips. Apart from this effect being incredible, it suggests something I am almost sure the author did not mean, namely, that this evil was visited on Lady Flora as a punishment for her sin of disbelief. This is out of character of the story, of Lady Flora and even of the gentle doctrine preached by Father Jacopo. After the completely convincing beginning and middle part of this story, the end is not only banal and incredible but, perhaps worse, misleading.

"The Blank Page." This is a gem, handled with consummate delicacy. It is a sensitive, imaginative, and most skillfully told miniature story. The unsoiled bridal sheet of purest flax hung in the hall of princesses reveals more eloquently the pathos of the life of the virgin Queen of Portugal than those framed sheets beside it, soiled with blood and seed. (Your question as to whether Carmelite nuns work at weaving flax is being investigated.)

"The Caryatides" is a mysterious tale blended out of reality and witchcraft with no resolution whatever. Yet it captures and holds an eerie mood and its people, like stone caryatides, are solid and chillingly real. Little wonder that Baroness Blixen subtitles this story "An Unfinished Gothic Tale." It is indeed unfinished, left dangling in midair. I wonder whether she had any intention of adding anything to it.

"A Country Tale." By her magical gifts as a storyteller Isak Dinesen can take the most ancient of tales—that of the royal changeling—and make it come alive with freshness and vigor. In this case it doesn't matter much that the loose ends are not neatly tied together, that strands of the story—Ulrikke, her mother, the fate of Lone or the uncertainty of the hero's parenthood—are left dangling. One is left in doubt about which of the two women to believe as the wet nurse and the old retainer contradict each other. But it doesn't matter; the effect, weird, compelling, surcharged with a sense of doom for the living man and the condemned man—all are here because of the spell created by a great storyteller. Dinesen can use archaic language mixed with modern locutions and always get a sense of the past relived and a kind of austere enchantment.

"Converse at Night in Copenhagen" is, for all its virtuosity, a dubious story about the imbecile and debauched young king and the too-fluent poet. Full of fustian (on the part of the poet) there are moments in which the story rises to a mad kind of nobility. Especially is this true of the three answers to the questions on the purposes of life. There is raillery in the story but it is not quite as sharp as the author thinks it is. A cast of characters consisting of a king, a poet, and a prostitute who are the spokesmen for the author (even though the prostitute remains silent) is quite a setup for some fancy moralizing, and the opportunity is not neglected. Nonetheless, this showpiece has a quality in the rough. I wish the author had worked it out more carefully.

So much by the way of comment on the six stories at hand in the manuscript of *Last Tales*...

In *Anecdotes of Destiny*, the first story, "The Diver," is a parable with two disparate elements: the one, the old story of Icarus retold in a new and strange setting; and the other, the tale of the pearl diver who learns wisdom from the fishes of the sea. Irreconcilable as the two parts of this moral lecture in fictional form are and as loosely bound together as they are (the passing identification of Saufe with the pearl fisherman), it is still a story that holds interest because even in her second-rate stories, the Dinesen touch is apparent. Suggestion: change title of story to "Mira Jama." This is the name of the teller of the tale, the artist who seeks its meaning. Besides, "Mira Jama" is euphonious and attention-compelling.

"Babette's Feast" is by far the best of the three tales so far available in this collection. The contract of the two prim and grim maidens with the French émigré servant who is a true artist is vivid. The dinner Babette prepares is her supreme achievement and it is brought about at the cost of everything she possesses. The old maid sisters are drawn as if in cameo and General Loewenhielm is done in full color, but it is Babette herself who stands most clearly etched. There is a statement in the story which points to a moral that is quite unforgettable: "Through all the world there goes one long cry from the heart of the artist: Give me leave to do my utmost."

"The Ring" has for its theme the old standby of fiction: a young woman's awakening from illusion to reality. Here a young bride encounters a sheep thief and she is so moved by his plight that compassion for him prevents her from betraying him. The story is brief and simply told. It is the stuff in old and almost-forgotten romances, yet the Dinesen touch saves it from being commonplace.

In addition to the above outlined stories, we have in our possession the following tales which are not mentioned in Baroness Blixen's table of contents: "The Ghost-Horses," "The Bells," and "Uncle Seneca."

"The Ghost-Horses" is a weird fable about a sick child made well by the powers of the imagination. The life force, this story implies, depends upon the imagination rather than the medicine of reality. The recovery of the child, Nonny, is brought about through the intervention of an artist who awakens her to belief by bringing her back to the magical world of ghostly horses and an Aladdin's treasury of jewels. This is a richly embroidered, imaginative tale, but it is quite inconclusive. Note queries regarding the time lapse on pages 1, 22, and 23. (7,000 words)

"The Bells" is not altogether a successful story. The history of the stolen treasure melted down first into a bell, then into a cannon and back to bells again becomes almost farcical rather than symbolic. There are echoes, very faint, of Bill Faulkner's

Snopes in the rise and decline of Jepperson-Sax-Sass, but not penetrating or funny. This story could well be omitted from consideration, as Dinesen probably intends it to be because she does not include it in her table of contents. We should, however, ask her what she intends to do with the three unlisted stories. (4,000 words)

"Uncle Seneca." It comes as quite a surprise that the mild-mannered Uncle Seneca should turn out to be none other than Jack the Ripper. The final irony is that when he dies he leaves all his money to the impoverished Melpomene, and Albert becomes subordinate to the revelation of Uncle Seneca's gruesome past. Incredible as this story is, it still has a quality of mystery and conflict—and always the Dinesen touch. (7,000 words)

I note that these three unlisted stories are summarized on your yellow sheet, notes made when these manuscripts arrived some six years ago. I also note that there is a summary of one story, "The Fat Man," which is not to be found among the manuscripts at hand. All the others are accounted for. All three of them were originally designated for the volume *Anecdotes of Destiny*, but are not mentioned in the latest table of contents. When you write to Baroness Blixen, please ask what her intentions are about these three tales.

The question of publication arises and the order in which these two books should be issued. The title *Last Tales* suggests that this volume be a kind of swan song and that *Anecdotes of Destiny* become our immediate concern. We could publish the latter in the fall of 1957 if Baroness Blixen would provide us with the missing stories . . .

Bob Haas's letter deals only with what Karen Blixen wanted to include, without spelling out reservations about any of the stories:

13 August 1956

Dear Baroness Blixen:

I have just returned to my office, which has given me my first opportunity to check carefully the material which we have on hand for your two forthcoming books and to try to get the whole situation clarified.

I imagine that you will want us to do *Anecdotes of Destiny* first and *Last Tales* following the first book at a reasonable interval. This sounds like a good plan to me, although, of course, if you have any other feeling in the matter, I would like to know about it.

Now as to the material for *Anecdotes of Destiny*. Your outline sent me recently lists the titles of seven stories.

The Diver
Babette's Feast
Tempests
The Immortal Story
Ehrengard
The Loyal Mistress
The Ring

Of these, we have "The Diver," "Babette's Feast," and "The Ring." The four which we lack, therefore are:

Tempests
The Immortal Story
Ehrengard
The Loyal Mistress

In addition to the stories mentioned above, we received from you three years ago others, listed at that time, as I understand it, for inclusion in *Anecdotes of Destiny*. The titles of those three are:

The Ghost-Horses
The Bells
Uncle Seneca

I also have a record of an additional story entitled "The Fat Man," but this manuscript we do not possess because I returned it to you at your request on 8 October 1951. I wonder what your wishes are about these last three stories (or four, if we are to include "The Fat Man").

Now we come to *Last Tales*. As I understand it, that is to be the title of the book and I am assuming (please correct me if I am wrong) that you have abandoned *Albondocani* as an entity and that the designation "Gothic Tales," as applied to "Caryatides" and "Echoes" is merely descriptive, as is the designation "New Winter's Tales" to "A Country Tale," "Copenhagen Season," and "Converse at Night in Copenhagen."

Of the eleven tales listed in your outline for inclusion in *Last Tales*, we have six in our possession. They are as follows:

The Cardinal's First Tale
The Cardinal's Third Tale
The Blank Page
The Caryatides
A Country Tale
Converse at Night in Copenhagen

Those still missing, therefore, are:

The Cloak
Night-Walk
Of Secret Thoughts and of Heaven
Echoes
Copenhagen Season

I would deeply appreciate some idea from you, if you are in a position to give it to me, as to when we may be likely to receive the missing stories for both books. I would also very much like to know what stories have been published in magazines or are under contract to magazines and which magazines specifically are involved. The reason that I ask for this information is that *The Atlantic Monthly* is interested in the possibility of publishing in its November 1956 Centennial issue some story of yours which has not yet appeared either in a magazine or in book form. In order to deal with them intelligently I must, of course, know what the magazine situation is.

As I wrote you from Vermont, Dorothy Canfield has now had your five new stories read to her—in fact I had the pleasure of reading "The Cardinal's First Tale" and "The Blank Page" to her myself. I know that she is going to write to you, but in the meantime, if you haven't heard from her, I thought you would be interested to know that she thinks you are writing perhaps more wonderfully and powerfully than ever. I thoroughly agree and I leave it to you to imagine how this delights me.

I hope you won't find it a burden to answer the questions in this letter. I look forward to receiving an early reply, but to be truthful, I look forward with even more eager anticipation to receiving the new stories. Whenever one arrives, I know I have a memorable reading experience before me and, I may say, a rare privilege.

Trusting that your health continues to improve and with very best wishes.

On September 25, 1956, the baroness replied.

I am very sorry that I have not till now been able to answer your kind letter of August 13 . . .

As to the order of publication of my two coming books you write me that you think it a good plan to do *Anecdotes of Destiny* first and *Last Tales* following the first book at a reasonable interval. I myself originally meant to have both books published on the same day! If, however, to a publishing firm this would involve difficulties of any kind I shall have to

change my mind here. But I should still want the two books
published within as short an interval as possible. Also, I want the
Last Tales to be published *first*. I hope you will understand my
view: that I do not want after such a long silence to reappear to
my readers with *Anecdotes of Destiny*—the which, although I
do not really consider this book to be of a lower literary quality
than *Last Tales*, to me myself is played on a different kind of
instrument to *Last Tales*, and does carry less weight.

Now as to the material for *Anecdotes of Destiny*, which is to
contain the seven tales enumerated in your letter. You write me
that out of these seven you have got "The Diver," "Babette's
Feast" and "The Ring," and that you are lacking four:
"Tempests," "The Immortal Story," "Ehrengard," and "The
Loyal Mistress." Out of these four, "Tempests" is written in
Danish, and I shall have to rewrite it in English. "The Immortal
Story" you have read, and you are mentioning it in your letter of
30 April 1953. "Ehrengard" is finished and when I have had it
copied out I shall send it to you. "The Loyal Mistress" is not
written yet, but it is a short tale, and I have got it so clear in my
mind that I shall probably be able to finish it in comparatively
short time.

As to the three stories "The Ghost-Horses," "The Bells," and
"Uncle Seneca," and the additional story of "The Fat Man," I did
indeed, as you write, at first mean them to be included in the
Anecdotes of Destiny. But I do not like them very much, so on
second thought I have decided to leave them out. It would
perhaps be the best thing to have the manuscripts returned to me.

Now we come to *Last Tales*. I have not really abandoned
Albondocani as an entity, but do on the contrary hope to get the
novel finished before my death. But if ever completed, it will be a
giant book, and all during last year, when I thought that I had
got but a short time left to me on this earth, I put aside the idea of
it, and decided to have the chapters already written included in
Last Tales. I take it that this will not harm the novel if eventually
published, since *Albondocani* is meant to contain about a
hundred such chapters. You write me that three chapters of
Albondocani—"The Cloak," "Night-Walk," and "Of Secret
Thoughts and of Heaven"—are still missing. But you have in fact
already received these, and have mentioned them to me in a
letter of 23 May 1955. If you have not got them, I shall send them
to you. Of the two tales which are to appear in *Last Tales* as
"New Gothic Tales," you got the "The Caryatides" a long time
ago. As to "Echoes"—the second "Gothic Tale"—I have been

working on it lately and should have had it finished by now, if
the unfortunate tax problem had not turned up. I hope, however,
to be able to forward it to you within a short time. "Copenhagen
Season" is written in parts, and I shall go on with it when I have
finished "Echoes."

Possibly I may include a further tale, "Tales of Two Old
Gentlemen," in the *Albondocani* group. This tale is finished, but
I have just got to make up my mind about it (it may be too
nonsensical!).

You write that you would like to hear from me as to when you
may be likely to receive the missing stories for both books. I
myself am very keen to get these books finished, and although I
am still partly in bed I have been working hard at them, and have
been glad to find that I have got some of my old strength back—
the work, I think, was really going well . . .

As to *The Atlantic Monthly*, I feel honored by its enquiry, and
should be very glad indeed to let it have a story of mine for its
November 1957 Centenary issue. But you will understand that
under the circumstances I do not see my way to meet them . . .

                                                    16 October 1956

Rungstedlund
Rungsted Kyst.

Dear Mr. Haas:

I am today sending you a story, "Tales of Two Old Gentlemen," which is to go into *Last Tales* as one of the chapters
from the novel *Albondocani*. . . .

I shall be sending you one more *Last Tale*, "Echoes," at the end
of this month.

You will find the "Tales of Two Old Gentlemen" a nonsensical
tale; so it is. But it ought to go into *Albondocani* in order to give
some kind of idea of what the whole novel will be like—not
altogether sad and solemn. . . .

In 1957 *Last Tales* was finally published, but Saxe's troubles with
the book were not over. The baroness wrote to Bob Haas:

I have been surprised to receive from Mr. and Mrs. Gould of
the *Ladies' Home Journal*, so long before the publication of the
book and while I myself have as yet had no copies, a copy of *Last
Tales*.

I much regret to say that this copy contains a number of errors
which I should most certainly have corrected if I had had the

opportunity of doing so, and which to my mind are misleading to the readers and sadly injurious to the book.

First of all I do not find in the book the table of contents which I am convinced that you have had from me, and of which I enclose a copy in my letter. Without the headings "From the Novel *Albondocani*," "New Gothic Tales" and "New Winter's Tales," the reader will get no comprehensive view of the main sections of the book, and much of the ideas of the stories will be lost. It seems to me obvious to anybody with a sense of literature that the seven *Albondocani* stories belong together and differ in style and idea from the two "Gothic Tales" and the three "Winter's Tales." With all sections of the book thus running into one another, the structure of the book is most seriously blurred.

I also find the summaries given on the flaps of the dust cover highly unsatisfactory. They contain a direct misprint in one of the titles, "Of *Seven* Thoughts and of Heaven." Also most of the resumes themselves are either positively misleading, or they give away the point of the story.

Why must it be stated beforehand about "The Cardinal's First Tale" that one of the twins dies? The resume of "Night-Walk": "Of the search for redemption and a strange way of finding it" to me looks as if it had been written by somebody who had not read the story. The same applies to that of the "Two Old Gentlemen": "Of the stratagems that sometimes succeed in preventing infidelity, but more often fail." The resume of "The Cardinal's Third Tale": "Of a giantess who had a great contempt for heaven and earth but paid a heavy price for her skepticism," as well as that of "The Blank Page": "Of a snow-white canvas symbolic of virginity" seems both coarse and insipid. "The Caryatides" according to the resume tells of a *secret* marriage, of which there is no question in the tale. The resume of "A Country Tale" states that the children are changelings, and does thus take away the suspense of the central talk between Eitel and Lone and destroys the whole idea of the author, who has wanted and endeavoured to keep the matter undecided. This resume particularly distresses me. In the resume of "Copenhagen Season" I should have wanted the period of the story, 1870, given.

There is in the book a good deal of confusion as to quotation marks. In "The Cardinal's First Tale" these are left out from the main part of the story, which to me seems the right thing. In "The Cardinal's Third Tale" they are repeated at the beginning of each paragraph. In case there had been any inconsistency in the manuscript I feel that I ought to have been consulted.

It is sad to think that I might have had most of these things put

right, if you had sent me page proofs of the book and a sample of
the cover. As matters now stand, I suppose nothing can be done
until the book is reprinted. I must then most firmly insist on
correction of the table of contents. I should also want to write
out myself resumes of the stories for the cover.

You will understand that I have been deeply disappointed by
what seems to me a grave negligence, which cannot but have
serious consequences for the presentation of a book on which I
have worked so hard and for such a long time. I have felt for the
first time that Random House has let me down. I take it that
there must be some particular explanation of the matter, I trust
that you will see to it that anything which might repair the
situation will be done, and I still hope that in spite of the errors
the readers may discover for themselves the idea and meaning of
my book.

There was another letter and a cable. Bob Haas apologized but
explained that it was not carelessness which led to the dropping of
the subheads in the table of contents.

                                                        28 October 1957
Dear Baroness Blixen:
    Your cable and letters have just arrived and I cannot
exaggerate to you the extent to which they had distressed me
because it really is too late for us to make any corrections in the
current edition. The publication date is November 4 and all the
books—nearly ten thousand of them—are already in the stores.
    I am particularly sorry that what you refer to as "errors" cause
you so much pain since I cannot believe that your evaluation of
their importance bears any relation to the publishing picture
surrounding the book here.
    I must tell you that the book was edited by the same editor
who has always concerned himself with your work and no one
could respect it more deeply than he. He has handled it
throughout the years with loving care and if, as seems to be the
unfortunate case now, he has made mistakes, I am positive that
no one could regret it more deeply.
    My own view is, for what it may be worth, that had the table
of contents been printed with the subheads as given, it would
have been somewhat confusing. I think our view here must have
been that the subheads were only included for our own guidance.
Don't you think yourself that to have used subheads "from the
novel *Albondocani*" might have puzzled people almost beyond

endurance since that novel is still nonexistent? Needless to say, I'm not trying to argue the point with you. I am simply trying to tell you the way it struck us and to reassure you that we acted as you yourself say we always have in the past—with the best will in the world and all good faith.

As to misprints, I can only apologize for them. They do keep happening but, obviously, that is no excuse.

I can only hope that you will not worry too much about these matters. They are not going to be noticed as much as you may think, if that is any comfort! And please do write summaries of the stories, won't you, and send them to me? Believe me, we'll be delighted to use them as well as to make all corrections in the next edition.

Nonetheless, the subheads were added in the next printing. And the jacket copy was changed—once Haas had corrected the baroness's errors.

William Faulkner and the Nobel Prize

When *Psychology: A Simplification*, which Saxe had written in collaboration with Lloyd Coleman, was published in 1927, the publisher sent a package of books to Saxe's home. Saxe was living with his parents at the time, and when the package arrived, they decided to make a ceremony of the occasion and waited impatiently for Saxe to return in the evening. When he arrived, Saxe, watched by his proud parents, unwrapped the books, which turned out to be six copies of a novel called *Mosquitoes*, by an author Saxe had not known until that moment. It was to be Saxe's introduction to the work of William Faulkner.

By the time Faulkner and Saxe met, in the mid-1930s, Faulkner had already produced, among other writings, *The Sound and the Fury, As I Lay Dying, Sanctuary*, and *Light in August*. Then in 1936 Faulkner brought his manuscript of *Absalom, Absalom!* to Random House, and from then until 1958, when Saxe died, Faulkner and Saxe worked closely together on the following books: *Absalom, Absalom!* (1936); *The Unvanquished* (1938); *The Wild Palms* (1939); *The Hamlet* (1940); *Go Down, Moses, and Other Stories* (1942); *A Rose for Emily, and Other Stories*, with a Foreword by Saxe (1945); *Intruder in the Dust* (1948); *Knight's Gambit* (1949); *Collected Stories of William Faulkner* (1950);

Requiem for a Nun (1951); *The Faulkner Reader* (1954); *A Fable* (1954); *Big Woods* (1955); *The Town* (1957). Before he died, Saxe was working with Faulkner on *The Mansion.*

The *Collected Stories,* the third such collection of Faulkner's tales to be published, had been Saxe's and Donald Klopfer's idea. Bill had resisted it at first, but later he wrote to Saxe: "You and Don were both right about the collection and I was wrong; I mean, about the time and place for it. I was worse than wrong: stupid. I didn't seem to understand what 'collection' meant. It's all right; the stuff stands up amazingly well after a few years, ten and twenty. I had forgotten a lot of it; I spent a whole evening laughing to myself about the mules and the shingles."

The collection came off the press in August 1950. Bill was in Oxford, Mississippi, attending to matters on his farm. Then one evening in late autumn Saxe pushed open the door of our apartment in New York and said, "What a day this has been! I've been besieged by reporters. The rumor is out that Bill Faulkner will get the Nobel Prize." At twenty past ten, the phone rang. It was a long distance call from Oxford, Mississippi.

This is a reconstruction of Saxe's end of the conversation: "Yes, Estelle, it's really wonderful! You got the news from the Swedish Embassy in Washington? What's the problem? Bill has no dress suit? Why, that's no problem at all. If he can't get one in Oxford, surely he will find one in Memphis on his way to New York. Did I hear you correctly? Doesn't want to buy a suit, wants to rent one!" There was a pause—then Bill came to the phone to tell Saxe he would call him at his office in the morning.

Don Klopfer recounted to me what happened the next day: "I was in Saxe's office when Bill called and asked Saxe to rent a full dress suit and a silk hat for him for the Nobel Prize presentation ceremony. At Saxe's request Bill proceeded to give his measurements—sleeve, shoulder to cuff, waist, trouser inside length, outside length, hat size and neck size."

Saxe went to Brooks Brothers, where he was told that they did not rent suits; but Brooks Brothers recommended a firm that provided tuxedos, cutaways, dress suits, silk hats, and all the necessary accessories. Off Saxe went to a shop called Fifth Avenue Formal Wear. There he met an affable little man. After Saxe explained his errand and gave him the measurements, the man said, "I got just the right suit for your friend. It's a blue black suit." "No,

no, no," remonstrated Saxe, "I want a black suit." "You no
understand," said the man, "there is a grey black and a brown
black, but a blue black is the best." A quick look assured Saxe that
the suit was all right.

He then gave the man Bill's hat size and the size for the white
shirt. All this was to be delivered to Random House as soon as Saxe
phoned him. Saxe also asked that someone come along with the
suit who could make such adjustments as might be necessary when
the suit and hat were tried on.

Just as Saxe was about to leave the shop, the man said, "You tell
your friend, he be happy in this suit 'cause Cardinal Spellman, his
nephew, he wear this suit last month when he go to Roma to meet
the Pope."

Saxe, like everyone else in Random House, was impatient for
Bill's arrival. Just as impatient were a few of Bill's drinking
companions. This time Saxe had to take a stand. "Why, Commins,"
they said, "this is a time for rejoicing!" "Yes, yes," said Saxe, "I
know all about that, but you've got to hold off this time, for Bill
must be at his best."

The first task that awaited Bill was the writing of the Nobel Prize
acceptance speech, which turned out to be a brief but eloquent plea
for the values "of love and honor and pity and pride and
compassion and sacrifice." Later, Bill gave Saxe the first copy off
the press.

The time for Bill's departure to Stockholm was drawing close.
The dress suit had been tried on, and this is what Donald Klopfer
told me about its subsequent history: "The clothes fit Bill reason-
ably well. However, when Bill returned from his momentous
journey, he told Saxe and me that he had noticed that the king had
two satin stripes on his trousers, while he (Bill) had only one. At
Saxe's suggestion Bennett and I presented Bill with the clothes he
had worn at the presentation ceremony, but not before Saxe had
had the extra satin stripe added to Bill's trousers."

On arriving in Stockholm, Bill and his daughter Jill were driven
to the Grand Hotel. There, the new laureates and quite a number of
former laureates stayed for the duration of the festivities. For the
two days following the presentation of the prizes, parties and
dinners were given to honor the new laureates. Then Bill and Jill
went off to Paris for a short visit before returning home to Oxford
in time for Christmas.

The following year, 1951, Bill received yet another award, an appointment to the *Légion d'honneur*. The ceremony of installation was performed by the French consul in New Orleans on October 26. Bill was in Saxe's office when news of the appointment came. Borrowing a note pad from Saxe, he sat down and wrote out a brief acceptance speech, in French. Later he inscribed "For Saxe Commins" at the top of the manuscript and gave it to Saxe to keep.

Long before Bill became a Nobel Laureate, he had talked to Saxe about trying his hand as a playwright. Certainly this would be a

Manuscript of William Faulkner's *Légion d'honneur* acceptance speech, inscribed to Saxe in the upper left corner new experiment for him. When they talked about a theme, Bill told Saxe that he would like to weave it around Temple Drake, the central character in *Sanctuary*. In the closing lines of that book, Bill had left her sitting with her father, Judge Drake, in the Luxembourg Gardens in Paris, that "gray day, a gray summer, a gray year." "Eight years have elapsed since," said Bill, "and I have been wondering what life might have done to her during those years." What Bill finally wrote—*Requiem for a Nun*—is partly a drama and partly a novel. It contains three acts, each of which is preceded by a long explanatory narrative. Temple was now Mrs. Gowan Stevens and the mother of two little children. From this starting point Bill unfolds a tale as harrowing and abhorrent as anything in *Sanctuary*, yet here one senses a feeling of commiseration as Temple engages in a fierce struggle for expiation and redemption.

While writing the narrative prologue to act 2, Bill sent the following note to Saxe asking about a possible subtitle.

What I wanted here was to paraphrase Eliot:

"In the beginning was the Word
Superfetation of τὸ ἕν ."

I don't know Greek.
Can we use

(Beginning Was τὸ ἕν)?

If not

(Beginning Was The Word)

Saxe provided the definition of the Greek ("the one"), but Faulkner decided against using the quotation from "Mr. Eliot's Sunday Morning Service." When *Requiem for a Nun* was published (1951), the prologue to act 2 appeared simply as "The Golden Dome (Beginning Was the Word)."

The book received mixed reviews. Faulkner had originally conceived it as a play, and after considerable negotiation, plans were made for performances in Switzerland, Germany, Spain, Sweden, Holland, France, Greece, and a number of other countries. In London, with Ruth Ford as Mrs. Gowan Stevens, the performance met with signal success. The play reached the United States in 1959, and again Ruth Ford won high praise in the title role.

Note to Saxe from William Faulkner proposing a subtitle for the narrative prologue to the second act of *Requiem for a Nun*

The play itself did not fare as well.

When Faulkner came to New York, he would stay at the Hotel Madison, which was near Random House. Bill would always wait for Saxe at the front entrance of Random House, knowing that Saxe was due to arrive from Princeton just before nine in the morning. They would then go to Saxe's office, where Bill had a desk and a typewriter of his own. Here Bill was interviewed; here Bill typed at some work in progress; here Bill would sit with his pipe in silence, perhaps thinking of a new work.

On one of these trips to New York, in 1951 or 1952, Bill brought with him the first hundred pages of *A Fable*—"the big book," as he called it—on which he had been working off and on for at least nine years. So that there would be none of the interruptions normal to an editor's office, Saxe brought Bill home, and here they worked, with stops for lunch or a walk into town or the countryside with our dog accompanying them. Then back to work again, with a break at tea time, more work, then a leisurely dinner at seven. And so the first hundred pages of *A Fable* were carefully gone over. Then the men returned to New York. At times Bill would disappear, to continue work in Oxford. But finally, on November 5, 1953, Saxe could write to Donald Klopfer from Princeton:

Dear Don,

   With this letter Bill is bringing the final, complete, ready-for-the printer manuscript of *A Fable*. Both of us feel, in the excitement and lift of working so steadily and to such wonderful purpose, that the script is as near perfection as we can make it. With what cuts we have been able to make (and there isn't a word we can think of to take out any more), the entire book runs to approximately one hundred seventy five thousand words, give a few thousand either way.

   I don't have to tell you how I feel about it as a work of art; what is important here is to set down a few suggestions for your guidance in handling the manuscript from now until we have the final book, or galleys at least.

   You will notice that all front matter is in place and ready for composition. On the copyright page, we have only to supply the Library of Congress Card Catalog Number. The 1950 date of copyright is to cover the copyright issued in Bill's name when *Notes on a Horse Thief* appeared as a Limited Edition under the imprint of the Levee Press in Greenville, Mississippi. The story itself is rewritten for the purposes of *A Fable*.

   On the acknowledgment page (which is vi in our front matter) you will see the precise manner in which Bill wishes to make the essential acknowledgments. We gave it a left-hand page, backing the dedication (also supplied) to save pages in front matter and not make it too conspicuous.

   You will see a note on the bastard title offering suggestions to the printer about the nature of the crosses used throughout the book—on jacket, binding, title page, half-title pages and even where two-line space breaks occur in the text. This is terribly important. We must avoid the use of denominational crosses and want simple, the simpler the better, wooden crosses throughout. Where the crosses appear at the opening of each of the ten parts, they must be quite large and so placed as to give the opening chapter page a great deal of sinkage. Where we indicate three little crosses to mark a lapse of time or change of scene we want the crosses to be no larger than the upper case of the regular type measure used for text, no larger than an ordinary asterisk.

   We would like to have a simple cross on a binding of blue for

the front of the book. The backbone will merely bear the title,
Bill's name, the Random House imprint, *but no crosses*.

Bill would like to offer the suggestion that the jacket be of a
dark blue at the bottom and gradually getting lighter and lighter
till at the top it is almost the color of a clear sky and imposed on
the top half again the simple cross, perhaps in white, and in
the dark blue section beneath

A Fable
William Faulkner

These are merely suggestions, and perhaps premature, but they
embody what we sat up all last night talking about after ten
steady hours of work at the script.

Our layout therefore will be as follows:

i	Bastard
ii	Ad-Facer (List of Bill's books)
iii	Title
iv	Copyright
v	Dedication (supplied)
vi	Acknowledgment
1	H.T.
2	Blank
3-?	Text

My guess is that we will come within fourteen forms of 32's or
448 pages or 480 at most.

You will notice that no provision is made for a note on the
author. This is at Bill's special request. It will therefore be
omitted.

At the end of the book there appears a three line date and place
notice, which we would like to have set in a small face, flush left,
somewhat like this:

December, 1944
Oxford-New York-Princeton
November, 1953

Whenever you decide to set, I will be responsible for all proofs,
if Bill won't be available to read them. If he is, we will do
them together.

You will notice that all the chapter heads except one—the last,
"Tomorrow"—bear date lines. We would want them set quite
inconspicuously, certainly not in caption style, as the days
themselves must be. The purpose of the date lines, obviously, is
to help keep the reader oriented in time.

In January 1954 Saxe began the reading of the galleys of *A Fable*, pausing from time to time to record his thoughts. One of the first notations was: "The work we did shows in the galleys. Bill wraps a scene around him and lets it unravel, once he gets a strong hold. It is interesting to see how much he allows it to rise out of the unconscious and get itself written down, without censorship, but with a general plan improved upon as the details are improvised."

Saxe spent days on the galleys, going over them again and again at home and in the office. The following are more of his notations, made at different times:

> On second and third and fourth reading, one gains a deeper impression of order rather than involution for its own sake or because it is so much what Bill himself is—involuted. Who isn't? Still a little bewildered by some of the rhetorical extravagances and the involuted progressions and regressions in the unfolding of a tale that is overwhelming and so simple, full of questionable coincidences and yet with a narrative substructure that holds the whole edifice from collapse.

> The dialogues are long, whether it is Magda, the runner, the German General, the quartermaster or anyone, except the Marshal. He is laconic always, coincidence is stretched, but it cannot be changed without pulling the whole novel from under itself. The great misgivings about the devised meeting between the Father (the old general) and Son (the corporal) with the deal offered and rejected. Only Faulkner would allow himself such a coincidence and make it almost probable by sheer force of rhetorical narrative.

> I acquire a nervous psychological block which makes it almost impossible to open its covers and see what we have wrought. There will be much to answer for—and I, not Bill, will be called on to answer questions.

On January 17, after working all day, Saxe finished going over the galleys, the equivalent of 450 pages. In one of his final comments, he said, "The best part—especially the resurrection—is deeply moving and reverent, if still macabre and funny as a drunken extravaganza. Strange humor our Little Lord Fauntleroy [Saxe's pet name for Faulkner] has, with a touch of necrophilia."

After dinner that night Saxe wrote Bill a long letter summing up his latest thoughts about *A Fable*, and two days later in a report to Random House he gave his estimate of the novel, a task that took him longer than expected. "To describe it properly," he wrote in part, "it would be necessary to describe the manuscript completely, if that ever could be done in so brief or even so long a sketch as the book itself." Unfortunately, the letter and the report have been lost.

The winter of 1953–54 had been a severe one, with much snow, sleet, and ice. The doctor had advised Saxe not to go to New York on bad days, and Don and Bennett had urged him not to come to the office more than once or twice a week. But Saxe could not resign himself to such restrictions, even though he could do much more work at home where he was not disturbed. The mere thought of curtailing his activities threw him into a state of deep despair. He missed the direct contact with the people at Random House, the impromptu lunches and discussions with authors and with his colleagues in the publishing world.

Professor Einstein, who was our neighbor in Princeton, sensed keenly what Saxe was enduring. He encouraged Saxe to drop by for a chat occasionally. When Saxe did visit, he was warmly received not only by the professor but by his daughter Margot and that devoted member of the family, Helen Dukas. Once, after a particularly stimulating discussion with Einstein, Saxe summarized the conversation in a notebook when he returned home: "We covered a good deal of ground, from moral absolutes to the limitations in science. Particularly interesting was the development of the thesis that it is necessary to put limitations on freedom, contrary to what all the eighteenth-century libertarians thought. When it becomes a question between security and freedom, pro-creation and freedom, we accept limitations. If we don't, our culture imposes them. When we ask what is freedom for, we get into the problem of values and metaphysics."

The talk between Einstein and Saxe was later brought to my memory by a certain passage in a letter from Faulkner to Saxe in September 1954: "Freedom, American style—the sort of misused freedom and liberty which produced the McCarthys and from which people like Oppenheimer [Dr. J. Robert Oppenheimer] suffer." Bill later amplified on this in an article, "Freedom, American Style."

The final proofs of *A Fable* arrived in late January, and once again the responsibility for checking them was Saxe's. On the page proofs, Saxe recorded his thoughts:

> I can risk the prediction that there will be elements in the tale, apart from its religious departures, which will come in for harsh criticism. The long arm of coincidence which embraces Father (Field Marshal) and Son (Christ), Martha's long speech to Bidet and also the quartermaster's, the ambiguity of Levine's role and death, the runner's final protest at the Tomb of the Unknown Soldier, the reliance on the story of the three-legged horse.

The next night Saxe wrote in his diary: "Finished page proofing of *A Fable* and wrote in all the running heads. They and all else have been my responsibility since the manuscript was completed in our home November 1953."

In 1954 our son Eugene was studying physics at the Graduate College of Columbia University. Now and then he would come home for the weekend. At one of those times Bill Faulkner was staying with us. Not wishing to intrude on Bill and Saxe's sessions, Eugene retreated to the kitchen, where he spread his papers on the kitchen table and proceeded to work on some problems in physics. Before returning to New York, he gathered up most of his papers but left a few work sheets on the table.

A few days later Saxe received a short note from Bill concerning the distribution of complimentary copies of *A Fable*. We were greatly amused to see that the note had been typed on the back of one of Eugene's work sheets!

A frugal man, our Little Lord Fauntleroy!

Since the stir created in 1931 by the publication of *Sanctuary*, Bill was much sought after by the movie people in Hollywood, and he developed what might be called a symbiotic relationship with Howard Hawks, the producer and director. "When I am hard up," Bill told Saxe, "I write to Hawks. When he needs writing, he writes to me." As might be expected, the novelist, though he wrote scripts for a number of movies, scarcely took film assignments seriously, and frankly admitted it.

Soon after Bill had turned in the final manuscript for *A Fable* to Random House, toward the end of 1953, he had a telephone call from Hawks urging him to fly to Paris. This was followed by a

Dear Saxe: What I wanted to know was, who in the east I might
have neglected to send a book to, so I can rectify when I come
up in May. Did I send Joan Williams (Mrs Bowen now) one: also
to sign books for any at Random House who should have one. But
mainly people outside Random House. If any sort of record of
the mailings was kept, I can attend to it.

       Please ask Harold to send the checks to me here. In
fact, I was glad to hear this part. I had a sort of recollection
that you gave me an envelope from him with a check in it while
I was there, but have not been able to find it. You didn't give
me such an envelope then, right?

                    Bill

Letter to Saxe from William Faulkner, sometime in 1954, typed frugally on the back of Eugene Commins's physics work sheet letter from Hawks, full of enthusiasm about Egypt and its history, for Hawks was planning to do a film about that country.

Saxe arranged for Bill's flight on December 5. Three days before he was to leave, Bill, who was in Oxford, called: "Saxe, I don't want to go to Paris, I don't want to go to Egypt. I'm not well; my back bothers me." I could hear Saxe say, "Bill, let's talk it over. Get on the first plane out of Memphis in the morning. I believe it gets in at the Newark airport at 3:30 or thereabouts. I'll be waiting for you there."

Bill was on that plane, but he was in a sorry state. There were deep rings under his eyes, and he looked harassed. The first thing to do was to quiet him. I phoned our doctor. He was out of town. I then called our good friend, Dr. Moolten, who lives in New Brunswick. He ordered a mild sedative. Bill took very little food, except some tea and toast.

The next day Bill was in a much better mood. The weather was beautiful, the air fresh and bracing. Even in December that year, trees were holding fast to their fall foliage; and when the men went walking in the woods, they went among shades of wine reds, russet browns, and golden yellows. On their return, I could see that Bill's tension had eased. At dinnertime there was no need to coax him to eat.

Late Sunday afternoon, Saxe drove Bill to the airport and stayed to make sure that he got on the plane. But for once the Hawks magic failed to work. Bill wrote from Cairo, "I don't think very highly of Egypt."

Faulkner's frequent visits with us were not only occasions for work with Saxe but also opportunities for Bill to unburden himself of the anguish and heartache that seemed to weigh him down. Certainly, such confidences as he revealed to Saxe during those visits could only be hinted at in his letters.

Tuesday

Dear Saxe:

No, I don't feel too well. My back gives me a little trouble, but not much; mainly, for the first time in my life, I am completely bored, fed up, my days are being wasted. It is just possible that I shall do something quite drastic about the matter before long. I have done no work in a year, do not want to, yet I have work

4 Jan 54

SUVRETTA HOUSE
St MORITZ

Dear Dorothy and Saxe.

The job here is going all right, but I was right about not wanting it. I am already sick to the teeth of rich American expatriates here in Europe too, who have moved intact their entire Hollywood lives to Europe. Got away from it Xmas, Stockholm and London & Paris, just got back tonight.

Have had no word from home yet, so I suppose everything is all right. Have made no arrangement about this money yet, so will you please transfer $2500 to my account, First National Bank. Oxford, Miss. Dont notify any one at Oxford: just make the transfer

I am well, not happy. Will keep you informed of new address. Love to all.

Bill

Letter to Saxe and Dorothy Commins from William Faulkner, January 4, 1954, from Europe

which I must do. We talked some of my giving myself six months
of absence, getting completely away from here and all my
familiar life. I think now it will take more than that. I think now I
may, to save my soul, something of peace, contentment, save the
work at least, quit the whole thing, give it all to them, leave and
be done with it. I can earn enough to live on, I think. I am really
sick, I think. Can't sleep too well, nervous, idle, have to make an
effort not to let the farm go to pot, look forward only with
boredom to the next sunrise. I don't like it. Maybe I will have to
get away, for at least a year, almost vanish. Then maybe I will
get to work again, and get well again. But I don't have enough
time left to spend it like this. That is, I still want what I have
always wanted: to be free; probably until now I have still
believed that somehow, in some way, someday I would be free
again; now at last I have begun to realize that perhaps I will not,
I have waited, hoped too long, done nothing about it; and so
now I must, or—in spirit—die.

I haven't quite reached the point yet, but I don't think I shall be
much longer. There will be scorn and opprobrium of course, but
perhaps I have already sacrificed too much already to try to be a
good artist, to boggle at a little more in order to still try to be
one.

Yours,
Bill

Or, in a letter headed, simply, "Saturday," and written, I
believe, in October 1953:

I will be frank: I would like to stay in Princeton with Dorothy
and you, not only because it will be good to work in the quiet,
and you and I can unravel the manuscript, but because of
money. I am worrying a little about money again; with the
drought we had this year, my crop was a failure and I shall have
to buy feed, etc.

I am trying to work on the manuscript here. My judgement is
still good; what I have done is all right, but very slow, difficult. I
must have peace again; I have almost got to teach myself again to
believe in it. I seem to have reached a point I never believed I
ever would: where I need to have someone read it and tell me,
Yes, it's all right. You must go ahead with it.

In March 1954 Northrop Frye, the literary critic, gave a series of
lectures at Princeton University, later published as *The Anatomy of*

Criticism. Saxe attended one of the lectures, in which the central question under discussion was, Does criticism in itself transcend what is being criticized? Should it be relegated to a subsidiary place and ultimately ignored, or should it be accepted as a necessary evil? Professor Frye offered this hypothesis: Literature is the human science, as mathematics is the speculative, and is to be appraised in critical terms.

Saxe, who came away skeptical, said,

> In all the years I have worked with creative men, there never was even a hint of what some critics insist is the creative process; it is something of which these writers were for the most part unaware. They—Theodore Dreiser, Sherwood Anderson, Wystan Auden, Eugene O'Neill, Sinclair Lewis, Walter van Tilburg Clark, William Faulkner, and all—wrote out of an indefinable necessity and a pride and a vanity and an understanding that surpasses all the evidence of such an understanding. One almost attributes the accidentalism of the creative process to the miraculous and stops searching for a key to the puzzle.

By late April 1954, Faulkner was back in town. Saxe found him one morning waiting at the Random House entrance, and as usual they went straight to Saxe's office. Bill did not seem at all well. He complained again of pains in his back and stomach. That evening Saxe brought him home.

Meanwhile, Saxe had been approached by a member of the Princeton faculty with word that the university wished to bestow on Faulkner an honorary degree at the forthcoming commencement ceremony. Bill's reply, as soon as Saxe told him about it, was an emphatic no. He felt he was not a university man and that such an honor should be limited to those who have achieved status in the academic world.

This was not the first time Bill had taken such a stand; he had earlier rebuffed universities in both Europe and this country that had offered him honorary degrees.

After a few days with us, Bill felt well enough to leave for Oxford in his Plymouth. He had left his car in Princeton for repairs before he had taken off for Europe and Egypt. A daring driver, he must have made the trip at a hazardous speed, for he wrote us that he reached home, some 1,188 miles from Princeton, within thirty-six hours. In the same letter he told us that his daughter Jill would marry Paul Delwyn Summers, Jr., of Washington, D.C., on

August 21 in Oxford and urged us to attend the wedding festivities. We of course accepted with pleasure.

Then came another letter, telling Saxe that the State Department had asked Bill to participate in the International Winter Congress to be held in São Paulo as part of the quadricentennial celebration of that city. Apparently Washington, having been under attack for its Latin American policy, hoped that Faulkner's presence would not only add enormous prestige but would be accepted as an expression of good will from this country. In assenting to Washington's request, Bill said that he would not accept a fee and that he would prefer going in the early part of August so that he could return to Oxford in time for his daughter's wedding.

The State Department did, however, arrange for his transportation there and back, while the Brazilian government expressed their intention to meet expenses. Once again Saxe was commissioned to make sure Fauntleroy would not embarrass his publisher or his country. Bill wrote:

> I will need my dinner jacket, the coat and pants hanging in Gene's [our son's] closet. I think the shoes were among the clothes I had stolen in Egypt. But in case, they are patent leather slippers, not new. If they are not in the closet too, can someone from R. House have a pair sent to me? I want English shoes, Church is the maker, evening shoes. There is a shop on the west side of Madison, somewhere between Fiftieth St. and Tripler's, I have seen Church shoes in the window, Tripler may have them, in fact, I think they have. If you could bundle the suit up and take it in with you, it and the shoes could be crammed into a packing box and sent to me, don't worry about creases as I will have it pressed here. I hate to have to worry you, but I didn't know about Brazil when I left the suit there.
>
> The shoes will be 6 1/2, B width or C, that is, not too narrow. That is, my foot is short, I can wear No. 6, D.

Bill was also occupying himself with writing at this time, though the heat was debilitating—and he was getting Jill's mount ready to enter a horse show at the end of July. Soon there was another letter, with an amusing reference to a very grand party held in Washington to announce Jill's forthcoming marriage to young Summers. "I'll write again later," Bill said, "I'll tell about Washington party later, damnedest collection of prosperous concerned stuffed-shirt Republican senators and military brass hats and the be-upholstered, be-coiffed beldames as you ever saw. Fortunately hardly any of them ever heard of me so I was let alone."

When he returned to Oxford, he found the first copies of *A Fable*. "They are very fine," he wrote to Saxe, "I am as proud as you are, if we are right and it is my best and not the bust which I considered it might be, I will ask nothing more."

Now the advance reviews began to pour in. I think that Saxe was much more concerned about the reviews than was Bill, who didn't even want to read them. He said to Saxe what he had said before, that once a manuscript of his leaves his hands, it is on its own and must face a kindly or a hostile world. Perry Miller of Harvard wrote as one who understood Saxe's anxiety:

Dearest Saxe and Dorothy:

If my sampling [of the reviews] is any indication, then you have simply got to comprehend your own meaning when you say that Faulkner exegesists have an unbroken record of comdemning at birth books they all regard as classics three years later. As for *A Fable*, it is clear they are simply bewildered. That performance of Geismar's in the SRL, for instance! He is just utterly non-plussed and could say nothing but the now orthodox doctrine of the previous books. All he or his tribe have to go on is the orthodox doctrine, and this book seems to shift the party line on them.

Most of these so-called reviewers are so much less than gnats that Saxe must see the utter irrationality of letting them bother him. I know it is your deep devotion to the craft—you would never admit it except obliquely, and when I try to tell you about it, you will only make obscene noises—that causes you to grieve at this spectacle of stupidity. But above all things, you must not—repeat NOT—let any implication, spoken or implied, that Faulkner's editor is at fault, you must NOT give it house room. You are too old a hand at this business not to know that the editor fulfills the writer's intention, and that is precisely what you did here. You could not so have tailored or altered the book in advance as to win the praises of Geismar et co., and still have had Faulkner's book. So, please stop beating yourself! Or your wife!!!

I don't suppose moral exhortation ever does much good, and certainly not when applied to such a moral reprobate as you are. I think you have got to understand something much more important, that this is a great book. It is just too damned big and complex to be understood for a long time; that great passage somewhere in Proust about how a major book has to create its audience certainly applies to this more than to any of F's books. That is simply going to take time.

I trust you were somewhat heartened by Carvel's [Collins] review. He tells me that Harvey Breit . . . cut it considerably, in violation of Brown's[1] agreement with Collins, but it seemed to me to come out fairly well.

As the time approached for our visit to Oxford, we had a number of cordial letters from various members of the Faulkner family. Saxe had been there once before, in October 1952, in response to a desperate plea from Mrs. Faulkner. Bill was then going through what might be euphemistically called a most trying period. Now Saxe and I were heading for Oxford under happier circumstances.

When our plane landed at Memphis on August 20, we were greeted by Mr. and Mrs. William Fielden, Estelle's daughter (from a previous marriage) and son-in-law, a very handsome couple. As we stepped into their air-conditioned car, we began to feel resuscitated, for the heat was blistering, the temperature hovering around 104°.

We were still unpacking at the Alumni House on the campus of Ole Miss when Bill came over to welcome us. "Right after the wedding," he said, "you are to move into my house. At the moment," he added, "it's crammed full with bridesmaids and groomsmen."

A number of guests had already arrived. Some were staying at a hotel and others were at the homes of friends of the Faulkners. The festivities began with a cocktail party at the home of Professor and Mrs. George Carbone. Already present as we joined the gathering were Estelle and Bill, her son Malcolm and his wife Gloria, Mr. and Mrs. Fielden and their daughter Victoria, and Mrs. Maud Faulkner, Bill's mother, locally addressed as "Miss Maud." We found her an engaging lady, perhaps a little over five feet tall, with dark hair showing a sprinkle of white. Bill had inherited the cut of her face, the shape of her forehead, mouth, and chin. When I told her, as one can't help doing, that I'd heard so much about her, the reply came quickly, "You wouldn't have, if it weren't for my Bill."

The room began to fill with in-laws-to-be, aunts, uncles, cousins, and assorted relatives. Soon we were most warmly taken into the

1. Editor of the *New York Times Book Section.*

family circle. A couple approached us and politely asked where we came from and added, "Are you kinfolk?" "No," we replied, "just good friends." With a drawl as broad as the Mississippi Delta, the man explained his relationship. "My grandnephew married Mrs. Faulkner's second cousin." For the rest of the day my mind kept puzzling over that relationship, trying to place it in the Faulkner genealogy.

That evening we all gathered at the Alumni House, where a magnificent dinner was served. There were many toasts, Bill's ending with, "Even strangers are made members of the family—and what an achievement to have made them cross the Potomac!"

Here again, as so often in Faulkner, we feel the characteristically Southern strength of kinship.

Bill next brought us to his home, Rowan Oak. The approach is up a cedar-lined drive. Built in 1844, the house is a typical Southern mansion of that period—a white two-storied structure with columns extending from the lower portico or porch to the roof, and a balcony set behind the line of columns.

After walking through a spacious hall, we came to what Bill liked to call his office, a large room with shelves of books and a work table on which were piles of papers. There we saw, written on one of the walls, what has now become an item of great interest in Faulkner's memorabilia—a day-by-day outline of the week's happenings in *A Fable*. As we stood before it, Saxe suggested that something should be done to protect and preserve it against the ravages of time. Couldn't someone in the art department of Ole Miss help with this problem? I am now glad to say that someone did.

After further prenuptial festivities the wedding itself took place at four o'clock that afternoon in St. Peter's Episcopal Church. It was a full-dress Southern wedding—lovely bridesmaids, a glorious bride, and even the bride's father in white tie and tails.

Saxe and I were now guests at Rowan Oak. During the morning, a succession of guests who had been housed elsewhere came to thank Estelle and Bill before leave-taking. Then Bill and Saxe stole off to Bill's "office" for a long talk while I occupied myself with reading. After an early lunch, Bill, Saxe, and I, with Estelle's son Malcolm at the wheel, went for a long drive past Oxford, as far as the Tallahatchie River. The country seemed burned beyond recovery by the drought. Everywhere the seared corn stood, a withered yellow. The beds of some streams were caked with red clay. It was as though the land lay panting and dying under the hot weight of the drought. Soon, however, as we drove about, the spell of Bill's imagination transported us to a more vigorous world of his own creation. For now we were in Yoknapatawpha County, a region he had peopled with the Sutpens, the Sartorises, the McCaslins, the Compsons, the Bundrens, the Snopeses and others, whose lives in one way or another are interwoven. Bill made an evocative guide in his own country. As we stopped at various spots, he pointed out where the different families of his mythical breed lived. When he pointed to the home area of the Compsons, I could hear the voice of that magnificent character Dilsey in a particularly poignant passage from *The Sound and the Fury*: "Dilsey made no sound, her face did not quiver, as the tears took their sunken and devious courses, walking with her head up, making no effort to dry them away even. 'I've seed de first en de last,' Dilsey said, 'I seed de beginnin' en now I sees de endin'.' "

Very few words were exchanged as we drove back to Oxford; I still lingered in a dream world and would have liked to remain there a little longer, as I thought, one at a time, of the unforgettable characters and scenes created by the magic of Bill's pen. On arriving at Rowan Oak, about an hour before dinner, I was asked to play. I played whatever came to my fingers, Chopin, Brahms, Debussy, till Bill, in a whisper, asked me to play the theme of Tchaikovsky's *Romeo and Juliet* music. I had to think quickly, since this tone poem is orchestrally scored. I improvised as best I could.

Before dinner Bill fixed himself a drink of whiskey and ice. Generally he took a drink or two before dinner, perhaps some wine during its course, and a drink or two before bedtime. Bill had once told Saxe that whiskey had been very effective in easing the acute pain he had suffered after a plane crack-up while he was in the Royal Air Force. He said he had enlisted in 1918 and had earned his wings and a commission as second lieutenant just as the war ended. Bill's squadron was lined up and told they could celebrate before leave-taking. What better way, thought Bill and his buddies, than to take one last flight? With permission granted, Bill took off. In his exuberance, he said, he misjudged and tore the roof off the hangar.

Bill could withstand the desire for drink for long periods; but when he was faced with emotional problems that he could not unravel, alcohol became an insistent urge and a means of escape. At dinner we watched him take one drink after another. Conversation at the table was distracted and desultory. Before long Saxe had to help Bill to bed. Standing by was Bill's faithful Wallace, who knew what to do.

But by morning Bill was comatose. Saxe had been with him for a number of hours, and late in the morning Malcolm came to take Saxe to the library to see the Mississippi Collection. There Saxe saw, in addition to many books by Mississippi writers, nearly a dozen cartoons by Bill, some of which show a strong influence of Aubrey Beardsley.

I stayed with Estelle, trying to divert her attention from her anxiety. Poor Estelle, poor Bill, poor everybody, all at the mercy of impulses and circumstances beyond their control.

12 William Faulkner as Cultural Ambassador

In late August of 1954, after we had returned from Jill Faulkner's wedding, hurricane Carol swept up the coast and vented her fury. Hardly had she left when New England was alerted that Dolly would soon follow. But Dolly never turned up; she veered toward Nova Scotia. A little more than two weeks later the Weather Bureau issued repeated warnings that hurricane Edna was heading toward the New Jersey region. By late afternoon of September 10 black clouds followed one another in quick succession over the Princeton area. Then came the cloud-bursts in a furious downpour and savage winds. Snug in our Princeton home, we wondered what havoc the hurricane was wreaking on neighboring communities. During the turmoil that kept us awake most of the night, we could hear the crash of breaking tree branches. At dawn we learned that Edna had spent herself and was moving out to sea and that we could expect a pleasant day.

In the morning, as we began clearing away the debris, our dog sat watching us. Suddenly she stood up, ears upright, and made a dash for the turn in the road; she had heard familiar footsteps. Bill Faulkner walked briskly toward us with our dog running alongside. He had slept poorly in New York and had taken the first train to Princeton. At breakfast I inquired about his mother, Estelle, the newlyweds, Malcolm, and Gloria, and everyone else in Oxford. They are all well, he reported, and remarked, "There was too much weddin'."

I asked how his mother's painting was coming along. "She ain't paintin' so good," he said. (Now and then Bill lapsed into colloquial expressions which didn't in any way fit his Little Lord Fauntleroy image.) He went on to explain that since she had had an operation to remove cataracts she could see better and entirely differently. He preferred the paintings done before the operation.

Saxe told Bill that we were due at Professor Einstein's that afternoon and urged him to come with us. A telephone call to the Einsteins confirmed the invitation.

Professor Einstein tried to engage Bill in conversation, but alas, the talk was unilateral, with Bill completely silent. He just sat there, his eyes never leaving Einstein's face. We had tea; then Einstein gave us an inscribed copy of his new book, *Ideas and Opinions*.

Beiden Commins mit herzlichen Grussen,
aber ohne Zumutung zu lesen.

Ihr
A. Einstein, 54

(To both Commins with heart-felt greetings,
but without obligation to read it.

Yours
A. Einstein, 54)

He also inscribed a copy for Bill. As we were walking home, Saxe asked Bill why he hadn't entered into the conversation. Bill replied, "What could I say to this great man that could possibly have any significance?"

Yet at times Lord Fauntleroy remembered his worth. In August 1953 Saxe wrote him of a plan by the New American Library to separate the two unrelated stories of *The Wild Palms* and issue them as two distinct volumes, one titled *The Wild Palms* and the other *The Old Man*. Bill had originally conceived the stories as running as alternate sections of one book. Saxe asked for Bill's approval, and Faulkner, who was finishing *A Fable* at the time, typed his agreement at the bottom of Saxe's business letter:

Dismembering *The Wild Palms* will in my opinion destroy the over-all impact which I intended. But apparently my vanity (if it is vanity) regarding my work has at last reached that pitch where I consider it does not need petty defending. Am so near the end of the big one that I am frightened that lightning might strike me before I can finish it. It is either nothing, and I am blind in my dotage, or it is the best of my time. Damn it, I did have genius, Saxe. It just took me fifty-five years to find out. I suppose I was too busy working to notice it before.

A recording company, under the direction of Béla Bartók's son, a sound engineer, had for some time been urging Bill to record readings from some of his works. In late September 1954, while he was staying with us, Bill decided to make the recording, and he and Saxe spent nearly three hours at the company's studio where he read from his Nobel Prize acceptance speech and from *A Fable*, *Requiem for a Nun*, *As I Lay Dying*, *Light in August*, and *The Old Man*. Yet when the records were sent to him, he returned them, saying he didn't want them and that, as a matter of fact, he didn't know why Saxe and some of his colleagues at Random House wanted them either.

On another day, while Saxe was busy in his office, "There was little Lord Fauntleroy," as Saxe told me later, "pecking away at the typewriter copying out a story he had written in first draft over the weekend." Two days later, just as Saxe was about to leave for Princeton, Bill handed him the story—a hunting story named "Race at Morning," in the manner of "The Bear," but briefer.

Early in 1955 Faulkner was in town working on a story entitled "Hog Pawn" which seemed to Saxe quite comical for its juxtaposition of two curmudgeons and their attempts to outdo one another. At the same time Saxe found some ambiguities that Bill would have to clarify. Very soon after, while the two men were lunching together, Bill spoke of putting together in book form a group of hunting pieces, leading off with "The Bear" and including "The Old People," "A Bear Hunt," and "Race at Morning," all to be interwoven with episodes and descriptive passages from his other works. The session ended with Saxe assigning Bill some homework on the interludes over the weekend.

The next day, as Saxe was driving back from the center of Princeton, attending to sundry errands, he was surprised to see Faulkner walking along the road. He stopped to pick him up. "I didn't phone," explained Bill. "It being Saturday, I thought I would most likely find you or Dorothy at home. If not, the dog and I would keep each other company until you returned."

Back at the house the two men agreed on a title for the new book—*Big Woods*. At this point Bill reached into his pocket and brought out a small sheet on which was written a dedication for *Big Woods*:

Memo to Saxe Commins
From: Author
To: Editor,   WE NEVER ALWAYS SAW EYE TO EYE
                  BUT WE WERE ALWAYS
                  LOOKING AT THE SAME THING.

This tribute could not have come at a better moment, for Saxe's spirits were pretty low. It was not solely a matter of the long hours he was working. The drain on his depleted strength was accompanied by a depression of spirit. He shared with Faulkner a pessimistic feeling about the quality of modern life. Bill, with his aversion to publicity, had written a diatribe about freedom of the press. Saxe had not been satisfied with it and had pointed out the defects. In the process of rewriting, the article had become "The American Dream: What Has Happened to It?" Somehow, now, the two pessimists cheered each other up while they recounted depressing stories of the sad shape the world was in.

I was overjoyed when Bill stayed the night and well into Sunday. The two men were a considerable help to each other. The mood that weekend was one of warmth and understanding and an inner serenity that eclipsed heartache and despair.

A few days later Saxe found a disgruntled Faulkner awaiting him at Random House. He had been asked to speak at the National Book Council award ceremony on January 25, where he was to be honored for *A Fable*. In addition to his dislike of interviews and the whole publicity circus, he thought it unfair to other writers that he should be given the National Book Award for fiction a second time; in 1951 *The Collected Stories of William Faulkner* had been chosen.

Bill wanted Saxe to represent him at the award ceremony since he expected to be in Hollywood in late January. However, Bill was still in New York on the 25th and did attend the ceremony and found it less grueling than he had anticipated.

When Bill received word several months later that *A Fable* had also won the Pulitzer Prize, he really balked at participating and begged Saxe to represent him. When the time came on May 2, Saxe stood in for him. That done, Saxe wired Bill, who was at the Brown

Hotel in Louisville, Kentucky, looking over the Derby entries prior to writing a commissioned piece for *Sports Illustrated*.

Early in June 1955 I had a letter from Estelle Faulkner asking whether I would consider giving a program in Oxford in the fall to help further the music scholarship fund instituted by an initial grant from Bill. Since I was scheduled to play in New York on November 17, I wrote Estelle telling her I would be glad to play and would repeat my New York program. The date for the concert was set for November 21 at the Fulton Chapel of Ole Miss.

A letter came from Bill dated July 6 which read in part, "I am undertaking the Japanese assignment for the State Department; expenses paid and some salary too, this time, and I will go on to Europe from there." Further in this letter Bill said, "Will leave here about July 28. I think to Washington first; don't think I will be able to come up, as I am due in Tokyo August 1." The last line reads, "I won't be able to see our book (*Big Woods*) this year until I reach home probably."

About a week after this letter arrived, Saxe learned in a call from Bennett Cerf that Faulkner had telephoned from Oxford to ask that Bennett's lawyers draw up a document investing Saxe with full power of attorney for Bill. On July 21 there was another call from Bennett, this time to say that an official-looking envelope addressed to Saxe had just arrived from Oxford and that Saxe had better come in to town.

On examining the contents, Saxe was surprised to find a document giving him complete and absolute power of attorney for Faulkner. Before the document was deposited in the Random House vault, a photostatic copy was made for Saxe. Back home, as he handed it to me, he said, "My fervent hope is that I'll never be obliged to use the authority it gives me!"

In the spring of that same year, Bill Faulkner had written to Bob Haas saying that "in the event of my death Random House is to continue as the publishers of all my literary work, previously published as well as what may remain unpublished." The next paragraph then conferred on Saxe what he may have felt was a much graver responsibility than dealing merely with Faulkner's material assets.

It is my wish that Saxe Commins have the final authority in connection with all material submitted for publication after my death. By this I mean authority as to what is to be published, how it is to be edited, deletions, corrections, etc. I would also like him to act in an advisory capacity in connection with any manuscripts of mine to be sold or given to museums or libraries. In other words, I would like Saxe to act as my literary executor and as editor for all my past and future literary work.

From the moment Bill stepped off the plane at the Haneda Airport on August 1, 1955, every hour in Tokyo, Nagano, and Kyoto was filled with lectures and other activities. On August 4 he arrived at Nagano to participate in the Summer Seminar in American Literature, sponsored by the United States Department of State. This was carefully documented by Mr. Robert A. Jelliffe in a book entitled *Faulkner in Nagano*, published by Kenkyusha Ltd., Tokyo. From Nagano he went to the University of Kyoto, and then back to Tokyo prior to his departure on August 23. A scrapbook compiled by Mr. Leon Picon of the United States Information Service covers most of Bill's visit in Japan. A microfilm of this scrapbook is in the Princeton University Library.

Bill's itinerary after Tokyo included stays in Manila, Rome, Paris, London, and Iceland. Instead of staying away until Christmas time, as he had thought he might, he was back in Oxford in October, and on October 21 he turned up in Saxe's office. They spent a good part of the day together; Bill recounted his experiences on the long journey.

Bill planned to visit us on Sunday, but an urgent call from Oxford summoned him home. His mother, now 80, was about to undergo a serious operation, the nature of which was not disclosed. On the following Tuesday Bill was to go to the State Department and report on his journey. Would Saxe phone the State Department and explain why Bill could not keep his appointment?

The day of my New York concert came and passed, and then I was on my way to Oxford for my concert there. Thinking I would be able to relax a bit, I took an overnight train to Memphis. What a mistake that was! The train stalled somewhere before we reached Baltimore. How glad I was that I had prevailed on Saxe not to come with me. The train ride alone would have undone him.

I was very tired when I reached Memphis more than two hours late. There I was met by Estelle and Mr. E. G. Bowen of the Department of Music at Ole Miss, and during the long drive to Oxford I heard all the family news. Bill's mother had made a miraculous recovery after her serious operation. Also Bill had been

delayed in New York and would arrive by plane in the early afternoon.

At dinner that night there were just the three of us—Estelle, Bill,
and I. A telephone call summoned Estelle away from the table.
When she came back, she was quite shaken. The caller, she said,
had threatened, "You tell your weepin' Willy, if we hear any more
of that talk of his, we'll burn his house down."

It was frightening! Bill had talked to a group in Memphis a few
days before, urging them to open the door of Ole Miss to black
students in gradually increasing numbers. When I asked Bill, "Why
do you continue to live here?" he replied, "My people live here, and
this is a problem we must solve, not run away from."

Our friend Perry Miller went down to Memphis from Harvard
around this time for three days of lectures. In a letter to Saxe, he
wrote:

> There were two incessant subjects of conversation, from
> Memphis to Natchez: segregation and Bill Faulkner. Only one
> family did I meet—one of the old Jewish families of Memphis—
> who have any idea that he is a great artist. All the rest denounce
> him for the 'bad press' that he gives Mississippi, for being a
> drunk, and a general damn fool. My hostess in Natchez was
> "dated" by him when they were undergraduates at "Ole Miss."
> She told charming stories about him—stories that, had we got
> them from someone who knew Shelley, would be part of the
> legend of poetry by now—in order to prove to me that he always
> was queer and nuts. (I have told them to Carvel [Collins], so
> maybe—if Carvel ever does write—they may be preserved.)
> People kept asking me, was I going to try to see him? I took great
> pleasure in explaining that if I wanted to intrude upon him, I
> could have had a letter from you, and that probably no letter
> would more open Faulkner's door than one from you, but that I
> would rather be burned at the stake than to ask for such a letter
> or to impose upon his privacy even if I had one. Most of my
> Southern friends (who otherwise were universally charming
> people) couldn't seem to understand what I meant (all except the
> aforesaid Jewish family), even though in the previous breath they
> had been berating him for vilifying the South!

My concert in Oxford went better than I had thought it would.
Sometimes anxiety and strain fall into the background when one
must face up to the demands of a situation. During the intermission,
a faculty member of Ole Miss stepped forward and announced that

out of the William Faulkner Scholarship Fund the sum of $500 would be set aside for the Dorothy Berliner Commins Music Scholarship. Early the next morning, Bill drove me to the Memphis airport. I was glad to return by plane. So much had been crowded into those three days—so much to think about during my flight; so much to tell Saxe when I got home.

In mid-December Saxe had a letter from Bill. "Doing a little work on the next Snopes book," wrote Bill, "have not taken fire in the old way yet, so it goes slow, but unless I am burned out, I will heat up soon and go right on with it. 'Miss' is such an unhappy state to live in now that I need something like a book to get lost in."

Early in January 1956, another letter from Bill arrived: "All well here. The Snopes manuscript is going pretty good. I still have the feeling I am written out though, and all remaining is the craftsmanship, no fire, force. My judgment might be extinct also, so I will go on with this until I know it is no good. I may even finish it without knowing it is bad, or admitting it at least. Am planning on maybe coming up for a week about 1 February, don't know yet."

Bill did get to New York the first week in February, and once there, he proceeded to drink himself into an unconscious state. What had precipitated this latest drinking episode was not hard to surmise. His recent letters had revealed how troubled he was about himself, about his home state, and about his writing.

One afternoon Saxe called me from his office. "I'm bringing Bill home with me," he said. "He needs a quiet time with us. Though he is better, he's still very shaky."

About two hours later the car drew up to the walk of our house and out stepped Saxe and Bill. I stood at the doorway to greet them. Hat in hand, Bill came forward and said, "Dorothy, I've misbehaved again." I could say nothing, but I raised my hands and held his face for a moment.

Saxe took Bill's trench coat and bag. That trench coat! I had seen it on Bill so many times. It was threadbare at the wrists. The inside rim of the collar was stained a brownish tan that no cleaning could remove. Not so his hat! That was a dapper little affair, alpine-shaped with a perky little brush peeping out of the band that encircled the crown.

We walked into the living room, where a fire was burning in the fireplace. "This feels good," said Bill. The darkness of night had already settled. The day had been raw and wintry with heavy clouds that promised snow. Bill seated himself in his favorite spot on the far end of the sofa near the fireplace. The conversation was fragmentary. Saxe and I knew Bill well enough not to force it.

At dinner Bill ate very little; he seemed to be coming down with a cold. He complained of pain in his lower back. This complaint was not new. It probably stemmed from the injuries Bill had sustained in his plane smash, compounded by falls from horses. When we left the table, Bill went back to his seat near the fireplace. He looked so tired! Before long he asked to turn in. He always preferred to sleep in the study. The day bed is very firm, and nearby is the typewriter. He was a light sleeper, and often he would get up during the night to jot down some thought.

While I was turning back the covers, Saxe came in with Bill's bag. He whispered to me, "I think I will give Bill a warm alcohol rubdown. It always helped that sore spot before." I looked at Saxe. "A rubdown with alcohol! After the bout he's been through! I think a couple of aspirins and some hot lemonade might be better."

In the morning the ground was covered with slushy snow. I hated to see Saxe go into New York on a day like that. He said he had told Bill last night that he had a 9:30 appointment he could not possibly put off. He would, however, take an early train back.

I started a fresh fire in the fireplace, pulled up a small table near Bill's seat, and went about tending to some chores. Bill came into the kitchen, expecting, as usual, to fix his own breakfast. It was meager enough—just coffee and toast and some sort of jam or marmalade. I said to Bill, "Do sit near the fire. I'll bring your breakfast to you; let me spoil you this once." He laughed and said, "I will if you will have some coffee with me."

He was wearing a full-length kimono that must have been handsome in its day. It was made of silk, a very dark purple. The hem was padded with cotton wadding to weight it down. Now the edge of the hem was so frayed that I could see bits of the wadding struggling to come through.

When we had finished breakfast, I offered Bill the *Times*, but he took up his pipe instead. Then began what always fascinated me; the filling of his pipe with his favorite tobacco (Blue Boar), the packing of it into the bowl, the deliberate striking of the match, and watching it take fire. Then a pause, a long pause, before Bill took a number of puffs. If Bill were in the midst of saying something, it would have to wait until this rite was fulfilled.

I looked at this kimono-clad figure and studied Bill's head. It was a distinguished head, and with the years it had become even more distinguished looking. His hair was now white and his mustache nearly so. The new lines etched on his face gave it more depth. His eyes were black and clear. His speaking voice was pleasant, pitched low, and well modulated. To many his detachment and aloofness were expressions of snobbery. But this was not true. He was innately fine.

For all Bill's ties with the South and all its traditions, he was a lonely man. Away from the South, he was even more lonely, and drinking offered him oblivion for a time. Perhaps during these drinking bouts the ideas he wanted to develop or the things he wanted to write about were incubating. Who knows? But this I do know: once he had come through one of these bouts (and they were severe), he was hard at work again and creating.

Saxe returned from New York in the early afternoon. His first words were "How's Bill?"

"He's in the study, typing away," I answered. Then I heard Saxe as he walked into the study.

"Why Bill," he said, "you look so much better. How do you feel?" The two sat there quite some time talking, and now and then I heard a bit of laughter. A little later I set up a tea tray near the fireplace and brought in some corn muffins just out of the oven.

The next morning was clear and crisp, and the two went off for an early walk. When they got back and had some coffee, Saxe extended the large oak table in the living room, which serves as a dining table as well. Saxe then brought in his brief bag, which contained what there was of the new Snopes manuscript, soon to be given the title *The Town*. The pages of the manuscript soon covered most of the table, leaving just enough room to make notes. Many pages were already spread on the floor. What a sight that was to see Bill and Saxe on their knees, moving from one page to another, marking, deleting, transferring passages here and there!

Following lunch, Bill, at Saxe's suggestion, lay down for an hour's nap. Then, in the early twilight, they went for another short walk. When they returned, we had dinner, and after that the table was quickly cleared and the work resumed. I left the room as Saxe was going over a portion of the manuscript and Bill was sitting in his favorite spot near the fireplace. Suddenly I heard Saxe pound the table with his fist.

"Bill," he said, "this won't do! You've said it before! It's redundant, and you are only weakening your premise."

Bill didn't say a word. Later, when Saxe turned in for the night, he said to me, "I wish Bill had talked back to me. He could have said, 'Goddamnit, this is my book; I want it that way!' Instead, he just sat there with his pipe."

In the morning, when I went into the kitchen, I noticed that Bill had already had his coffee and toast and that in Saxe's place at the table there were four newly typed pages with the old version pinned underneath. Evidently Bill had stayed up half the night revising the pages. When Saxe read them, he was delighted.

Bill was in a better frame of mind and spirit when he returned to Oxford. He approached his manuscript with a fresh burst of energy. Still perturbed about the racial situation, he wrote his "Letter to the North" contained in the March 5, 1956, issue of *Life* magazine; and the March 15 issue of *The Reporter* carried an interview with Bill on the subject of segregation.

One day in June, Saxe found Bill waiting for him in his office. He had come to tell Saxe that he had received a letter from President Eisenhower asking him to be chairman of a group of writers of his choosing who would travel abroad as ambassadors of American culture.

June 1956

Dear Mr. Faulkner:

I am writing to ask your help.

Our Government, as you know, has relatively modest apparatus for trying to make the United States' objectives and principles better understood throughout the world. I have asked Congress for additional funds to strengthen this activity during fiscal '57.

But, clearly, there will never be enough diplomats and information officers at work in the world to get the job done without help from the rest of us. Indeed, if our American ideology is eventually to win out in the great struggle being waged between the two opposing ways of life, it must have the active support of thousands of independent private groups and institutions and of millions of individual Americans acting through person-to-person communication in foreign lands.

Secretary Dulles and Mr. Theodore C. Streibert, Director of the U.S. Information Agency, join me in this conviction that there is something important which every U.S. Citizen—man, woman and child—can do to help make the truth of our peaceful goals and of our respect for the rights of others known to more people overseas.

In a very real sense, to be successful we must wage peace with all the vigor and resourcefulness and universal participation of wartime.

It is my intention to call upon all U.S. citizens to help their Government in this task; but before doing so I would like to bring together at the White House a group of distinguished American leaders to assist with the organization of various phases of the work. I earnestly hope, therefore, that it will be possible for you to participate as one of these leaders and assume the chairmanship for writers' activities.

In accepting this appointment, you will be undertaking an assignment demanding of some time and effort on your part to make it successful. But it is patriotic work and work which I am convinced is of vital importance to our national interest. I seek your help confident that you will be able to impress this fact upon leading authors throughout the country and convince them that by taking part in creating understanding abroad they will contribute to lessening world tensions and to helping solve our problems.

With kindest personal wishes,

Sincerely,
Dwight D. Eisenhower

In setting up his committee, Faulkner sent each writer a copy of the president's letter. Presumably Saxe had suggested that the appeal might be made more sophisticated, less blatant, for in a letter to Saxe, Bill wrote:

I would make no change in the letter, nor attempt to rectify anything except a glaring untruth, even if I needed to. To change a written statement is to become a censor, and any censor is a dictator, or wants to be.

I would suggest that, as soon as Miss Ennis has an answer from everybody, she notify me and send me any further comments like mine above, and I will send my copy of the letter, with the comments, in a covering personal letter to the President of the United States, whose committee we are.

Then I don't know what more we can do. Though as loyal citizens and cognizant by our craft of world conditions, he himself already knows he has only to call on us further.

At this time *The Town* was about one-third complete. Bill sent the unfinished manuscript to Saxe with a letter saying, "The committee business will interfere, but I will keep at the manuscript typing, cleaning it up. I hope to have it all in by December 1, maybe sooner." Then he added, "I still can't tell, it may be trash except for certain parts, though I think not. I still think it is funny, and at the end very moving; two women characters I am proud of."

Bill did complete *The Town* ahead of schedule, turned it over to Saxe in mid-October, and soon he was talking to Saxe about the next Snopes book, *The Mansion*. In this Bill would bring to a close the saga of the Snopes family, that rapacious tribe that took root in Bill's legendary county of Yoknapatawpha in 1908 and carried forward their predatory activities through sixteen novels, covering a period of forty-odd years. Early in 1957 Bill brought the first pages of *The Mansion* for a brief conference with Saxe.

Saxe had persuaded Bill to deposit some of his manuscripts and other related papers in the Princeton University library. James B. Meriwether, who was then a graduate student at Princeton, working on Faulkner's writings, suggested that an exhibition of Faulkner's work, including the deposited items, would be important. Bill loaned his manuscripts from the Random House storage vault, and Saxe added some of his papers. The exhibit was beautifully organized by Meriwether, with the technical advice and aid of Alexander Wainwright of the Rare Book Department of the Princeton library. Bill and Estelle visited the exhibit in May.

Despite so much expenditure of Saxe's energy, he found time not only for writers whose works were not published by Random House, but for students at the university, especially those interested in Faulkner, who rang our doorbell and asked, "May we speak with Mr. Commins?" Saxe always made them welcome.

Saxe told Professor Whitney J. Oates about this, and they both felt it would be a fine thing if Bill would talk to the students. This was broached to Bill, who was most receptive to the idea. Professor Oates then arranged a program in which Faulkner would participate in several graduate seminars, as well as with small groups in undergraduate courses in American literature. This program was to be carried through in the following spring term, from March 4 through March 14, 1958.

Postlude

In the fall of 1957 Saxe entered Princeton Hospital for a check-up and was put through all the paces. When the report came through, he was told that he would have to undergo surgery. On October 23 our son Eugene and I drove him back to the hospital.

Saxe had been asked to speak at the Eugene O'Neill Pipe Night that was to take place on November 10 at the Players Club at Gramercy Park in New York. He had to forgo that, but Mike Oates had his secretary take down what Saxe had planned to say, and this was read by Don Klopfer. It traced the events from Saxe's first meeting with O'Neill to the subsequent events that led up to *Long Day's Journey into Night*. In addition it explained why Random House had been honor-bound not to publish *Long Day's Journey into Night* until twenty-five years after the author's death.

The evening at the Players Club came to a close with lines spoken by the actors who had performed in plays by O'Neill: Ward Costello as Robert in *Beyond the Horizon*, Frank McHugh as Ole in *The Hairy Ape*, Alan Bunce as Matt in *Ah, Wilderness!*, Jason Robards, Jr., as Hickey in *The Iceman Cometh*, Fredric March as the father in *Long Day's Journey into Night*. All this was reported to Saxe by Louis Sheaffer, who was writing a biography of O'Neill, and Russell Crouse, the journalist, playwright, and producer, who was an old friend of O'Neill.

With the approach of spring, Saxe seemed to have recovered from the operation and was in good form, looking forward to Bill Faulkner's seminars. In March Bill's visit was indeed successful, and Saxe acted as moderator at a number of the sessions. Before Bill went back to Oxford, he was asked to return for the fall term and was immediately scheduled for sessions running from November 18 through November 26, 1958.

Our son Eugene had met Ulla Grip, a Swedish girl who worked at the United Nations, and before long he came home to tell us of their intention to marry. Saxe and I thought it would be a lark to attend the wedding in Sweden, see a bit of Scandinavia, then make our way to Paris to meet some of the French publishers, and after that to visit our French relatives. We even spoke of taking a peek at the tiny attic atelier we first lived in at 9 rue Falguière and the lovely studio apartment at 11 rue Schelcher that held so many memories for us.

Our doctor thought a leisurely boat trip would do Saxe a great deal of good, so we purchased our tickets, bought new luggage, and had our passports attended to. Edgar Snow, who was with us at the time, remarked, "You both behave like kids who have never left home." Indeed, I don't think I had had a holiday with Saxe in years. His vacation time was usually spent working at home on manuscripts that needed more attention than he could give them at his office.

A few weeks before we were to sail, the parents of our son-in-law gave a party for Ulla and Eugene and us at their home in Morristown, N.J. It was a glorious June day, with a profusion of flowers everywhere. Saxe looked well; I even teased him and told him he looked like Beau Brummell. It was a happy party.

While we were driving home through rather dark country roads, I heard Saxe say, "I have a pain between my shoulders." I urged him to stop the car. "No," said he, "it's better to drive on to a spot where there are a few houses."

Soon there was one in sight. I ran toward it and got an ambulance to come. When we reached the hospital, it was determined that Saxe had had a mild heart attack.

By July 4 Saxe had rallied sufficiently to be permitted to sit up a bit in his hospital bed. He grew restless and clamored for the

Kirchstetten (West Bahn)
Hinterholz # 6
Niederösterreich
Austria

Oct 8ᵗʰ

Dear Mrs Commins:

I have just heard from Mr Bloomfield of
Saxe's death. I don't see American papers
in Europe, and nobody in Random House let me
know. I should have written a letter to
the New York Times, attempting to express what
I am sure every author who has the privilege
of working with him, must have felt. Efficiency
of mind and goodness of heart are rarely combined
in equal measure, but in Saxe they were. It is
much for an author to know that his most tiresome
requests will be listened to courteously and respectfully,
and that everything will be done to turn out his book
as he would wish, but it meant a great deal more
to me to feel, every time I entered Saxe's office,
that I was in the presence of a good man.

Knowing this, it would be impious of me to try to
express in words my sympathy for you in your
personal loss. I do hope, though, that if you come to
New York at all (I return Oct 26ᵗʰ) you will come
and see me.

    your affectionately
    Wystan Auden

Letter to Dorothy Commins from W. H. Auden, October 8, 1958

Dinesen and Snow galleys. I remonstrated, but to no avail. "Please
try to understand," he said. "These books are scheduled for
publication in early fall, and the corrected galleys must be at
Random House on schedule."

I spoke to the doctor about this. He thought that to withhold
them might even do harm, but we were to see to it that Saxe did
only a few pages at a time. I brought the galleys. The Dinesen
stories now bore the title *Last Tales*, and Edgar Snow's manuscript
had finally been given the title of *Journey to the Beginning*.

On July 16 the checking of the galleys was finished. When Saxe
handed them to me he said, "Please package them and take them to
the post office before it closes, and be sure to insure them. Random
House should have them by noon tomorrow." I attended to all that
and returned to the hospital, staying as late as I was permitted to
stay. I walked home.

As dawn broke the next morning, the doctor drove up to tell me
that Saxe had died.

When he heard, Bill Faulkner sent the following telegram:

THE FINEST EPITAPH EVERYONE WHO EVER KNEW SAXE WILL HAVE TO
SUBSCRIBE TO WHETHER HE WILL OR NOT QUOTE HE LOVED ME UNQUOTE
BILL FAULKNER

Index